SENSING GOD'S SPIRIT IN ALL THINGS

by
Ross L. Bortner

Ross L. Bortner
6 East Rhodes Avenue
WEST CHESTER, PA 19382

Scripture quotations are as follows: Those marked NIV are from the *Holy Bible, New International Version,* copyright © 1973, 1978, 1984 by the International Bible Society. Used by permission of Zondervan Bible Publishers. Quotations marked KJV are from the *King James Version* of the Bible. Quotations marked P are from *Phillips: The New Testament in Modern English,* rev. ed. © J.B. Phillips 1958, 1960, 1972. Used by permission of Macmillan Publishing Company. Quotations marked RSV are from the *Revised Standard Version of the Bible,* copyright 1946, 1952, © 1971 by the Division of Christian Education of the National Council of the Churches of Christ in the U.S.A., and are used by permission. Quotations marked TEV are from the Good News Bible, the *Bible in Today's English Version,* copyright © American Bible Society 1966, 1971, 1976. Quotations marked TLB are from *The Living Bible,* copyright 1971 by Tyndale House Publishers, Wheaton, IL. Used by permission.

Quotations marked NEB are from *The New English Bible,* © 1961, 1970 by The Delegates of the Oxford University Press and The Syndics of the Cambridge University Press. Quotations marked NKJV are from *The New King James Version* of the Bible, copyright © 1979 by Thomas Nelson Publishers. Quotations marked NAB are from the *New American Bible,* copyright © 1970 by Confraternity of Christian Doctrine, Washington, D.C. Quotations marked NASB are from the *New American Standard Bible,* copyright 1960, 1962, 1968, 1971 by the Lochman Foundation. Quotations marked JB are from the *Jerusalem Bible,* copyright © 1966 by Doubleday and Company. Quotations marked MLB are from the *Modern Language Bible* (The New Berkeley Version in Modern English), rev. ed., copyright 1945, 1959 © 1969 by The Zondervan Publishing House.

Note: In some Scripture quotations, more than one version/translation has been used to give the text a richer and more complete meaning.

To *JEANNE*—my wife of forty-two years—for her open communications, her generous loving spirit, her steadfast gentle faith—and whose criticisms of my writings keep me humble.

To *DAVE* and *CINDY*—our son and daughter-in-law—who are a delightful joy in our lives through their constant caring and sharing, and showing loving concern to others.

To *MY PARENTS*—for encouraging the development of my spiritual life at an early age—mostly by setting a worthy example.

To *A HOST OF PEOPLE*—relatives, friends, and acquaintances—mostly Christians—who, by displaying the fruit of the Spirit in their lives, have inspired me to continue growing in the Spirit.

ACKNOWLEDGMENTS

I am deeply grateful to HELEN GRIER for her expertise in typing my manuscript; her ability to decipher my scribbled handwriting; her total commitment to this project; and her personal friendship.

I am also deeply appreciative to DR. RALPH C. PRESTON, my doctoral dissertation chairman at the University of Pennsylvania—and now Professor Emeritus—for his deep involvement in reading the entire manuscript and making many helpful written comments; his keen critique of the contents; his insightful encouragements along the way; and his overall sensitivity to the "things of the Spirit."

CONTENTS

PREFACE

This book is written for people of all ages who want to enjoy the excitement of living each day as a new adventure—despite all the frailties of human nature, the uncertainties of world conditions, and the frequently held dim views about God and His all-powerful, all-knowing, and always-present Spirit in the world.

Whatever the circumstances in life, there will come a time in our lives when we reach the extremities of our own resources to solve all of life's problems, and we will seek the help of Almighty God. At such times, we cry out: "Help me God. You've got to help me. I don't know where else to turn. Connect me to your Spirit."

God is Spirit. God is Holy Spirit. God did promise, if we ask, to help us by sending His Spirit whereby we might be guided and comforted through truth and love into living a more abundant life, a kind of "Life in the Spirit" right here on earth *and* akin to having "one foot on earth and one foot in Heaven" much of the time—and getting some foretaste of living the heavenly life while still here on earth.

Sensing God's Spirit In All Things was written to help all seekers of His Spirit realize this ideal state, for in fully appreciating and enjoying the things of earth that touch us—and in overcoming life's problems and fears by the power of God's Spirit—we will be increasingly granted illuminated foretastes of the heavenly life to come even in our present bodies.

Within the broad spectrum of living, significant areas have been selected that most of us experience from day to day. These writings are arranged in ten chapters that reflect the idea of *personal growth* throughout a lifetime, with special attention given to the development of spiritual awareness in all things (even in so-called worldly areas). Most of us want to live confident lives in tune with God's Spirit, rather than insecure lives separated from God's help.

Sensing God's Spirit in the worldly environment most of us live in—a highly complex world with many competing (lesser) spirits—is not an easy task. Therefore, to aid us from a Biblical perspective, over 150 Bible references relating to the topical contexts are included, which contain spiritual insights, even if only in a single compelling sentence.

In making hundreds of daily decisions that directly affect our personal growth, we become keenly aware of the continual need to keep our physical bodies and minds under control. Unless God's Spirit permeates our lives so that our thoughts and actions are guided by His Spirit ("Spirit over mind over body"), much of our searching for a better life will be in vain. God's Spirit uniting with our spirits is the best life.

On a more personal note, I have been interested in spiritual things since an early age, but have become increasingly more interested in wanting to live the "life of the Spirit" since doing my doctoral thesis in education at the University of Pennsylvania in 1957 on *Teaching Spiritual Values in the Public Schools*. One of the thrusts for that study grew out of the fruit of the Spirit cluster found in Gal. 5:22–23, NIV: "The fruit of the Spirit is love, joy, peace, patience, kindness, goodness, faithfulness, gentleness, and self-control."

It is my hope that although some of the writings are straightforward and hard-hitting, with some surprises, there will be enough love, humor, and sensitivity showing through in other pieces so that a judicious balance of the earthly and the heavenly will prevail—and that the fruits of the Spirit will shine through many of the sections to help give a spiritual perspective to your everyday living.

It is also my hope that you will find most of the book interesting, encouraging, and uplifting as you live, move, and have your being somewhere between the natural visible things of earth and the supernatural invisible realms of Heaven.

ROSS L. BORTNER

IN THE BEGINNING GOD...

In the beginning God created the heavens and the earth...
By the seventh day the whole universe was completed
    in all its vast array...
For the foundations of the earth are the Lord's;
    upon them He has set the world.

God created male and female in His own image...
What is man, O God, that you should think of him;
    mere man, that you should care for him?
You made him a little lower than the angels;
    you crowned him with glory and honor,
    and put all things under his feet.

In the beginning was the Word...
And the Word became flesh and dwelt among us,
    full of grace and truth;
We have beheld His glory,
    glory as of the only Son from the Father.

God has made everything beautiful in its time.
He has also set eternity in the minds of men;
    and formed the spirit of man within him.
Yet, man cannot see the whole scope of God's work
    from the beginning to the end.

However, since the beginning of the world,
God's invisible qualities—His eternal power and divine nature—
    have been clearly seen.
Being understood from what has been made,
    so that all people are without excuse.

But it is the Spirit in a man,
The breath of the Almighty,
    that gives him understanding...
The Spirit of God has made him;
    the breath of the Almighty gives him life.

Have you heard that there is a Holy Spirit?
Did you receive the Holy Spirit when you believed?
    Where can you go from the Spirit?
    Where can you flee from its presence?
Or can you find someone in whom is the Spirit of God?

The Spirit searches all things
    even the deep things of God...
If the rulers of this world had understood
    the hidden wisdom of God,
They would not have crucified the Lord of Glory.

Has God not made foolish the wisdom of this world?
For the wisdom of this world is foolishness in God's sight...
The world at large cannot receive God's Spirit,
    for it can neither see
    nor recognize that Spirit.

However, your Father in Heaven
    will give the Holy Spirit
To those who ask Him...
Those who are led by the Spirit of God
    are the sons [and daughters] of God.

Those who live in accordance with the Spirit
    have their minds set on what the Spirit desires.
The mind controlled by the Spirit
    is life and peace...
The Spirit gives life,
    so live in the Spirit.

In The Beginning God...
    The aforementioned quotations are from the Bible, with the following taken from: Gen. 1:1; 41:38; 1 Sam. 2:8; Job 32:8; 33:4; Eccles. 3:11a; Zech. 12:1; Luke 11:13; John 6:63; Acts 19:2; Rom. 1:20; 8:5,6,14; 1 Cor. 1:20; 2:10; 3:19 (NIV). The following selections are taken from: Gen. 2:1 and Ps. 8:4,5b (TEV); Ps. 8:5a, Eccles. 3:11c, and John 14:17a (TLB); Ps. 8:6 (NAB); John 1:1 and Gal. 5:25 (KJV); John 1:14 (RSV); John 14:17b and Rom. 1:20a (P).

CHAPTER I

EARTHY TOUCHES WITH SPIRITUAL HINTS

The first man (Adam) is from the earth, earthy; the second man (the Lord) is from heaven....And just as we have borne the image of the earthy, we shall also bear the image of the heavenly.

—1 Cor. 15:47,49 (NASB)

A HOUSE...AND A HOME

What type of place would you like to live in?

A modern, luxurious, prestigious Park Avenue apartment in New York City that requires letters of recommendation for its prospective tenants, and "impeccable credentials"?

A suburban split-level rancher that has "curb appeal" through the handsomely landscaped lawn and shrubbery that enhance the beauty of the earthy stone and white-clapboard house?

A white-stuccoed country house (circa 1780) topped with a wood-shingled roof and three broad chimneys of stone, nestled by a stream, with old shade trees and mature plantings, and a stone-walled patio that opens to a low fence of roses?

A historic gentleman's farm-estate of twenty acres featuring a fieldstone and stucco residence with additions and terraces, a handsome barn with horses, a springhouse, a swimming pool, a garden, an orchard, and professionally landscaped areas of lawns, trees, shrubbery, and flowers?

And what would you like the *interior* of the house to contain? Mellow random floors? Open-beamed ceilings? Wide windowsills? French patio doors? Chandeliers in the reception hallway? Spiraling staircases? Paneled library? Charming dining room with harvest table? Lovely fireplaces with mantels? Plush wall-to-wall carpeting, or braided colonial rugs, or exciting orientals? Skylights in selected areas? Open, sunlit kitchen? Custom bath vanities? Jacuzzi package? Central air-conditioning? Your preference of types of furniture, lamps, draperies, wallpaper, paint colors, paintings?

Then there are all the personal touches that give a distinctive charm to a house and help provide a warm, cozy, livable atmosphere—perhaps a Norman Rockwell painting, an old Country Garden quilt, stained glass in the hallway, a stereo unit throughout the house, hand-carved antiques, a grandfather clock, Windsor chairs, family collections, sparkling Lismore Waterford crystal, gleaming silverware, delicate china, fruit bowls and floral arrangements scattered throughout the house.

With such an array of exterior and interior design features and furnishings to choose, it's a delight to know that with the touch and decorative ideas and skills of the individual owner, each house can become a unique place of beauty.

But...

A house does not a home make.

Home is where the heart is.

It takes a heap o' livin' in a house to make it a home.
—Edgar A. Guest

Home's not merely four square walls,
Though with pictures hung and gilded;
Home is where Affection calls—
Filled with shrines the Heart hath builded.
—Charles Swain

Where we love is home,
Home that our feet may leave, but not our hearts.
—Oliver Wendell Holmes

This is my home of love; if I have ranged,
Like him that travels, I return again.
—William Shakespeare

Mid pleasures and palaces though we may roam,
Be it ever so humble, there's no place like home…
An exile from home splendour dazzles in vain,
Oh give me my lovely thatched cottage again;
The birds singing gayly, that come at my call,
Give me them, and that peace of mind dearer than all.
—John Howard Payne

Give a man a book he can read:
And his home is bright with a calm delight,
Though the room be poor indeed.
—James Thomson

This is the nature of home—it is the place of Peace; the shelter,
not only from all injury, but from all terror, doubt and divisions.
—John Ruskin

The house that looks to east, to west,
This, dear one, is our home, our rest.
—Richard Watson Gilder

The image of *Home* contains not just the idea of a place, but
beliefs, values, understandings, traditions of the past, and visions
of the future.
—Timothy B. Cogan*

*Timothy B. Cogan, Memorial Address given on Alumni Day in Princeton
University Chapel, Feb. 24, 1974.

"For we know that when this tent we live in—our body here on earth—is torn down, God will have a house in Heaven for us to live in, a home He Himself has made, which will last forever." (The Apostle Paul, 2 Cor. 5:1, TEV.)

What credentials and letters of recommendation will we need?

"WE'RE STAYING AT THE FITZWILLIAM!"

I have long suspected that many people taking vacations (or on other traveling occasions) often stay at "name places," prestigious places that bring a certain amount of pride and status to the occupants. After arriving back home, when we are asked, "How was your vacation?" by inquiring relatives, neighbors and friends, we can answer with justifiable pride, "O fine! We stayed at the Ritz in Paris"; or "Just great—we stayed at the Palace in Gstaad"; or "Terrific—we stayed at the Savoy in London"; or "I'm glad you asked—we stayed at the Grand in Rome."

The seasoned traveler will immediately recognize this as name-dropping of discriminating places to stay for superb cuisine, opulent accommodations, and headquarter places to see international celebrities in luxurious lobbies, but more importantly, as places of distinction that will enhance the guests' (clients') prestige. There might even be the "too much to resist" temptation to send postcards from the top-drawer establishment to people back home that you want to especially impress, even in advance of your own arrival home.

However, it may come as a great surprise to you (as it did to me) that a small, unpretentious historic inn located in a small, unpretentious village in rural southern New Hampshire might be unwittingly in competition with far more sophisticated, ultrachic world landmarks. I discovered the Fitzwilliam Inn while reading about country inns of New England.

Fitzwilliam, New Hampshire is a beautiful village of several hundred residents that contains antique shops, one grocery store, a small house for a post office, a house library open three days a week, and no bank. The central triangular village green is bordered by a white colonial church and an exquisite town hall. The village's modesty would prevent boasting about itself; albeit, its town hall is one of the most architecturally beautiful edifices of its type to be seen anywhere.

In addition to its town hall, the small village could also boast about its historic Fitzwilliam Inn (1796) located at the head of the village green, and the hub of its social life. The inn has 22 rooms, 12 with bath (the Savoy has more than 500 rooms, all with bath). There is no elevator (16 steps to the second floor, 15 steps to the third floor). It is without wall-to-wall carpeting (exposed foot-wide wooden planks instead). The innkeeper, who is also the chef, looks like Ernest Hemingway or Orson Welles. In the cozy living-room-type dining rooms, all menus are tacked to little bread boards. The Fitzwilliam Inn has no descriptive brochures about itself, nor does the town hall, but it can best be described as an unpretentious, warm country inn that offers "comfort, friendliness, and informality more than fanciness."

The Fitzwilliam may not be one of the best-known establishments among the jet set, but it does have its own fiercely passionate devotees and proud clientele. A distinguished guest who has international connections among the royalty of Europe was overheard, on telephoning some of her friends in New York City and Cape Cod, to say excitedly and proudly, "We're staying at the Fitzwilliam!"

So, too, I say as one who has strolled leisurely through the lobby of the Savoy, but never *stayed* there; or as one who has eaten in the Ritz garden restaurants, but never *stayed* there; and as one who *stayed* in Gstaad, but *not* at the Palace:

We didn't stay at the *Ritz*
but proudly
We stayed at the *Fitz*william!

TRAVEL

Taking trips to experience *the thrill of discovery* is one of the real joys of earthly living—and to read and plan ahead for them is often as great a joy as taking the actual trips themselves.

It's educational fun to plan auto trips across America. I have found the seven regional editions of the *Mobil Travel Guide* to be extremely helpful in locating outstanding dining and lodging establishments, and worthwhile attractions to see. Four extensive cross-country trips have been taken by our family to the West Coast, and each trip has been a photographer's delight in seeking to get a collection of memorable pictures of our beautiful country. I think of America in a series of moving pictures from East to West, North to South, that includes these photos:

- Colorful fall foliage and historic country inns of New England.
- Rugged rockbound coast of Maine and the beauty of the Bar Harbor area and Acadia National Park.
- Unspoiled chaste beauty of Vermont's red-barn farms, white church steeples, and crisp, clean countryside (no billboards).
- Serenity of New York's mountainous lakes.
- Overpowering immensity and sparkling beauty of Niagara Falls.
- Unbelievable city of Manhattan with its simplicity of street designs (you can't get lost), and its multiplicity of attractions (you can get overwhelmed deciding what to take in).
- Rich Amish farmlands around Lancaster, Pennsylvania.
- Abundance of significant historical sites along the East Coast, including such smaller cities as Annapolis, Maryland; Williamsburg, Virginia; Wilmington, North Carolina; Charleston, South Carolina; and Savannah, Georgia.
- Paradise charm of Florida, owing mainly to its warm, sunny weather during the winter months.
- Magnificent mansions and grounds of the Southern plantations.
- Peaceful nature of the forested Appalachian Mountains and its national parks.
- Thrill of crossing the legendary Mississippi River with its vast tributaries for the first time, expecting it to be broader than it is.
- Singular beauty of the ripened golden wheat fields in the Plains

states, with tall grain elevators identifying towns miles in advance of them.

• Rugged majesty of the snow-capped Rocky Mountains (and the excitement on first sight of them), and the natural wonders contained within its extensive ranges—especially the National Parks: Glacier, Yellowstone, Grand Teton, Rocky Mountain, Yosemite, Redwood, Grand Canyon, Zion, Petrified Forest, Pikes Peak, Royal Gorge, Mt. Rushmore, Mt. Rainier, and Mt. Hood.

• Vastness of open space in western Texas and the dry, warm Southwest.

• Naked beauty of the lonely desert areas of Utah and Nevada that leave us vulnerable and dependent.

• Wonders of the West Coast, particularly charismatic California with its generous offerings of sunshine and varieties of climate within a couple driving hours—from enchanting San Francisco at the Golden Gate to Lake Tahoe perched high in the Sierras; and from cool San Diego on the Pacific to the hot sunny sands and decorative mountains of relaxing Palm Springs.

In addition to seeing America by automobile, there are also the joys of discovery to be found in traveling overseas, especially to Europe, the ancestral home and lineage of many families in America. Most people fly to Europe these days, sometimes for extended weekends to London, Paris, or Rome; or for longer stays in England to visit such splendid cathedrals as Coventry, Salisbury, and Wells; or on lengthy trips of a month or more where both rented autos and Eurail passes (railroad tickets) are used to roam wherever one desires on the mainland of Europe. Be sure to stop in at least a few fun cities (such as Amsterdam, Copenhagen, Hamburg, Munich, and Salzburg) that feature open fairs and art festivals, musical concerts and operas, flower markets on street corners, and balloon sellers on busy streets, as well as to see the historical cities and their shrines.

Whatever the mode of transportation, I have found Fielding's *Travel Guide to Europe* to be an excellent, almost foolproof bible in searching out superior accommodations, gourmet dining spots, and fine shopping places.

Whether traveling by car or camper or mobile home to see the United States, or by ship to the Caribbean to visit some lovely island spots like Bermuda and the Virgin Islands, or by train to see Canada or Europe, or by plane to fly around the world—and whether traveling on business or vacation, to a convention, or on a honeymoon to Tahiti in the South Pacific— it's always fun to anticipate the abundance of thrills to be found in discovering new places and new faces, different foods and peoples and habitats.

It's somewhat heavenly to be always dreaming of traveling to some far-away places you've never been before—like Australia, New Zealand, Egypt, or the Bible Lands ("to walk where Jesus walked"), or maybe just go to some nearby spots to discover hidden "acres of diamonds" in your own hometown environs.

If you're one of those rare persons who has taken forty or more trips around the world and "seen everything," or happen to be one who is fussy about going to places that pose current threats of terrorism or violence—you might want to try a visit to Johnstown, Pennsylvania. Johnstown has the lowest crime rate in the nation, primarily because, as written in *The Philadelphia Inquirer* (September 19, 1982): "The city has strong ethnic and family ties, and the rules and regulations established in the home carry over into the community. If people see someone breaking into your car, they'd chase him and hold him until the police came.... People aren't afraid to walk the streets at night."

At the base of its incline railway is Johnstown's flag plaza, where there is a flag for the country of each of the city's thirty-nine ethnic groups, representing the many ethnic neighborhoods as well (a small United Nations).

In addition to being a picturesque town nestled in a series of deep valleys surrounded by mountainous hills, and situated at the confluence of the Conemaugh and Stony Creek Rivers, Johnstown has a handsome "big-league" ballpark at the mouth of its two tributaries. There is a downtown central park with lots of park benches amid trees and flowers that invite easy conversations among its people.

Johnstown, often called an "all-American city" by its natives, is a town of 35,000 people that also has the highest unemployment rate in the country because of its past heavy dependence on coal and steel (both depressed industries now). Yet, despite the loss of jobs, banks report that the rate of savings is going up (1983), and church donations have never been higher.

The people of Johnstown are legendary, chiefly because they have fought adversities again and again, and have always come back. They survived three devastating floods—1899 with 2,200 killed; 1936; and 1977 with $250 billion in damages.

But through it all, Mayor Herbert Pfuhl, Jr. says with humble pride: "This town has lived with adversity. If it's not a flood, it's a steel strike. If it's not a steel strike, it's a recession. People here don't give up. They don't panic. They stay close together. They know that no matter how bad things get, there is always hope that things will turn around and get better."

So for a different kind of trip that's worth its weight in moral and spiritual values, visit Johnstown and its people—who, because of an unusual amount of adversities, seem to possess an unusual amount of hardworking simple virtues and disciplined tough convictions, and an uncommon amount of good common sense and boundless hope for the future.

BIG CITIES

In this day of fast traveling from one section of the country to another, big cities are either flown over by plane or bypassed by cars using interstate highways and beltways around the cities. Then, too, some people prefer the country and small towns, and avoid entering a big city at all costs. Such folks would *never* entertain the thought of ever living there—even for a day. They tend to seek out such places as Peacham, Vermont; Plains, Georgia; Oakley, Kansas; Steamboat Springs, Colorado; Big Sky, Montana; New Meadows, Idaho; Arlon, Belgium; Wiveliscombe, England; or Rossiniere, Switzerland.

Furthermore, the temptation is strong nowadays to see the country as God's place, and the city as belonging to the devil. Yet today, 90% of the earth's inhabitants live in 5% of the earth's area. In the United States at least 60% of the people live in cities.

Let this effort, then, be a resounding round of praise for big cities.

Visiting big cities by train is the ideal way to get right into the heart of a city—with minimum loss of time and energy. Upon leaving the station, you're immediately downtown where all the action is—big hotels, famous restaurants, lots of people.

Flying by plane will usually land you *miles* from the center of town, necessitating a bus or taxi to get there. Flying over or near cities at night, though, is worth the inconvenience—just to look down, so it seems, upon thousands of inverted silver stars nailed to the earth, and whose lights depict the shape of the city in a beautiful constellation pattern.

I have seldom regretted taking the extra time while traveling, usually by car, to visit a big city. On such ventures, travel guides and road maps are invaluable tools to be used diligently in plotting out what sights and sounds are to be visited.

So it is that I have visited the heart and center of the 100 largest cities in the United States, from Boston to San Diego, from Miami to Seattle—and the largest cities in Canada and Europe.

Why all this appetite for visiting big cities?

Big cities represent the best in cultural atmosphere and achievements that mankind has ever produced. It's an intellectual and emotional rendition of a people collectively sharing their finest and best—from the modern, sleek, skyscraper office buildings that can create a beautifully harmonized architectural skyline from afar (Atlanta, Denver, Houston, Minneapolis, Pittsburgh)—to the more historic, gardenlike cultural buildings of an art gallery, botanical garden, cathedral/church, historical society,

11

library, music hall, opera house, or science museum (Boston, Chicago, New York, Philadelphia, Washington, D.C.).

Then there's the hustle and bustle of a big city. You see people of all cultures, ethnic groups, and races dressed in a great variety of traditional garbs and colorful costumes. It's great fun and excitement looking into the individual faces of rapidly passing people of all ages, wondering who they are, where they live, what they do, why they're in the big city now. Will I ever see that face again, even if only for a fleeting second?

Studies have been done periodically by researchers to determine the "top forty" or the "top ten" best cities in the United States to live, considering such varied factors as climate and terrain, housing, health, crime, transportation, education, the arts, recreation, and economic outlook.

Other listings have been compiled of the favorite American cities of tourists, based on actual head counts of annual visitors. In such listings, points of interest often include historic, man-made, recreational and scenic factors.

So here is my own list of the "top three" favorite big cities of America to visit, based on little scientific research but on a tremendous amount of "emotional feel" and warmth for them:

- *New York City.* Still considered the crossroads of the world. A truly cosmopolitan city, with peoples from every continent. Has everything imaginable—the United Nations, Times Square, Broadway, Wall Street, Fifth Avenue, Rockefeller Center, Greenwich Village, Yankee Stadium, Statue of Liberty, and skyscrapers galore.

- *San Francisco.* "A glowing white city set on many hills that cannot be hid," except at times by fog, which only adds a touch of mystery to this angelic-looking sophisticated city. A beautiful harbor entrance, fashionable shops, famous restaurants, dramatic bridges.

- *Washington, D.C.* A beautiful city filled with many parks, gardens, and handsome homes. It looks a lot like Paris, with its many broad avenues, fountained circles, floral gardens, and stately governmental buildings, and it is of course a center of political activity.

Other big cities deserving a special visit, with consideration given to such factors as scenic beauty, the arts, climate, historic sites, creative urban renovation, and friendliness of its people include Atlanta, Baltimore, Chicago, Cincinnati, Denver, Indianapolis, Kansas City (Missouri), Louisville, Minneapolis, Nashville, Philadelphia, Pittsburgh, St. Louis, St. Paul, Salt Lake City, San Antonio, San Diego, Seattle, and Tucson.

It should be noted that America is not the only country with exciting big cities. Neighboring Canada has beautiful Montreal near its eastern end, delicately situated on an island in the middle of the St. Lawrence River and uniquely perched in front of some rising hills, giving it a fairylike look at night from across the river. It has a thoroughly international flavor, with a charming blend of the old and new.

At the western end of Canada is Vancouver, situated so majestically on a peninsula with high-rising hills forming a beautiful backdrop for this clean, modern, exciting city.

Of course, one can never forget the "big three" European cities of London, Paris and Rome. Each has everything—beauty, charm, elegance and lots of people, millions of them.

My personal favorite of the three is London, perhaps because of the easily understood language and our common historical heritage, but there's a bigger reason. The people of London are so extremely courteous and helpful to perfect strangers. They take time to answer visitors' questions, are extra-polite, and delighted to be of help, just as though it's the first visitor they've ever met.

But I still yearn to go to faraway places—and other big cities. I've always dreamed of going to such beautiful majestic places as Sydney, Australia—with its stunning harbor; Capetown, South Africa—with its 3500-foot Table Mountain as a spectacular backdrop; Hong Kong—with its fascinating harbor and ships bringing imported goods from all over the world, and also exporting from a port that is surrounded by high mountains; Bangkok, Thailand; Rio de Janeiro—said to have a breathtakingly beautiful harbor by day or night, with majestic Sugarloaf Mountain and another 3400-foot mountain with a huge 120-foot statue of Christ with hands outstretched, looking benevolently over the harbor from its lofty peak; Constantinople; and Cairo—with its ancient Egyptian culture and its famous nearby pyramids. And oh, *Jerusalem!* The ancient Biblical city—Mount Zion, the Holy City—with many sites sacred to Jewish, Christian and Moslem faiths.

If I forget you, O Jerusalem, let my right hand wither! Let my tongue cleave to the roof of my mouth, if I do not remember you, if I do not set Jerusalem above my highest joy! (Ps. 137:5,6, RSV.)

Spiritually, I believe that life in Heaven will be like living in a big city—the City of God, the Heavenly Jerusalem. There will be crowds of people there—millions and millions of people with their faces covered with love, along with millions and millions of angels. I can envision unending art festivals; spirited conversations; loving interchanges; harmonious communions; angelic choirs; domed cathedrals; herald trumpets; harpists; wedding banquets; many mansions; vast crowds from every nation, of all tribes, peoples and languages worshiping together as one congregation and singing hosannas and hallelujahs!

As the Apostle John wrote in the Book of Revelation:

> I saw the Holy City, the new Jerusalem, coming down out of Heaven from God, prepared as a bride beautifully dressed for her husband....The City shone with the glory of God, and its brilliance was like that of a very precious jewel, like a jasper, clear as crystal....The City [was found to be] 1500 miles in length, and as wide and high as it was long. (Rev. 21:2,11,16, NIV, TEV.)

Now you know why I really like big cities!

FOOTBALL STADIUMS

What is the ultimate fascination that a football stadium holds in our American culture over any other sports complex—be it a baseball stadium, basketball arena, or soccer field? Some families when taking auto trips across the United States have even been known to give football stadiums *top priority* while visiting a city, ranking it ahead of city hall, art museums, music halls, libraries, science museums, and cathedrals.

Apparently this fascination is not entirely the province of sports lovers, for whenever other groups want to hold a really big event with anticipated tens of thousands of people—like a Billy Graham Religious Crusade—the organizers will head for a football stadium.

College football stadiums, in contrast to their modest baseball fields, are usually the ultimate in location, beauty, and design, often exceeding the modern sports complexes that professional teams use.

Historic memories of unforgettable football games played in certain football stadiums will heavily influence individual decisions on choice of gridirons. Ivy League fans will doubtless remember historic games played in Yale Bowl, Harvard Stadium (oldest in the United States), Palmer Stadium in Princeton (second oldest), and Franklin Field at Penn. Other university followers will lay claim to classic encounters in larger stadiums, such as Memorial Stadium at the University of California in Berkeley, Memorial Stadium at the University of Nebraska, University of Michigan Stadium, Notre Dame Stadium, Neyland Stadium at the University of Tennessee, Owen Field at the University of Oklahoma, and Beaver Stadium at Penn State University.

The Bowl Games on New Year's Day are usually played in beautifully designed stadiums. The best of them all is the Rose Bowl! It is also the largest, seating about 105,000 with the lower rows of seats hugging the playing field. It's a perfect horizontal oval shape, just like a football. Everybody can see everybody else (with binoculars), and with a large stadium, the greater the cheering crowds. It's like a big edition of a "cheer-along" extended family celebration!

Open-air football stadiums seem to really come alive on sunny Saturday afternoons with blue skies, when there is a nip in the air and the leaves are turning bright colors. There is a spirit of joy outside the stadium before the game in seeing happy faces of all ages coming from all directions to descend with single-minded purpose on the stadium, many dressed in their finest tweed and suede collections in fall colors of rust, yellow, orange, green and brown; on rare occasions there may be a lady or two wearing a fur piece, or sporting a big yellow mum as a corsage.

Once inside the stadium, the excitement of the game is often surpassed by the halftime shows of ceremony and pageantry put on by colorful marching bands playing halftime spirited arrangements, performing intricate maneuvers that sometimes rival Hollywood productions, and crowned by the singing of alma maters by the fans. This inscription, found on the outside walls of Memorial Stadium at the University of Illinois, might serve as a fitting benediction for all true stadium lovers everywhere:

> May this stadium ever be a temple of sportsmanship inspiring athletes of the University of Illinois and those who cheer them as they play, always to uphold the spirit and tradition of Illinois athletes and to play manfully and courageously to the last no matter what the odds—to play fairly within the spirit and the letter of the rules, to win without boasting and to lose without excuses—may these ideals of manliness, courage, and true sportsmanship find expression not only within the stadium, but throughout the life of the university. Above all, may the stadium always be the symbol of a great united university, drawing closer together in common bond and spirit all the men and women of Illinois.

Maybe the stadium is not quite a cathedral, but it is a truly hallowed place nonetheless!

THE ROAR OF THE CROWD

Football enthusiasts love to hear the roar of the crowd game after game, season after season, whether it is the roar of thousands at a high school or small college game, or the bigger roar of 100,000 or more in the largest stadiums.

As kickoff time for the game approaches, the bands and cheerleaders from both sides continue to whoop it up with cheers and songs, getting the fans involved through a crescendo of yells and applause as starting players are introduced by name, number, and position. At the moment of kickoff, it's just as though the whole world is waiting for this exact moment. There is no place in the whole universe you would rather be.

If good fortune smiles upon you, and the game seesaws back and forth with no distinct advantage to either side, it may be the very last play of the game that finally sends your body reeling with frenzy. So it happened in 1979 on the last Saturday in October in the University of Michigan Stadium. The score was tied 21–21 between the University of Michigan and Indiana University, with only six seconds left to play. Michigan had the ball near midfield. There was time for one last play, with a possible Rose Bowl bid hanging in the balance. Even though there were over 100,000 partisan fans in the stadium, there was dead silence and stillness at this moment. (For you must know that Indiana had been a two-touchdown underdog and had just rallied to tie the score with 55 seconds left on the clock.)

Michigan's reserve quarterback, John Wangler, took the snap from center, faded back beyond midfield, and threw the ball 20 yards to his speediest receiver, freshman Anthony Carter. He caught the ball on the run in the middle of the field, eluded a pair of tackles at the 20 yard line, and outran another last defender who made a desperate attempt at a flying tackle at the 5 yard line. The speedster just managed to free his left leg from the attempted tackle and high-stepped into the end zone as time expired. The sellout crowd of 104,832 burst into an instant roar that was at once completely deafening and acutely electrifying.

The crowd was ecstatic, slapping one another and tossing caps, while the teammates of Carter mobbed him and nearly crushed him in the end zone. The goalposts were nowhere to be found among the hordes of fans swarming onto the field. Thus, the final score stood: Michigan 27, Indiana 21—with no try for the extra point ever attempted, nor was one needed after such a thrilling finish.

The instant roar of this crowd of over 100,000 had said it all, and, among this writer's earthly experiences, stands to receive the decibel award for the loudest crowd roar ever heard.

It may be ultimately exceeded, however, when we hear the roar of that larger Heavenly Crowd upon gaining eternal victory!

WINTER OLYMPICS

The Winter Olympics are just the right medicine for the mid-winter doldrums. They give a lift to the spirit and send it soaring to capture some of the adventure and enchantment of the winter games. There is a special electricity in the air that you can feel before certain events take place, even if not there in person but watching by satellite television.

There are twelve broad categories of events, with some offering more beauty, excitement, spills, and thrills than others. Ski jumping, alpine skiing, and figure skating would seem to qualify as the top glamor attractions.

In the winter of 1980, I was fortunate enough to attend the Winter Olympics at Lake Placid, New York, a hauntingly beautiful village nestled in the Adirondack Mountains. I was able to secure tickets in advance to attend the 1500-meter speed skating event for men in the morning, and the women's figure skating short program in the afternoon. It was thrilling to see smooth, muscular Eric Heiden win his fourth gold medal in the 1500 meters amid softly falling snow in the outdoor oval rink (Heiden was destined to win every men's speed skating event at Lake Placid, handily winning five gold medals); to see spectators and athletes from thirty-seven nations dressed in multicolored woolen winter capes, sweaters, caps, ski jackets, ski pants—and boots of many designs; to see a host of brightly colored national flags furling in the breeze outside the Olympic Center; to see people of all ages trading pins, patches, posters, and souvenirs, buying gifts, munching on hot dogs and sipping hot chocolate—and saying a cheery "hello" to one another in a variety of languages as they passed (and sometimes bumped) into one another on the crowded, S-curved main street; to talk to fabled Jack Kelly and Sandra Worley; to hear the majestic names of Intervale, Mt. Van Hoevenberg, and Whiteface Mountain called over the loudspeaker in the center of town for bus departures to those skiing event places; and to witness the impressive Awards Ceremony in the evening on the ice of Mirror Lake.

For sheer color, international flavor, togetherness, personal closeups, and warm, friendly feeling, a day at the Winter Olympics is worth even more than the competition of the games, or knowing who may have won the medals.

In the Winter Olympics of 1984 in Sarajevo, Yugoslavia (the site must have been selected in part because of the melodious sound of the historic town's name—and fittingly arranged as a closing ceremony song), there

19

were strides made by the sports commentators in creating greater interest and appreciation for the less glamorous events like the luge, biathlon, and cross-country skiing. One commentary piece on cross-country skiing catapulted the event, normally thought of as a slow, tedious, painfully fatiguing individual contest, into the glamor category by labeling it among the best of aerobic exercises—right up there with swimming, jogging, and aerobic dancing. That's enough to give the spirit an extra lift, to know that cross-country skiing can now be thought of as a glamorous event in our culture. Even vicariously, one might easily imagine how taking a brisk daily walk in the neighborhood would now be turned into an "aerobic, olympic event" with a practiced longer stride of the legs and a longer swing of the arms to simulate the alternating ski pole push-offs.

Ski Jumping. This looks like a neat event to enter. Granted, there are some serious accidents on occasion, and people trying this event would make out better if God had made people with wings. Nevertheless, even without wings, ski jumpers report that it's "just like floating on a bed of air." What a grand feeling that must be!

Alpine Skiing. This exciting downhill event is freewheeling at its daring best, as mastered in the more recent past by the American "Wild Bill" Johnson at Sarajevo in 1984, by the Austrian Franz Klammerer at Innsbruck in 1976, and the Frenchman Jean-Claude Killy at Grenoble in 1968. Nor who could easily forget West Germany's Rosi Mittermaier and her exciting ski runs at Innsbruck in 1976. Many times during these runs the skiers were literally "flying through the air," sometimes landing in a frenzied manner, with one ski under control, and the other pointing skyward—attaining speeds of over 70 miles an hour while executing sharp curves and bends. A real test of all-out speed and courage!

Figure Skating. Now here's agility, beauty, grace, and elegance all combined in one event, often accompanied by musical selections that are moving in themselves, like selections from *Scheherazade, Bolero, Barnum,* "Memories," "America The Beautiful" (Ray Charles), and "Amazing Grace." The female skaters usually wear glittering, chiffon outfits that are flimsy enough to move in the breeze during the faster-moving free dance numbers.

Past American winners in figure skating seem easy to recall. Dick Button (twice), Hayes and David Jenkins—all were consecutive champions from 1948–1960. Among the female skaters, the ice queen winners were Tenley Albright in 1956, Carol Heiss in 1960, Peggy Fleming in 1968, and Dorothy Hamill in 1976. (Of course, Norwegian Sonja Henie was the first of the queens, and the grandest of them all—winning three gold medals.) It would appear that all these female gold medalists had two things in common beyond physical coordination: a beautiful figure and a pretty face.

Skating to Perfection. The ultimate achievement of perfection, however, was attained in the Winter Olympics of 1984. Jayne Torvill and Christopher Dean, an ice dancing pair from Great Britain, put on a dazzling display of ice dancing to the strains of Ravel's *Bolero*, receiving perfect scores of 6.0 on artistic impression from all nine judges for their free-dance program, something that had never occurred in Olympic competition. In addition, of their nine scores in the technical merit category, three were a perfect 6.0. The four-minute performance by the blonde couple was imaginative, romantic, luminous, and electrifying and included slow, bending movements and more dramatic movements that incorporated bits of gymnastics. One move saw Dean lean way back while skating backward with Torvill reclining on his extended leg. As the end of the *Bolero* performance approached, the couple were seen kissing one another, and performing a sensual, gradually building ballet that climaxed like an opera with both of them sprawled deathlike on the ice. A deeply moving experience!

"When it's done right," Torvill said, "it feels like the last breath of life has gone out of you."

In retrospect, Torvill and Dean appeared to glide effortlessly through their program, handling twists and turns deftly, smiling throughout. Their skating in complete unison and harmony appears so easy. Yet, a closer look will reveal that some basic principles of life are beautifully woven into their performance of aesthetic grace and skill.

• Self-discipline. According to their coach: "They practice ten to twelve hours each day, seven days a week, every week of the year." Comment: Think what that type of self-discipline could do in the spiritual realm whether you are practicing the life of prayer or promoting God's Kingdom on earth.

• Total commitment. In ice dancing, it is required that the ice dancing pair must skate with each other all the way through the number, never separating from one another more than five seconds at a time. It's as though the two perform in such perfect synchronization that they appear to be one. Comment: What a beautiful spiritual parallel in marriage: "A man will unite with his wife, and the two will become one" (Eph. 5:31, TEV). And if a total commitment is made to one another, as Torvill and Dean do in their dance, then more marriages would work out successfully.

21

• Perfection. The Biblical admonition to "be perfect" is seldom seen in human form on this earth. Torvill and Dean, through their single-minded self-discipline and their devoted total commitment to one another, are the best earthly example I know to show us how to achieve perfection (completeness). Comment: Winning the gold medal was not their biggest Olympic achievement, nor did it seem an adequate reward for their near-perfect performance. They were skating beyond the gold medal and into the triumphal spiritual realm where the integration of body, mind, and spirit to achieve a single-minded goal is the ultimate crowning fulfillment of living!

WHEN ATHLETES CRY

It is a moment that will remain locked forever in one's memory. It's the moment that John Cappelletti, former star running back of the Penn State Nittany Lions, received the Heisman Trophy as the nation's outstanding college football player in 1973. Before a battery of TV cameras and sports writers in New York City, John gave his brief acceptance speech, all the while crying unashamedly with tears that fell to the podium. He said he was accepting the trophy on behalf of his kid brother Joey who was at that moment fighting for his life with leukemia. He also said that he would give the Heisman Trophy to Joey who, in his weakened body of pain and suffering, had exhibited more qualities of courage and character while battling for life than he had with his strong body on the football field while battling for touchdowns.

There were not many dry eyes in the assemblage that night when John Cappelletti so spontaneously, so obviously heartfelt, humbled himself before a national TV audience like an innocent child, and in the process became a giant of a man. Joey must have been proud of his big brother John that night for baring his soul on his behalf. It was a simple, pure, and true act of brotherly love.

Others may recall a riveting moment in the 1984 Summer Olympics when Jeff Blatnick, a hulk of a man, won the gold medal in the super-heavyweight division of Greco-Roman wrestling. As the referee raised Jeff's arm in triumph, Jeff dropped to his knees, clasped his hands, and raised his eyes heavenward.

What a sight to see this giant down on his knees to give thanks to God—amid sweat and tears streaming down his face. For, you see, Blatnick's triumph arrived just two years after he had been diagnosed as having Hodgkin's disease, and having his spleen removed. Jeff, after winning the gold medal, wanted to thank God, his parents, and all the people who had seen him through his cancer ordeal, rather than strut around as a conquering hero with his fists in the air.

Other old-timers may recall the gut-wrenching emotional moment when Lou Gehrig, the handsome "Iron Man" first baseman of the New York Yankees, stood at home plate in Yankee Stadium in 1941, waved his baseball cap across his frail body that had been struck with what has since been called "Lou Gehrig's disease" (nerve deterioration), and bade his huge crowd of friends farewell. There were tears in his eyes, for he knew he had played his last game as a Yankee. Everybody in Yankee Stadium must have been crying right along with Lou on that unforgettable day when he said: "I may have been given a bad break, but I have an awful lot to live for. With all this, I consider myself the luckiest man on the face of the earth."

(Lou died in 1941, at age 38, after having played in a record 2,130 consecutive games.)

Amateur and professional athletes never stand taller as heroes than when we see them cry unashamedly.

"WE'RE NO. 1!"

Everybody likes to be a winner, or be associated with a winner—whether it is in sports, politics, or warfare. We want our team, our side, our nation to come in first. And what's even more heady, we somehow manage to delude ourselves into believing that "our side" won as a direct result of our having rooted for them. Out of such giddy misconceptions, it is no small wonder that many of us "grow up" to become fanatic hero worshipers of teams and superstar personalities; and the longer our team remains No. 1, the more frenetic, overbearing, and unlovable we become.

Then, too, many of us have become painfully aware over a period of years and decades that the team, politician, or country that is "at the top" for the present may just as quickly become a loser, fall out of favor, lose power, and even in time become just another underdog.

Do you remember the days (1936–1956) when the New York Yankees were almost unbeatable? Or when the Pittsburgh Steelers were Super Bowl champs four times within six years (1975–1980)? Both teams have had their share of losing years since then.

Sometimes the opposite occurs, as we recall the total defeat of Germany and Japan in World War II, and their subsequent rise to become two of the world's leading economic powers today.

Since sports teams often become a way of escape for us from the perplexing nitty-gritty problems of the world, it becomes all the more urgent to follow a team that is No. 1, or has a good chance of reaching the top soon. We want to experience "the thrill of victory" rather than "the agony of defeat."

Yet, there is something to be said for the other side of the coin, although learning to cheer lustily for a losing team "at the bottom" takes some uncommon soul-searching to effect such a dramatic change in attitude and spirit.

The sports enthusiasts from England have maintained for centuries that "it's easier to lose graciously than to win graciously." Accordingly, rooting for a losing team must bring greater rewards in building desirable character traits than does cheering on a winner.

So I've decided to finally make the switch!

This coming fall I'm going to root "with all my might" for Gainesville High School in Missouri to win its first game in seven years. Their record was 0–57; and only twice in the last three years have the Gainesville Bulldogs led at halftime. In those two games, the coach theorized that "they didn't finally win because they didn't know how to handle a lead going into the second half."

Come on, sports fans! Aren't you tired of always wanting to be No. 1? No. 1 teams don't need you anyway. Go where you're needed.

Let's get on the Bulldog bandwagon and root for a real legitimate underdog and build some worthwhile character traits in the process—like long-suffering and suffering long.

NUDISM

We're all nudists to a degree; we were all born nude, we all take show-
ers and baths in the nude, and we sometimes sleep in the nude on warm
nights.

Other nudists go a step farther and sunbathe in the nude at nudist camps
and sunshine parks. They seem to have overcome their fear of being seen
in the nude by others outside their immediate household—and can even
eat, play volleyball, and converse with perfect strangers without feeling
the need for "covering up."

Clothing manufacturers and clothing stores would generally not be in
favor of wholesale nudism, nor would certain moralists. But there are
some things to be said for nudism (being naked) that seem to be embodied
in psychologically sound principles of good mental health (and spiritual
growth). These are my observations:

All attempts at cover-up are gone.

All pretenses are gone.

The naked truth is revealed—because there is nothing more to hide.

Most vanities disappear, especially those involving clothes.

Without clothing one appears destitute—in need of outside help.

Conversations are more open and honest, for there is less need to
rationalize.

One feels less need to justify oneself, to inflate one's own ego, to
gain status.

Humbleness is generally the accepted order of the day—with no
need of violence.

There's more to be said for nudism than having a body totally immersed
in sunshine and an "allover" suntan.

CHAPTER II

IN SEARCH OF SELF-CONTROL

When I want to do good, I don't; and when I try not to do wrong, I do it anyway.

—Rom. 7:19 (TLB)

The person who lives in fear has not yet had his love perfected.

—1 John 4:18b (P)

ALL YOU CAN EAT!!!???

It is reported that some of the Hunza people in the high mountains of Asia live to the age of 140. Those not reaching 140 usually die of old age and not of diseases.

Do you believe that the Hunza people live such long lives by practicing health habits that include "All You Can Eat" meal signs? Definitely not. Doctors who have studied their longevity secrets report that they have relatively clean bloodstreams in large part because they eat moderate amounts of fresh fruits and vegetables, dried apricots, nuts and grains, soybeans, legumes, and yogurt. They drink lots of water and avoid overindulgences.

Do you avoid overindulgence? Or do you frequent restaurants where large placard signs above the serving lines read "All You Can Eat!"?

Having been in such a "pig-out" restaurant recently, the images are all too vivid. People of all ages, many with waistlines already protruding into overhanging stomachs, both male and female, wait in line at the salad bar to build themselves a compost heap topped with rich creamy dressings— then back again to wait in line for an array of meats and gravies—on to another line for buttered, highly seasoned vegetables, mashed potatoes, and more thick gravies—and finally to the most coveted line of all, the revolving dessert carousels featuring dozens of pies with whipped creams, cakes with sweetened icings of all colors, varied cheeses, and twenty-eight flavors of calorie-laden rich ice cream. If you're a true-blue, fun-eating patron of the "All You Can Eat" club, you'll balance several plates in both hands and take at least six desserts to top off your stomach's fill-up, and also get your "money's worth" at the one fixed price.

By ironic contrast, later in the evening in this same "good and plenty" restaurant downstairs, there was a seminar being conducted on "How to Keep Healthy and Happy." Here moderation in eating was stressed, along with avoidance of fat and sugar. Emphasis was placed on eating foods containing proteins and carbohydrates, and meat three times a week. The white meats of turkey or chicken, and fish were highly recommended, as was the eating of fresh fruits and vegetables—particularly dark leafy vegetables such as broccoli, spinach, and romaine lettuce. Selective foods recommended to buy were plain yogurt, whole grain cereals, nuts and seeds, garlic, okra, sprouts, celery, carrots, and lemons. "Eating the proper balanced foods can be your best preventive medicine in staying well," we were told.

A delightful, colorful drink was served to all participants that was mixed in a blender and contained carrots (bright orange), celery (bright green), and lemons (bright yellow). Such a beautiful concoction has got to be good for you.

On leaving the seminar, I noticed that most of the participants already had waistlines that were smaller than their hips, undoubtedly as a result of having had some previous years of "lean cuisine."

Someone has said that if we can't gain victory through self-control over something as relatively simple as the type and amount of food we put into our bodies, how can we gain victory in the more difficult problems of life.

Smorgasbords? Family-type restaurants that fill dishes as quickly as they are emptied?? Fixed one-price restaurants where you are encouraged to "eat all you want"??? Houses of gluttony???? Heaven forbid!

Have you forgotten that your body is the temple of the Holy Spirit, who lives in you, and is God's gift to you? (1 Cor. 6:19, P.)

Whatever you eat or drink should be done to bring glory to God. (1 Cor. 10:31, P, [my paraphrase].)

THE MIND AND IRRATIONAL FEARS

We all long to have a mind that thinks clearly, is able to separate the important things from the unimportant (the wheat from the chaff), and draw sensible conclusions for a future course of action when difficulties arise; a mind that is single-minded and stable, yet can weigh multiple alternatives; a mind that is unhurried, uncluttered, unconfused, and so at peace that it sleeps easily at night and functions like a nimble computer during the day.

Minds do not become sharp and focused automatically, or without cultivated care. The oft-repeated phrase regarding computer programming and printouts—"garbage in, garbage out"—is graphically true in terms of the functioning mind.

A neurosurgeon recently discovered that within the brain of a human being there is a small section that serves as an absolute recorder of all past thoughts, feelings, and experiences. A reputable hypnotist can clearly demonstrate the truth of this finding by taking hypnotized people, through the power of suggestion and their subconscious minds, back to their childhood days and have them recall and act out events just as experienced many years ago. If the events recalled were happy ones—like seeing Christmas presents under the tree at age three—the hypnotized person will react accordingly. But if a recalled event involved a negative, fearful experience—like losing a father through death or divorce at age six—the reaction will be one of stress and anxiety.

It's just as though all one's meaningful experiences were duly recorded on the microfilm portion of the brain, like a scroll that can then be unrolled at a given command for recall and review.

Reactions to specific events in life do help shape and condition the mind. The death of a spouse, divorce, or the death of a close family member are guaranteed to create a certain amount of stress in all individuals, and load the mind with extra uncertainties. At such times, the mind needs to have an abundance of faith fed to it, and needs to have its confines loaded with love and the other fruits of the Spirit of God in order to adjust and make the necessary changes so that soft landings can ensue.

It is the irrational fears that frequently occupy too many adult minds, however high their native intelligence, that should give us cause for greater concern in our society. Such unwarranted irrational fears in adults produce unreasonable mind sets that greatly interfere with their normal thinking processes, cause them to jump to unwarranted conclusions and often make them look foolish and absurd.

As Jack Mabley of the Chicago Tribune Service has said:

> Most of us fear the wrong things for the wrong reasons. It's far riskier to step into your bathtub than to step onto an airliner. It's more dangerous to ride a bicycle around the block once a week than it is to live next door to a nuclear power plant. We may not like cigarettes, but we do not fear them, yet they are responsible for 350,000 deaths every year.

Apparently risk taking and irrational fears are related to irrational psychological perceptions and faulty mind sets: (1) If the event feared is one big single event (like an air crash or a Three Mile Island type of disaster), we fear it more than separate, scattered events like auto accidents and cigarette-related deaths. (2) If the risk taken is under our direct control (for example, when we drive an auto, ski, skydive, or smoke cigarettes), we deny its risk compared to risks taken when we are not in control (flying in an airplane, or driving with someone else at the car wheel). (3) If the risks involved are familiar dangers, no matter how great the danger, it becomes hard to fear them (taking heroin or cocaine, smoking marijuana, and having promiscuous sexual partners). Unfamiliar threats, though, are almost impossible not to fear.

The media, who should possess sounder minds and know better, are not exempt from taking "irrational fear" positions, and putting dangerous situations in habitually scary perspective.

When all the aforementioned three elements are put together, one can better understand why the deck is stacked, for example, against the nuclear power industry, in part because so many irrational people fear it—including certain elements of the media who seem to thrive on helping perpetuate the irrational fears of highly emotional, insecure people.

But the mind is made for rational thinking—we have minds that usually think positive, optimistic thoughts, that think through all sides of an issue, and are held in a ready state of relaxed alertness, for clear decision making. We need to guard our minds and the quality of its input and output—just like computers—and to be freed of irrational fears.

If the input data going into our brain is biased, skewed with false motives, and filled with irrational fears, then the output received will be in kind. If, however, our input has to do with the things of rationality and reasonableness and intelligent understanding, then the output will be in similar measure.

In a spiritual sense, we are told in Rom. 8:5 (KJV) that those who walk "after the flesh do mind the things of the flesh; but they that are after the Spirit, the things of the Spirit." In like manner, if the input into our minds

33

has to do with the things of the Spirit, then the output will be the things of the Spirit.

In Phil. 4:8 (KJV) we are exhorted to fill our minds with thoughts of things that are "true, honest, just, pure, lovely, of good report, [of] virtue and [of] praise." This is the mind set for the input and output of the things of the Spirit—and for conquering irrational fears.

"I KNEW I SHOULDN'T DO IT...BUT I 'DOOD' IT ANYWAY!"

This oft-repeated comment by comedian Red Skelton became a trademark of his radio and TV shows. It could also serve well as a trademark to identify where a lot of us are at, and how we can so easily be deluded in our thinking. We even read in the Scriptures: "For what I know is wrong—that I keep on doing! (Rom. 7:19b, NIV, [my paraphrase]).

From a would-be dieter: "I know I shouldn't eat sweets, but I just love Hershey's Chocolate Kisses so much that I eat a dishful at a time."

From an alcoholic: "I know my family wants me to stop drinking, but I need it to get me going in the morning, and get me through the day."

From a compulsive gambler: "I know the odds of winning the lottery are against me, but I just might win a million if I play long enough."

From a convicted lawbreaker: "I know that stealing doesn't pay, except that I didn't expect to get caught."

From a patient with cirrhosis of the liver: "I knew that the doctor wanted me to stop drinking my 12 cups of black coffee a day, but I would rather die than give up my enjoyment of coffee."

From a lung cancer victim: "I knew smoking was harmful, but I didn't think it would harm me, so I continued smoking."

From a drug addict: "I knew taking cocaine was habit-forming, but I didn't think it would hook someone as strong as me, so I kept on taking it."

From a divorced parent: "I knew 'stepping out' on my spouse was not the right thing to do, but I got more attention and compliments from other partners, so I continued playing the field until I got trapped by someone else."

What is the answer to these and other delusions we all have in some form at various times in our lives?

In Rom. 12:1–2 (NEB) we read, *I implore you by God's mercy to offer your very selves to Him: a living sacrifice, dedicated and fit for His acceptance, the worship offered by mind and heart. Adapt yourselves no longer to the pattern of this present world...*

To arrive at this optimum result may require a heap of helping from understanding and compassionate friends and relatives along the way, as well as appreciative church and community support groups. But the most important thing for each of us to understand and accept is that we don't want to be deluded, and if we are enslaved by some strong delusion, to honestly admit our entrapment to ourselves and others and to seek spiritual counseling so that we can comprehend more fully the total picture before us.

Therefore, since we are surrounded by so great a cloud of witnesses, let us lay aside every weight (delusion), as well as every sin to which we cling and that so easily entangles us, and let us run with perseverance the race marked out for us, looking to Jesus, the author and finisher of our faith. (Heb. 12:1–2a, RSV, NIV, NKJV.)

PROCRASTINATION

Any of us who have ever tried to lead a more spiritual life here on earth can well identify with this terse, albeit true, Bible verse found in Romans 7:19a—*"For the good that I would, I do not"* (KJV).

Many of us can lay out five-year plans in our jobs with ease, but have difficulty putting into practice even modest one-year goals when it comes to planning and executing any spiritual goals we may have set for ourselves, such as: (1) reading the Bible through in a year (three chapters a day); (2) visiting shut-ins on a monthly basis; (3) having a regular time for daily prayer; or (4) extending our spiritual fellowship.

It's much more difficult to discipline ourselves to do something on a regular basis than to slip up frequently, and erroneously excuse ourselves by saying, "Well, at least what I half-accomplished is more than what most of my colleagues do; they haven't even made an effort to begin."

To succeed in anything, such as improving one's golf score or tennis game, a full commitment needs to be made to the task at hand, requiring self-discipline, perseverance—and an organized timetable. Questions such as "Do I have to do what I want to today?" are to be asked only by indolent procrastinators.

But just get serious about starting any such spiritual self-improvement program, and see how quickly you will be tempted to procrastinate and "put off its implementation" until tomorrow. Not today...Not now...Tomorrow...Tomorrow...

Some may say that the most insidious sin in the world is pride. For many of us, *procrastination* is just as insidious and even more persistently devilish. Most of us will need the help of the Holy Spirit to conquer this roadblock to joyful inner peace.

FEARS AND MORE FEARS

If one were to be so inclined, there are enough fears being voiced in a week to fill our minds all of the waking hours and even manage a few sleepless nights as well.

Fears about new foods and medicines that have been found to cause cancer, fears about inheriting certain diseases, fears about the spread of AIDS (for which no cure has been found), fears about blood transfusions and their possible ill effects on immune systems.

Fears about being able to go to sleep.

Fears of speaking before an audience, meeting people, going outside, high places, closets, elevators.

Fears about snakes, rats, poison ivy, bee stings.

Fears about air pollution, water shortages, drought, lightning, hurricanes, earthquakes, and other natural disasters.

Fears about accidents and disasters on air, land, and sea—airline crashes, expressway accidents, chemical spills, nuclear plant malfunctions.

Fears about unemployment, a stock market crash, bankruptcies, loss of social security, muggers, car bombings, terrorism, and nuclear warfare.

Fears of divorce, being alone, being disliked by others.

Fears of failure in general, and of God in particular.

And the ultimate fear—death.

Most of our fears concern the unknown future—fear about what an uncertain tomorrow may bring. If the telephone rings, will it be bad news?

How can these fears be brought under control?

Through love, love, love!!!

God did not give us a spirit of fear; but of power, and of *love*, and of a sound mind. (2 Tim. 1:7, NIV, KJV, italics mine.)

There is no fear in love, but perfect love casts out fear, for fear has torment. This means that the person who lives in fear has not yet had his love perfected. (1 John 4:18, NKJV, P.)

God is Love, and anyone who lives in love lives in God, and God lives in him. (1 John 4:16, TLB, NIV.)

My prayer for the fearful is David's prayer found in Ps. 34:4—"I sought the Lord, and he *heard* me, and delivered me from *all* my fears" (KJV, italics mine).

DECISIONS, DECISIONS, DECISIONS

"Multitudes, multitudes in the valley of decision!" (Joel 3:14a, KJV.)

What an apt description for most of us in our daily life. We're continually surrounded with having to make a plethora of decisions—in the valleys or on the hilltops—from early in the morning to late at night.

We must decide when to awake in the morning, and when to retire at night—when to work and when to play—when to joke and when to be serious-minded, and give answers to all the who, what, when, where, how, how much, and why questions.

Nothing is more crucial to the success of our earthly pilgrimage than making the right decisions at the right times—knowing what is best for all concerned before determining a course of action.

There are a few things in life about which we do not have the freedom of choice: our birth date, our ancestry, our birth order in the family (even being an only child), and our death date (save suicide).

Beyond that, God has ordained that we should have free will to decide what actions we should take in our daily lives both in small things and on larger issues. We are not puppets on a string, yet there is a delicate fine line between exercising your own will and doing God's will.

Here are some daily choices to be made that many would consider routine, yet they are vital to your well-being, and essential in helping to discipline yourself if you are to make the right decisions on larger issues:

- Eating the right foods
- Planning balanced meals
- Exercising properly
- Wearing attractive clothes
- Doing needed household chores
- Shopping carefully
- Managing time wisely ("When we are young and look forward, time seems to march so slowly, but when we look back how swiftly time goes by."—Leslie B. Flynn)

While mowing the lawn, I sometimes think about the mundane things of life that need decisions, like making a list of the football games I plan to attend during the football season, and which ones I will see on television; and indulging in that wonderful late Saturday afternoon pastime of watching the scores come in from all over the country on "College Scoreboard."

At other times when mowing the lawn, I think about the deep things of life, the "what-if" questions that demand a response: What if there was no God? What if there was no resurrection (Easter)? What if Heaven was unheard of? What if there was no hope of eternal life beyond death? What if there was no Bible? (I'd search out all the libraries to find such a book that contained the message of eternal life.) What if God's Holy Spirit was not present on earth?

Making the wrong choices usually brings grief—whether it is playing the lotteries (with the chance of becoming an instant millionaire as the come-on, and with most people overvaluing their chance of gain and undervaluing their chance of loss)—or people making the wrong judgments about themselves, wherein they make themselves their standard of measurement and judge their own value from comparisons with other people (rather than using God's standards for measuring themselves)—or allowing vain, impure thoughts to get lodged in one's mind, resulting in intimate sex with the wrong person.

Making the right choices usually brings inner joy—whether in a career, marriage partner, house, car, children, pets, financial investments, church affiliation, or volunteer organizations. Here are some major decisions to be made that could be considered crucial choices (you provide the yes and no answers):

• Do I know what God's will is for my life as to vocation, geographic location, marriage, children?

• Have I made an unconditional surrender of my life to God?

• Is there any sin in my life that has not yet been confessed?

• Do I have any damaged relationships with others that need mending?

• Do I believe that Jesus Christ is God's revealed Son?

• Am I being continually guided by God's Spirit?

• Is there a disciplined quiet time to read the Bible, meditate, and pray?

Everything in this world should take a backseat to knowing God—to being God's man or woman—for the sake of yourself and others you meet.

Elizabeth Achtemeier writes in her book, *The Committed Marriage* (Westminster Press, 1976): "By Christian I mean those faithful ones who, through weeks and months and years of disciplined practice in prayer and study and worship, have absorbed the Word of God into their bones and

40

have come to know the presence of God with them as a constant reality....*They are the persons on whom one can depend*, persons whom one knows will always try to do the right thing, as that right is defined in Scriptures."

Joni Eareckson, who became a quadriplegic as a teenager in a swimming pool accident, says straightforwardly in her book, *Joni* (Zondervan Press, 1976): "Before my accident I didn't 'need' Christ. Now I needed him desperately. When I had been on my feet, it never seemed important that he be part of my *decision making*—what party to go to, whether to go to a friend's house or a football game. It didn't seem that he would even be interested in such insignificant things. But, now that my life was reduced to the basic life-routines, he was a part of it because he cared for me. He was, in fact, my only dependable reality."

MONEY, MONEY, MONEY

There is no topic more universally discussed than money. It seems you either have too much or too little.

"How can I make *more* money?" is asked all too frequently by most of us. We never seem quite satisfied with what we have. Even if there is no good reason why we *need* more money, it almost becomes an obsession to want more—to make a game or chase of it—as in gambling, buying lottery tickets, or playing the stock market.

The Bible, often misquoted on this point, says that it is the *love* of money, not money itself, that is the root of all evil (see 1 Tim. 6:10).

Most of us would need to plead guilty on both counts: we want more money, and once we get it, we're not satisfied; we want more and more—if for no other reasons than to brag about our monetary successes to others, or to buy more worldly possessions to show others, or perchance to get our names in the papers. We really don't need more money for the basic essentials of living.

If each of us were confined to living alone on an island, there would be no need or desire to make more money since there would be no one to hear about our successes, see our newly bought possessions, or read about us in the entertainment, sports, financial, or society pages.

It has been said cynically that many of us spend our lives doing work that we don't like, to make money we don't need, to buy things we don't need, in order to impress people we dislike.

Many of us who are tempted to get more and more money are also plagued by the temptation to get it as fast as we can—the instant-rich syndrome. The chance to become an instant millionaire is the big attraction of the lotteries and the gambling casinos. The high-risk entrepreneur in the business world hopes to make millions; if not instantly, then in a few years. If you're not a millionaire by the age of thirty, you're traveling in the slow lanes and not using all of your "smarts" to outwit your competitors.

In sports-crazed America, football and basketball players, if superstars in college, can become instant millionaires in their early twenties before ever playing one professional game if they have aggressive agents and sign with the teams having flauntingly wealthy owners.

Entertainers command even higher salaries than sports figures, although they may not get them as quickly. It is said that Johnny Carson pulls down $1.5 million *a month* for his occasional appearances on "The Tonight Show."

Someone has teasingly suggested that if you really want to get rich quickly—in thirty days or less—get one penny and have it double each day for thirty days. This simple strategy will net you over $5 million after only thirty days.

There is another condition in our society that helps to put money matters in further perspective—it is that most of us are judged by the amount of money we have, not by our sterling inner character traits. "He (or she) makes good money" is often the most telling thing we can say about someone. We seem to measure a person's worth or degree of success in the world by that statement. Seldom do we hear "He (or she) is a loving, caring person," or "He (or she) really takes the time to help others" in lieu of the more prevalent assessment of a person's monetary earnings.

Accumulating piles of money, whether instantly or by taking the more circuitous route of long preparation and hard work, or "being at the right place at the right time" when job openings occur, or making shrewd investments, or through inheritance—whatever—I've been told by those who "have it" that figuring out how to dispose of your money while still living, particularly if you want to continue to exert some earthly control over it (a natural inclination), often presents more problems than did the prior accumulation of the wealth.

But is that all there is to life—the scrambling and rushing to get more and more money as fast as possible—even at the expense of others?

Thankfully, there is a flip side to this *greediness* for more and more money.

There are many people who make money the old-fashioned way—they earn it by working steadily at unglamorous jobs year after year, content with receiving just enough money to provide for the necessities of life and later retirement.

Blessed are the people who are contented with the amount of money they are making and receiving; and blessed are they who enjoy spending it as much as they enjoy getting it; and doubly blessed are those who enjoy giving their money away to help others, even more than they enjoy receiving it. They are helping to fulfill the Biblical example stated in Acts 20:35: "It is more blessed to give than to receive" (KJV).

Happy are the persons who have learned to tithe their monies, and to plan as diligently for its wise distribution as they have for its eager acquisition. Some persons in the $20,000 to $30,000 income bracket have been known to tithe 30% or more of their adjusted gross income, and to make contributions to as many as forty different charity organizations by December 31 of each year. Others have learned to give through making faith promises to God, not knowing at the time how they would get the money to give as promised, but depending on God to receive it at the due time and in the right amount.

Prayerful decision making is needed to choose among the hundreds of worthy charitable causes and organizations desirous of your money. Starting with sizeable love gifts to your own church or synagogue, wise choices will bring rich rewards of inner peace and joy in the Spirit. There can be no greater satisfaction in money matters than to know that the giving away of your monies freely, without strings, to help others is the will of God for you.

As Jesus said in the Sermon on the Mount: "Do not store up for yourselves treasures on earth, where moth and rust destroy, and where thieves break in and steal. But store up for yourselves treasures in Heaven, where moth and rust do not destroy, and where thieves do not break in and steal. For where your treasure is, there your heart will be also." (Matt. 6:19–21, NIV.)

So let us eagerly desire to give our money away cheerfully to help others, especially since we know that God loves a cheerful giver! (See 2 Cor. 9:7.)

OUT OF CONTROL

It's said of some athletes, even the best superstars, that on certain "bad days" they seem to be playing "out of control." The baseball pitcher's throws to the batter are wild and completely out of the strike zone, while hitters "in a slump" will swing at bad pitches and be off balance. Basketball players will sometimes play "out of control" by trying too hard to do it all by themselves, and taking poor shots that never even hit the rim of the basket. Golfers will lose their rhythmic swing and hit slices to the right and hooks to the left. Downhill skiers often ski to the limit, right on the edge of control, and sometimes ski "out of control" and take a spill.

There are times in our personal lives when things seem to get totally out of control. Despite our best efforts to remain "in the groove," some days turn out to be a series of adversities from dawn to dusk. Nothing seems to go right—a faulty light switch, a flat tire on the car, a missed appointment, a letter of inquiry from the IRS, a larger-than-anticipated (nonitemized) plumbing bill, a disgruntled spouse, a confrontation at the office, a threatened strike by employees at work, a road detour, complaints by children, a rabbit eating vegetables in the garden, a steep drop in the stock market, a neighboring dog's deposit on the front lawn—any random combination of these incidents is enough to ruin one's day.

On such days of misfortunes, one has to learn to be thankful for the smaller things in life that have not gone haywire, and are still "in place" and under control: the house is still standing at the same address, the front entrance doorway has not moved, the kitchen appliances are still working, the clothes closet still has your favorite clothes, and the bathroom still has its familiar location, with the toothbrush in its customary spot.

Sometimes, however, what we may consider "bad days" or "lost days" with little hope in sight, may seem relatively small with the passage of time, or when viewed in the perspective of larger world events that at times engulf us. These events seem not only to be "bigger than life" and "beyond our control," but are "out of control" for many people at the time of their happening.

Such a list of "out of control" occurrences came within a relatively short two hours of morning news in early summer of 1985 following release of the thirty-nine Beirut hostages held for seventeen days, and drove home to me the mighty force of the meaning of the phrase, "out of control."

News Item 1: There have been over 200 terrorist bombings of business buildings abroad since 1970.

News Item 2: Dozens of fires in nine Western states destroyed over 200,000 acres and over 200 houses.

News Item 3: Israel's inflation is at an annual 400% rate in 1985.

News Item 4: The interest on the U.S. federal debt is mounting rapidly to $8,000,000 an hour.

News Item 5: New York City has only enough water to last six months under present rainfall conditions.

News Item 6: The worldwide drought of 1985 could result in the potential deaths of 100,000,000 people.

With news events at home and abroad filling us daily with items that seem to be increasingly beyond our control and "out of control," it behooves us as individuals to stay "in control" as much as possible and to be a source of encouragement, comfort, and hope to those about us.

May the God of hope fill you with all joy and peace in believing, so that by the power of the Holy Spirit you may abound with hope. (Rom. 15:13, RSV.)

IRRITABILITY VS. RIGHTEOUS INDIGNATION

Some people never seem to get irritated at anything. They always seem so "cool, calm, and collected," even under trying circumstances, and never raise their voices in anger or protest.

There are others who might be tempted to be irritable over certain happenings, but remembering they were taught that they should always act like mature ladies and gentlemen, they would prefer to use the term "righteous indignation" to justify their ruffled feathers.

Then there are those of us who are willing to admit the necessity for exercising our feelings in both categories with forthright aplomb, and without any apologies. However, as Dorothy Storck, columnist for the *Philadelphia Inquirer* points out, a distinction needs to be made early on between what is an irritation and what is righteous indignation. She writes in the October 13, 1983, edition:

> Irritation is the feeling you get when you go to a public washroom and find it filthy, or you find all the doors locked until you produce a dime. Righteous indignation should be reserved for those things that have the weightier force of public opinion—such as lenient judges, the IRS, welfare fraud, and communists.
>
> I think there is use for instant irritation, instantly expressed. Not a lengthy exchange of invective that may get the adrenalin flowing but that tends to obscure the message. I mean the sharp expression of displeasure, adroitly delivered, with the option of moving out of range instantly. An apt expression of irritability ought put a stop to such nonsense that, gone unchecked, could well cause irritation for the next person to come along. Looked at this way irritability is positively altruistic.

In this altruistic spirit, here is a partial list of things I will continue to get irritated about by speaking up when the occasion demands:

• Neighborhood dogs that do "their business" on everyone's property but their owner's.

• People who push piles of snow from their private driveways onto public streets.

• Smokers in restaurants who allow their smoke to drift across your table.

• Multiple mailings of identical materials from organizations due to miniscule computer variations of your mailing address.

• The thoughtless littering of streets, sidewalks, lawns, parks, and countryside with candy wrappers, bottle tops, can opener lids, broken glass, cigarette butts, sticky gum, and sputum.

• Municipal leaders who become self-righteous and self-serving.

Here is also a partial list of appropriate subjects for displaying righteous indignation periodically:

• Violence on TV
• Nuclear weapons buildup
• Terrorist attacks on innocent people
• Neighborhood crimes (burglaries, holdups, vandalism)
• Drunk drivers
• Pollution of the air and water
• Choose one: (1) abortion; (2) pornography; (3) homosexuality

CHAPTER III

GROWING UP—BODY, MIND, AND SPIRIT

Trust in the Lord with all your heart
   and lean not on your own understanding;
In all your ways acknowledge him,
   and he will direct your paths.

                              —Proverbs 3:5–6 (NIV)

But the Counselor, the Holy Spirit...will teach you
[believers] *all things*.

                       —John 14:26 (NIV, italics mine)

NO BIGGER THAN A PINHEAD

Did you know that all of us began our existence at fertilization, with the joining of a male sperm (one of millions) with a female egg, a united single cell that was formed at the moment of conception, and that at conception we were no bigger than a small pinhead?

Isn't it amazing that in a short time this minute single cell soon divides into two cells, then a body of four cells appears, then eight, sixteen, thirty-two, and so on and on?

And isn't it completely fascinating to be told that during the first four weeks of the continuous division of the cells of the embryo that the various bodily structures and organs are already being formed and that the heart is already beating?

By the end of eight weeks the human embryo is about an inch long, and the head, facial parts, and the extremities can be readily distinguished. There is already a brain, and fingerprints on the hands have also been formed—and will never change, except for size.

And by the sixteenth week the embryo is about five inches long, yet already possesses a definitely human form, with fingers and toes fully separated and having soft nails, and the external genitals are already well formed so that the sex can be determined.

The growth of the fetus continues until the end of the fortieth week, which is usually the time of birth. The average length of the newborn infant is about twenty inches, and generally weighs about seven pounds.

Isn't it absolutely awesome that during this prenatal period of growth all the millions of necessary parts for our body are being formed to operate in complete harmony—and even more miraculous, that all parts of our body grow in exact symmetrical proportions—so that the left leg is no longer than the right leg, and the arms don't grow faster than the legs, and the right eye matches the left eye? And that all cells in the embryo know where to go and what to become? And that each of us has an inner, personally programmed genetic chart that determines our ultimate height, frame, physical features, and mental capacities?

"The Spirit of God has made me, and the breath of the Almighty gives me life." (Job 33:4, NIV.)

The birth of a baby and its later growth and development of body, mind, and spirit from infancy through adulthood has to be the grand climax design of all creation—even greater than the sun, moon, and stars (whose creations are also well beyond the complete comprehension of most of us). After all, didn't God, the master architect, create us in His own image?

What could be better than that?

No bigger than a pinhead at conception, but what potential lies hidden in that tiny, mysteriously sealed pregnant seed—what a loaded, prepackaged, preordained, well-protected pinhead—that will quietly and quickly burst in size from one cell to trillions of cells before birth.

"Know that the Lord is God; it is He that has made us, and not we ourselves." (Ps. 100:3, NKJV.)

Despite whatever earthly accomplishments and pride we may have accumulated along life's way, and however big and tall we may become physically, it's a humbling experience to remember that at one time we were all no bigger than a pinhead.

WHAT MAKES PEOPLE TICK?

What is it that causes people to have distinctive characteristics that make each person a unique individual, with a life-style that is different from any other person on earth—and yet at the same time to have needs, hopes, and aspirations that are common to the whole human race, and bind us together?

It would seem that our distinctive individual uniqueness is determined by a conglomerate mix of *genes* (heredity and family trees determine the color of our eyes, hair, skin, sex, and other physical and mental features); plus a healthy sprinkling of *family relationships* (parents, grandparents, other family ties) over which the growing infant and child has little choice or control (the family is the setting for experiencing initial emotional and social contacts and impressions—for feeling loved and wanted, or unloved and rejected); plus a host of other outside forces over which the developing child likewise has little control—*world conditions* (warfare, depressions) and *cultural influences* (national, regional, ethnic).

It takes several years of growing up before a child begins to exert some control over his environment, begins to make friends on his own, and engages in neighborhood activities.

It is in the interaction of the growing individual with his environment that *personality traits* (talents, abilities) are developed; and it is in the growing commitment to a set of values and beliefs that *character traits* are formed.

In adolescence, it is important that the youth chooses *friends* wisely, develops *hobbies*, and applies his mind and heart to *instruction*. (Prov. 4:13 says: "Hold on to instruction, do not let it go; guard it well, for it is your life."—NIV.)

Later on, continued wise choices will need to be made concerning possible *colleges, marriage partners, homes, jobs, expanding friendships*, and *community activities*.

With such an influx of currents and crosscurrents from birth through adulthood, and with millions of other individuals having their own set of predetermined factors and conditioning experiences along the way of life, it's simply amazing that we grow up in one whole piece at all, and that we continue to tick, if on only half the cylinders at times—for 20 years...40 years...60 years...80 years....

What keeps us from blowing up completely, body and soul, in our complex interpersonal relationships? What keeps us sane in the multitudinous ebbs and flows of history's currents, some of which are decidedly devilish

52

and insane? What keeps us from becoming unglued and straying from a relatively even keel as we make hundreds of choices each day?

The creative force that keeps us from splitting apart into shattered pieces, that gives us a center of gravity, that gives us a basically positive, optimistic outlook on life rather than a negative, pessimistic one, that gives us a hope beyond death, and that binds us together as one on this earth (as in times of natural disasters, national catastrophes, and personal tragedies and losses) is the *Love of God* as manifested by the Holy Spirit and fulfilled in Jesus Christ.

People tick best, however individualized their personalities and lifestyles, when they are united with others in a common cause that is bigger than themselves to which they can give their bodies and souls completely and without reservations.

It's the complete surrender of self to God that really makes people tick at their fine-tuned best!

NIGHT WATCH

Everyone should have enough night-watch experiences in their lives, preferably alone, to help answer the three basic questions the soul continually asks: (1) Who am I? (2) Why am I here? (3) Where am I going?

The daytime is for rejoicing and affirming; the nighttime is for asking questions—deep questions. Night watches are the best times for asking questions, especially when you are all alone with your Creator.

Who am I? This question comes most rapidly while stargazing on a clear, cold, dark winter's night, or viewing a comet, meteor, or northern lights. The flash of a lightning bolt at night, the moon in all its phases, the configuration of the constellations—all these have visual stories to tell us and remind us that the universe is an orderly and awe-inspiring place, not man-made, but creatively designed with an economy and efficiency of operation that is still a mystery, even to astronomers.

Possible Answers to Question:

When I consider thy heavens, the work of thy fingers, the moon and the stars, which thou hast ordained;

What is man that thou art mindful of him? and the son of man, that thou dost care for him?

For thou hast made him a little lower than the angels, and hast crowned him with glory and honor.

Thou madest him to have dominion over the works of thy hands; thou hast put all things under his feet. (Ps. 8:3–6, KJV)

Why am I here? This question comes most readily if you are doing guard duty on "the graveyard shift" (2 to 4 A.M.) in the military, or if you are unable to turn or sleep in the middle of the night (following hospital surgery), or if you are on a lonely night prayer vigil in a darkened church, or if you are doing an early morning watch at the bedside of a loved one nearing death.

Possible Answers to Question:

To comfort those in any trouble with the same comfort we ourselves have received from God. (2 Cor. 1:4, NIV, [my paraphrase].)

To know Christ and to experience the power of His resurrection, to share in His sufferings, and become like Him in His death. (Phil. 3:10, NEB, MLB.)

To be able to discern the will of God, and to know what is good, acceptable, and perfect. (Rom. 12:2, NEB)

To glorify God, and to enjoy Him forever. (*Shorter Catechism,* United Presbyterian Church.)

Where am I going? This refrain of the soul is a longing to be "at one with the universe," to never lose our state of consciousness, and to always have an identity with God our Creator. This question can be asked at all ages, but probably begins around age five or six, and is not limited to night watches. As one's conscience begins to dawn, one of the first questions asked of one's self is, "What would happen to me if I were no longer alive in my body, if I were to suddenly die, and have no more earthly relationships, no more todays and tomorrows?" Many of us spend the remaining decades of our lives trying at various times and places to find a satisfactory answer to this pervasive question.

Possible Answers to Question:

Now we know that when we die and leave our earthly bodies, we have a building from God, an eternal house in Heaven. (2 Cor. 5:1, TLB, RSV, NIV)

Our citizenship is in Heaven! (Phil. 3:20, NIV)

Rejoice that your names are written in Heaven. (Luke 10:20, NIV.)

This is the promise that He Himself gave us, the promise of eternal life. (1 John 2:25, NEB)

SLEEP, DREAMS AND VISIONS

Maybe the reason many of us are not getting sweeping visions and dreams like Daniel did, with clear understanding and interpretations of them as well—or dreaming exciting dreams like Jacob did at Bethel when he experienced the awesome dream of seeing angels of God ascending and descending a ladder from earth to Heaven, and receiving the Lord's promises for himself and the house of Israel ("In thy seed shall all the families of the earth be blessed." Gen. 22:18 KJV.)—is that we are not getting enough good sleep to properly relax our subconscious minds and let the Spirit take over during sleep.

Sleep is precious, and yet statistics tell us that millions of people need pills to induce sleep, and to help eliminate "counting sheep" or some other mental gymnastics. Some sleep experts recommend self-hypnosis phonograph records, while others suggest "relax-sleep" exercises that incorporate listening to music, like Beethoven's Sixth Symphony.

The less *unfinished business* we have on our agendas at bedtime, the more easily we will fall asleep—and the more spontaneously and freely our thoughts will flow in our dreams.

Many of us have experienced the common dream of anxiety ("unfinished business" items). Often this represents some internal conflict. In the dream we are being inhibited from reaching our goal by some external force, thus making us late for an important event, or missing it altogether.

On the other hand, the daily practice of saying prayers at bedtime, even in the relaxing, humbling position of being on one's knees, and turning over our wearied bodies and minds to God's care is psychologically sound and redemptive. The practice of also offering our love and praise to God at bedtime, however tired we may be, also engenders relaxed sleep that is heavenly.

There can be little question that a good night's sleep is a greater healer of body, mind, and spirit, and provides a fertile seedbed for producing dreams and visions that are at times surprisingly reassuring and revealing—and if not resulting in heroic visions, perhaps providing clairvoyant dreams that will sprout creative impulses and intuitions for creative people, like artists and writers.

Not all visions occur at night while sleeping. In the Book of Revelation, the Apostle John had his Isle of Patmos vision apparently during the daytime, for he writes, "I was in the Spirit on the Lord's day.... and I saw..." (Rev. 1:10, KJV).

During our daytime conscious hours, it is doubly important that we think basically positive, optimistic thoughts so that when bedtime arrives, the switchboard of our brain has not been overloaded with too many negative waves and unresolved issues.

Mary Beth Zimmerman, a most recent dramatic success story in women's golf, visualizes herself winning on the golf course with positive thinking. It involves many of the principles of self-hypnosis—total relaxation exercises, deep breathing techniques, and visualizing herself making all the shots. "I play the course in my head the night before, and think positively," she said. "If I get down on myself, I can pretty well assure myself a bad round."

What a beautiful parallel there is in the spiritual world. To live the life of the Spirit, whether at work or in leisure, we must concentrate on the things of God and visualize ourselves doing His will in our lives. Negative thoughts can rob us of His love, joy, peace…and self-control.

A final thought about sleep: Some Christians believe that our nightly sleep on earth (and waking up each morning after what sometimes seemed just a moment of sleep, even though it really was seven or eight hours) is a foretaste of what the death of our bodies will be like.

Martin Luther expresses it like this:

Only A Night's Sleep
What is our death but a night's sleep? For as through sleep all weariness and faintness pass away and cease, and the powers of the spirit come back again, so that in the morning we arise fresh and strong and joyous, so at the Last Day we shall arise again as if we had only slept a night, and shall be fresh and strong.

HOW CAN I KNOW THE WILL OF GOD?

There can be no more pertinent question to ask of oneself during our earthly pilgrimage than this one. The great majority of serious-minded people not only ask this question (often silently to themselves), but really are intent on wanting to know the answer.

Writers have pointed out that there are three basic kinds of wills in the universe. In the beginning there had been one will, the will of God, the Creator. After the rebellion of Lucifer there had been two wills, that of God and Satan. And since the sin in the Garden committed by Adam and Eve, there is self-will whereby each person has turned to his own way. God's will, Satan's will, and self-will. But because of self-will, there are now more than three wills—there are billions of wills. There are more than two billion wills in this world alone—one for each person on this earth.

What most of us yearn for is not following our own will—which fits us for a life of self-centeredness, ego trips, and inflated, unrealistic opinions of ourselves as being the center of the universe around which everything else revolves (which we abhor in anyone else)—or a following of Satan's (or the Devil's) will, which few people want to consciously admit following (we would rather follow the wills of our own choosing), yet do so unwittingly and deceptively at times anyway—what we yearn for is an honest-to-goodness following of God's will for our lives. We want to be in tune with God, to feel the power of His presence and guidance, and to be "at one with the universe" through our Creator. What greater privilege and opportunity is there?

But how can I know God's will for my individual life? Maybe I need to be convinced before asking that question that God even knows I exist as some kind of small dot, or bleep, or glitch on this earth; and furthermore, that He cares about whether I ever exist or not, or that He has a unique road map and *will* laid out for me that is especially designed just for me and my future.

Someone has suggested that we need to first discover God's *sublime* will, in which we can then discover His *specific* will for our lives—so that we can become fully the persons we were meant to be.

George Müller, founder of an orphanage in Bristol, England, has written a masterpiece on "How I Ascertain the Will of God" that is just as simple, clear, and timely now as it was when it was written over a century ago. In a brief but encompassing outline, here are his pithy, practical thoughts that may be just as helpful to you as they were to him:

• *Surrender your own will.* I seek at the beginning to get my heart into such a state that it has no will of its own in regard to a given matter. *Nine-tenths of the trouble with people is just here.* Nine-tenths of the difficulties are overcome when our hearts are ready to do the Lord's will whatever it may be. When one is truly in this state, it is usually but a little way to the knowledge of what His will is.

• *Do not depend on feelings.* Having done this, I do not leave the result to feeling or simple impression. If I do so, I make myself liable to *great delusion.*

• *Seek the Spirit's will through God's Word.* I seek the will of the Spirit of God through, or in connection with, the Word of God. *The Spirit and the Word must be combined.*

• *Note providential circumstances.* Next I take into account providential circumstances. These often plainly indicate God's will in connection with His Word and Spirit.

• *Pray.* I ask God in prayer to reveal His will to me aright.

• *Wait.* Thus, through prayer to God, the study of the Word, and reflection, I come to a deliberate judgment according to the best of my ability and knowledge and *if my mind is thus at peace and continues so after two or three more petitions,* I proceed accordingly. In trivial matters and in transactions involving most important issues, I have found this method always effective.

It has been suggested that taking one-half hour in the morning and one-half hour in the evening—for two weeks—would be one way of making an honest attempt to discover God's will for our lives.

Jesus was the first person to be completely obedient to God's will. At the proper time we will have the gift of the Holy Spirit to give us the guidance and help we need—so that at life's end, we will know that the maximum achievement in our lives was to have done the will of God.

Do not conform yourselves to the standards of this world, but let God transform you inwardly by a complete change of your mind. Then you will be able to know the will of God—what is good, and is pleasing to Him, and is perfect. (Rom. 12:2, TEV.)

Prayer

O Gracious Lord,
Forgive us for our wayward willfulness;
Help us to surrender our selfish will to your sovereign will—
So that Your will may be done through our wills;
Here on earth, and through Eternity.

Amen.

PERFECTION!

"Be ye perfect, even as your Heavenly Father is perfect." (Matt. 5:48, KJV, RSV.)

I used to be haunted by this admonition from Jesus. I would try at all times to be perfect, and when I brought home more A's than anything else on my report card, I thought I was getting there.

There were other isolated moments in my life when I thought I was approaching perfection—like the time I apparently played "Falling Waters" flawlessly at a student piano recital—or the time I played short-stop in an adult church league softball game and stopped every ground ball hit between second and third base, threw perfect strikes to the first base-man from whatever fielding position I was in, and leaped several feet into the air to snare some line drives hit in my direction, seemingly undaunted by the pull of gravity; at bat, I hit safely every time up; and I ran the bases like a gazelle. I thought I had achieved perfection, and was headed for the Big Leagues at last. But I found out later on that this "near perfection" I thought I had achieved was short-lived—sort of a one-time phenomenon.

Apart from one's own personal attempts at achieving perfection—whether in the physical, mental, moral, or spiritual realms—where does one turn to find perfection in other persons here on earth? Does one turn to politics for example, or education, or nations, or governments, or the law, or medicine, or Wall Street, or Hollywood, or history, or the Bible, or fine arts, or sports?

Arriving at perfection is difficult to measure in the moral and spiritual realms. In matters of honesty, how can you measure whether someone is 100% honest, or maybe just 80%? Or is 100% truthful in 90% of the decisions, but is not completely truthful in the other 10% of them?

Achieving mental perfection is likewise difficult to measure. To achieve a perfect 1600 College Board score (800 Verbal, 800 Math) is a rarity, and to arrive at a 200 I.Q. test score is just as rare—and few have attained them, except a few geniuses.

In the field of music, history tells us that Wolfgang Mozart is regarded as one of music's greatest geniuses. From the time he was six years old, he played piano and composed brilliantly. Beginning at age eight, Mozart composed more than forty-one symphonies. At age twelve he composed an opera that was performed in Salzburg, Austria. In all, Mozart composed more than 600 works in his brief thirty-five years of earthly life. His last three symphonies, several of his concertos, and his chamber music seem especially to reach perfection.

In aviation, the precision flying of the Thunderbirds (five matched Air Force planes) in various formations approaches perfection.

In the sports world, physical skills seem easier to measure than in any other realm, for they are all tied to a mathematical base that usually has an exacting time (seconds, minutes) and space (feet, miles) relationship. Records for each sporting event are kept, and it is assumed that when a new record is achieved (like breaking the "four-minute mile" barrier in track) that the new champion has "almost" achieved perfection. I am convinced that this keeping of past records, and the eternal attempt to always want to break them in whatever the sport, is one of the perpetual fascinations of the sports world for writers, players, and fans alike—and is one of the reasons the sports world perennially attracts so many enthusiastic followers.

In baseball, "near perfection" seemed to have been reached in the summer of 1941 when Joe DiMaggio, the Yankee Clipper, hit safely in 56 consecutive baseball games for the New York Yankees. As Joe was establishing new records with his hitting streak, fans everywhere (but especially in The Big Apple) would rush between classes or work shifts (most games were still played in the afternoons then, the way baseball was meant to be played) to crowd around a public radio to hear if "Di Mag" had kept his "perfect" streak alive. As the streak passed fifty games, opposing pitchers would pitch with extreme caution to Joe, and on several occasions walked Joe the first few times at bat, leaving all the dramatics until the ninth inning for Joe to deliver a base hit and go "1 for 1"—drawing a mighty roar from the hundreds of students (including me) surrounding the full-blasting radio in Hartley Hall at Columbia University (just a few miles away from the stadium). For the records, after a one-game miss, Joe did hit safely in the next twenty games also. So except for one "near miss," Joe's consecutive hitting streak of 56—which many baseball experts consider to be a "nearly perfect" record, and the most unlikely record in all of baseball to be broken—could have been an even more unreachable 76.

Bill Bradley, U.S. Senator from New Jersey, was considered by many to be one of the greatest college basketball players of all time. He was a pure (almost perfect) basketball shooter (6'5" forward) who once scored 58 points in an NCAA playoff game against Wichita State to help Princeton gain a third-place finish in the NCAA finals in 1965. One day during practice Bill noticed that his baseline jump shots, which he practiced with meticulous care, were not "swishing the nets" at the one end of the court with the regularity to which he had become accustomed. The basketball was continually hitting the back edge of the rim, narrowly missing. He requested that the height of the basket from the floor be checked. It was found to be 1/16" too low—and hence interfering with his "attempts at perfection" results.

In football, there have been quarterbacks who have come close to perfection in pass completions for a game, in some cases completing the first fifteen passes thrown, only to have the next two passes fall incomplete.

In wrestling, the closest thing to perfection must be the unbeaten record of friend Richard ("D.B.") DiBatista, who never lost a wrestling match—with a perfect record of 82–0 at Penn, and winning two NCAA titles (175 pounds) in 1941 and 1942. What a wrestler!

If perfection is difficult to achieve in performance of athletic skills that are measurable, how much more difficult it is to even attempt to measure (and achieve) perfection in the moral and spiritual realms.

As some of us grow older, we may attempt to console ourselves with the thought, propagated from some books and pulpits, that the word *perfect* means "complete"—so that we don't need to be perfect anymore (morally or spiritually); all we need to do is to be complete. At first hearing, this sounds like "blessed relief"; we don't need to be perfect any more, only to be a complete person. On second thought, however, what is the realistic difference between being perfect (100%) or being complete (say, maybe 99.44%)?

A far more meaningful and comforting Biblical insight might be helpful to us at this point as we aim for "perfect, complete" maturity. It is this: We are not going to achieve full perfection, or completeness of personality and/or character on this earth, but we hope to achieve perfection in Heaven because of what Jesus, the Heavenly Father's Son, did for us in living the only perfect (sinless) life known to earthlings. All we need to do to be perfect is to believe in Jesus, the perfected one, and let Him live His life in us—starting with life on this earth, and then attaining its full perfection when we are translated into our fully completed new spiritual bodies in Heaven (see Gal. 2:20; Phil. 1:21).

ROLE MODELS

How many different role models have you had in your lifetime? People that you respect and admire, and would like to emulate? Probably more (if you were to count them) than you might have guessed initially.

If my passage milestones are correct, I've had at least fifty role models over a period of sixty-five years to significantly guide and enrich my life. Astounding!

In early childhood, my projections changed quickly from broadly wanting to be a fireman...a policeman...a truck driver—to that of imagining I was a storekeeper...a doctor...a teacher—all while engaged in child's play.

During later childhood and adolescence the images of my role models became more sharply focused and less fleeting. For instance, I can remember thinking I was Cecil Travis (shortstop for the Washington Senators in the late 1930s) for several baseball seasons. I adopted his batting stance at the plate, tried to follow his hitting style by slicing line drives to the opposite field, used his autographed glove to scoop up grounders at shortstop (I still possess that well-worn Cecil Travis glove—I just can't throw it onto the rubbish heap), and always imagined my uniform to be the same number 5 that he wore.

In later baseball years, when my fielding finesse exceeded my hitting prowess, I took on the role models of the slickest fielding shortstops in the Big Leagues at that time—Phil "Scooter" Rizzuto of the Yankees, and Marty Marion of the Cardinals. (I even imitated his perpetual habit of picking up minute pebbles around him.)

Competing in neighborhood football games during adolescence, I envisioned myself being anything from a crushing runner like Bronko Nagurski of Minnesota—to a dazzling, sidestepping, straight-arming runner like Elroy "Crazy Legs" Hirsch of Wisconsin, or swivel-hipped Tom Harmon of Michigan—to a smooth, accurate slingshot passer like Sammy Baugh of the Washington Redskins.

There were more serious role models beyond those in sports.

In choosing my career of education and teaching, for example, I was heavily influenced in a nondirect way by my father, who loved teaching so much that he taught for forty-three years (most of them in a one-room school), followed by ten more years of substitute teaching until age eighty. My dad's love of his pupils, as well as his thorough knowledge of the subjects he liked to teach, undoubtedly provided a strong positive role model for me—and a later desire to enter such an exciting and self-fulfilling profession as teaching—just as my older brother Leon had done.

Throughout my several decades of schooling from first grade through a doctorate in education, I have had more than a dozen inspirational teaching models to emulate: a fifth-grade female teacher, a male chemistry teacher, a female algebra teacher, a male music professor, a female student teaching supervisor, a male biology professor, and a male doctoral thesis advisor. All the above-mentioned role models had one thing in common—they took a deep personal interest in me as a person and wanted me to excel as a student. They also asked tough probing questions that challenged my thinking and enlarged my horizons.

During later adulthood years, role models last longer, are not usually connected with hero worship, and often are related to close, cherished friendships. We enjoy having social relationships with people of all ages (including some relatives) who are open-minded and objective about issues, think basically positive and optimistic thoughts, and who consistently display the fruits of the Spirit in their walk and talk. We seem to be drawn to such people like magnets.

If we are growing spiritually as persons, and displaying a maturing faith that attracts other people toward us in wanting "what we have"—we should be thankful for the opportunities of unwittingly becoming role models for those in our magnetic field, especially our peers and the younger generations. What an awesome privilege and responsibility!

The ultimate role model for Christians, of course, has to be Jesus Christ—our revered example for earthly living, and our lively hope for eternal living in Heaven.

REUNIONS

"It's great to see people you haven't seen in years, and reunite with them again in bonds of friendship. It brings back a flood of memories of times, places, and people."

Such a comment might well cover a multitude of reunions—from the annual summer get-together of family clans and World War II units to the five-year celebrations of high school and college graduation classes.

There is always the anticipatory joy of these affairs that almost surpasses the reunion day itself.

Annual family reunions have their customary share of unknown news items to announce: Who has been married during the year, and to whom? Who has been divorced? Who has the youngest baby? How many people have died during the last year, how old were they, and what caused their death?

With the five-year class reunions, the large turnouts develop slowly. The fifth-, tenth-, and fifteenth-year reunions bring back few alumni, for most recent graduates are apparently too busy getting established in jobs and families. By the time of the twenty-fifth-year reunion, however, far greater numbers turn out, often accompanied by postadolescent daughters and sons. Then by the thirty-fifth-year class gathering, alumni have achieved financial security and are willing to make large contributions to their alma maters. Soon all eyes focus on hoping to survive and make it to the golden fiftieth-year reunion, a kind of geriatric milestone.

Also, in five-year class reunions there are always a number of big surprises, and the questions often become more coquettish and fanciful: Who will be there? If my old girlfriend appears, will I recognize her? Will she recognize me? Who will look the oldest? The youngest? The fattest? Who will be the shapeliest? The most vivacious? In later reunions, the questions are family and work oriented: Who will have the most children or grandchildren? Who will be judged to be most successful? Who has been divorced the most often? Who will have died in the last five years?

We do seem to enjoy reunions for a variety of reasons: the gossip, the pleasing dress and good looks of people who "back there then" were pure wallflowers, the slippage from grace of some of the popular, good-looking "top of the class" kids who now appear to be lonely, downcast, and "old looking." In short, it's a brief time in which to make quick comparisons of maturing growth (or the lack of it) among former classmates.

Finally, reunions afford one to take a brief longitudinal look at familiar people over a period of time to see what makes them tick, and how their value systems may have changed. We seldom are afforded this opportunity in life except for immediate family members—to follow them from teenage years through retirement years—a possible fifty-year observational study!

Fascinating!

P.S. This love for reunions must be a foretaste of a larger, more permanent future reunion in the skies—but with a different agenda of questions and subject matter.

FAMILY TREES AND BUSHES

Many of us have grown up in America within families that have a long ancestral family tree—with a family coat-of-arms from the old country, and family histories predating the DAR and the coming of the Mayflower.

The family tree looked like a tall sturdy oak that could trace back its descendants to Adam and Eve, or so it seemed looking at it for the first time. Genealogies could be traced back several centuries, however—on both sides of the family—with some grandparents becoming great, great, great, great grandparents. There were many branches of aunts, uncles, and cousins.

Also, there were names and titles to be memorized, especially so in families that perpetuated namesakes—so that it was most important to remember if this was William Buckley Senior or William Buckley Junior, or Henry duPont the III or Henry duPont the IV.

A favorite after-dinner family pastime (before TV) was the spirited attempt to recall names of living and dead relatives and determine who they married, where they lived, how many children they had, who the children married...ad infinitum. Usually a juicy story or two developed along the way—like Uncle Harry living with twin sisters, while supposedly being married to only one of them; or Aunt Lizzie being a socially approved housekeeper (live-in) for a man she was not married to. Generally, though, most everything fit together into a biological family tree.

With the onslaught of more divorces, remarriages that included children from former marriages, sometimes a second divorce, and then a second remarriage with additional children brought along, the traditional pattern of drawing family trees has been changed to drawing extended family bushes.

Ellen Goodman, syndicated columnist for the *Boston Globe*, in an article on August 20, 1983, states it well:

> The reality is that divorce has created kinship ties that rival the most complex tribe. There are not always easy relationships. The children and even the adults whose family lives have been disrupted by divorce and remarriage learn that people they love do not necessarily love each other. The extended family does not gather for reunions and Thanksgivings.
>
> But when it works, it can provide a support system of sorts. I have seen the nieces, nephews—even the dogs—of one marriage welcomed

as guests into another. There are all sorts of relationships that survive the marital ones, though there are no names for these kinsfolk, no nomenclature for this extending family.

Not long ago, when living together first became a common pattern, people couldn't figure out what to call each other. It was impossible to introduce the man you lived with as a "spouse equivalent." It was harder to refer to a woman your son lived with as his lover, mistress, housemate. (Note: A friend once described her daughter's male friend in such an arrangement as "her sin-in-law.")

It's equally difficult to describe the peculiar membership of this new lineage. Does your first husband's mother become a mother-out-law? Is the woman no longer married to your uncle an ex-aunt? We have nieces and nephews left dangling like participles from other lives and stepfamilies entirely off the family tree.

From another perspective, some family agencies, in attempts to prevent further family breakups, are putting more emphasis on strengthening the role of the father in the family. Commenting on this, Judge Armand Della Porta, of the Court of Common Pleas in Philadelphia, offers this disquieting perspective:

The father is the one who has more often than not abdicated his authority and responsibility in the family. Almost every youth who has come before me charged with a serious offense had either no father at all or had a drunkard for a father. Whatever semblance of family has been left is due to the efforts, of heroic proportion at times, of the mother or grandmother.

From family trees to family bushes to family gaps—without a father; maybe that's why there is a Heavenly Father to fill in all the gaps.

A SIMPLER LIFE-STYLE?

One is sometimes haunted by the thoughts of living a simpler life-style on earth (especially on hectic days)—something like Gandhi did, or Einstein, or St. Francis of Assisi, or the Amish, or Mother Teresa.

But questions quickly arise: Would it mean giving up my good job for less pay? Would a simpler life-style mean giving up prized property and possessions? Would it mean giving up all modern conveniences—dishwashers, washing machines and dryers, refrigerators, air conditioners, microwaves, automobiles? Would it include giving up most of our social club memberships and friendships? And would it mean leaving our country?

Most of us, however spiritually-minded otherwise, would be hard put to give up most of these things, especially the modern conveniences—for from another perspective, they help us do household tasks quicker and better, thus freeing us for doing more creative things and theoretically "helping our neighbors in need" more often.

Then, too, most of us would face extremely difficult decisions if we were to stop accumulating material possessions, or not continue to hang on to what we already have stockpiled. Instead, through love for one another, we would put everything we have into a common pool with others of like mind and spirit—like the early disciples—and not be concerned if someone has more than we have. We would treat each other as "one big family," giving all our surplus goods to help feed the poor and less fortunate. Now that is tough "disciple discipline" (see Matt. 19:21).

Perhaps a simpler life-style is something we all secretly yearn for many times, dream about, and give lip service to, but when faced with the hard reality of practicing it on this earth, we would prefer postponing its implementation until later in life. Perhaps at retirement, when it is rumored we will have more time to do things more leisurely and graciously, and be less hurried.

And if in our retirement years a simple life-style does not clearly emerge, and we still have great difficulty getting rid of our material possessions (even sometimes adding that "I'm going to keep my things as long as I live, and when I'm gone somebody else can fight over them") or we continue to join things, and hurry, and worry—then there's little hope left for us on this earth to ever live a simpler life-style.

On rare occasions one hears of someone who has done advance planning during preretirement or retirement years for the orderly disposition of many nonessentials for living (jewelry, china, silverware, collections,

70

antiques, etc.). Such decisions bring added satisfaction to the donors, knowing that while still living their gifts were joyfully being transferred to appreciative loved ones or charities. Although rare, such instances would tend to lead toward a simpler life-style and the "lightening of the load" in gradual preparation for our eventually "leaving everything" at death.

Soldiers in the army learn to travel lightly. All they own—eating utensils, clothing, and a pup tent—are all carried about in *one* duffel bag. Most of us will never travel that lightly on earth unless forced.

However, for most of us who are reluctant to part with anything while on this earth—including useless books and stacks of filed materials that have been unused for decades, and loads of unneeded clothing and trash items in closets and offices—it would make sense to start "cleaning house," throwing things out, and giving away valued possessions while we still have all our faculties.

For those who will never be led to lead a simpler life-style on this earth, but still yearn to do so—take heart. There is still hope for us in the next life, in the spiritual life prepared for us in Heaven. For we are led to believe that in Heaven there will be no interferences by way of material possessions, worries, power plays, social status, or temptations to covet and hoard.

It will be a rarefied privilege to *travel lightly* in Heaven, with no excess baggage (not even a duffel bag), and to *finally* live a simpler life-style in the joy of the Spirit!

TIME

Most of us would agree that there is not enough time to do everything we'd like. There's not enough time in a day, or a week, or a year, or a lifetime.

We are told in Scripture (see Ps. 90:10) that the average length of life on this earth is seventy years—and by means of extra strength, eighty years and beyond. Since the life span of most Americans is increasing each year, let's envision a life expectancy of seventy-five years. The first fifteen years are spent in childhood and early adolescence, twenty years are spent sleeping in bed, and roughly another twenty years in eating and watching television—that leaves us precious little time to live creatively as adults.

Since most of us also have jobs during adulthood, figure another fifteen years aggregate on the job and waiting at red lights to and from work—and that cuts us down to five years for free-time thinking, meditation, and creativity—and improving our characters.

Our *time* is short!

What is your life? It is even a vapor that appears for a little time and then vanishes away. (James 4:14, NKJV.)

Since time does pass so quickly, it becomes essential that only the planned priorities in our lives be done. Each of us has been given the same amount of time—1,440 minutes a day, 168 hours a week. It is important that we manage it wisely.

This is God's day that he lent to me,
That I may use for good or ill.*
—Annette Wynne

Our *managed time* is also short!

That's why the concept of eternity is so vitally important. God is from everlasting to everlasting. He never had a beginning; He never had an end.

One day is with the Lord as a thousand years, and a thousand years as one day. (2 Pet. 3:8, KJV.)

We will never have enough time, even if well-managed, to do all the things we would like to do on earth in the time allotted to us—meeting people and going places and doing things—but in eternity there will be endless time of infinite duration—to meet loving people, to go to heavenly

*From *This Is God's Day* by Annette Wynne.

places, and to do spiritual things.

For we know that if this earthly frame that houses us today should be destroyed, we have a building from God, a house not made by human hands, *eternal*, and in Heaven. (2 Cor. 5:1, NEB, RSV, italics mine.)

We want our transitory life on earth to become absorbed and transformed into the life that is eternal (never-ending) in Heaven.

CHAPTER IV

FUN TIMES

A cheerful heart does good like medicine. (TLB)
Being cheerful keeps you healthy. (TEV)

—Prov. 17:22

Always be cheerful. (MLB)
Be happy in your faith at all times. (P)

—1 Thess. 5:16

Trust…in the living God, who gives us richly *all
things* to enjoy. (NKJV, italics mine)

—1 Tim. 6:17

FUN ON THE FARM

Farming is getting to be Big Business with lots of mechanized equipment and thousands of acres to manage, and big agribusiness operations involving hundreds of thousands of dollars. It's something beyond my full comprehension.

My traditional view of the farm is that of farmers walking the fields behind a plow that is pulled by horses or mules, without any high-tech tools, far less acreage, and minuscule dollars.

In fact, the all-purpose farm I grew up on over fifty years ago was about fifty acres with eight fenced fields, one deep woods, one meadow that initiated (through five springs) its own meandering strong stream, one fertile truck patch, one fruit orchard, and one richly-manured garden.

The farm also had two strong horses, a herd of milking cows, a collie dog to chase the cows back to the barn, a hog pen full of squealing pigs, several chicken houses of egg-laying white leghorns, and a few scattered ducks, geese, and guineas.

The early 1930s were the Depression years, so that making money was not the chief goal of farming; survival, with enough food for the family, was the essential thing. Farmers who tilled the soil for planting wheat and corn appeared to enjoy their work, and seemed satisfied with having just a little money left over each harvest season for buying family clothing and a few toys for the children. They were always concerned about the weather—that there might be just the right amount of rainfall and sunshine to nourish the crops in the growing season. When dry spells appeared, farmers looked anxiously to the skies for God's help.

A chief satisfaction each year came from having enough new hay to store in the barn, threshing enough wheat, and husking enough corn, so that all the animals would have sufficient food for the winter months.

The sources of income were shipping milk by rail to a creamery in Baltimore, selling eggs to an "egg man" who collected them in a truck, taking a few extra bushels of wheat by wagon to the local miller for grinding into flour, and in the summer hauling some fresh fruits and vegetables on a loaded truck some six miles into town for "peddling on the streets."

Growing up on a compact, cozy farm near Marburg (York County) Pennsylvania was lots of fun and hard work. But the real joys of being a kid on a farm far outweighed the griping about doing the backbreaking chores, such as cleaning stinking chicken houses in the winter and picking string beans all day in summer's hot humid weather.

Here are some of the fun times I remember while living down on the farm as a kid:

• Fast sledding rides down long hills over hard crusts of snow on a Flexible Flyer.

• Taking rides on horse-drawn sleighs through a snowy woods on a cold winter's night to visit neighbors.

• Tracking wild animals in fresh snow, especially foxes and raccoons.

• Trapping for muskrats along a stream that was landscaped with many muskrat holes and well-defined muskrat meadow paths, with the holes sometimes creating new mysterious tunnels for the water to follow.

• The abundance of colorful spring flowers in fields and meadows, dominated by red carpets of Indian paintbrushes.

• The smell of new-mown hay in the meadow, affording opportunities for lying flat on one's back on a pile of hay and gazing at the white puffy clouds.

• The special thrill of picking and tasting luscious red strawberries on a sunny hillside, and the leisurely savoring of clusters of grapes from a loaded grape arbor that looked like a shaded wigwam retreat.

• Playing hopscotch, and shooting marbles in piles of dust by the light of the moon.

• The fascination of seeing animals born, especially a calf—and seeing little chicks hatch from eggs, and later cradling them in my hands for days.

• The thrill of discovering a rabbit's nest with bunnies in a field, a squirrel's nest high in a tree, and an intriguing Baltimore oriole's nest on a high branch.

• Standing high on a hill on a clear sunny summer day, and holding a visiting girl's hand for the first time at age ten—and thinking I had discovered a whole new sensory world of touch.

• Picking all manner of fruit from trees in the orchard and from bushes along fence lines—cherries, apples, peaches, pears, raspberries, huckleberries.

• Threshing time in hot July when a bunch of farmers in sweaty suspenders moved in for a couple of days with a threshing machine rig and tractor to separate "the wheat from the chaff" in a noisy, dusty operation—with the serving of cold root beer from the spring-house to the threshers during brief rest periods.

• Flying a kite on a windy day and thinking it might lift me into the sky—overalls, straw hat, bare feet, and all.

• Looking up at "thousands of stars" on a crystal clear night—with no artificial lights to interfere—and thrilled when shooting stars and the northern lights sometimes appeared.

• Harvesting all kinds of vegetables and fruits—with a special eye on having the women jar many of them and preserving them for eating during the winter.

• Husking corn while seated Indian style in a family circle on soft corn shocks, and engaging in warm light-hearted conversation under a bright autumn sun—hoping to find and husk a rare red-grained ear of corn, an especially happy achievement.

• The butchering of hogs on the day after Thanksgiving—with the involvement of all five senses throughout the day—and highlighted by the unbelievable use of the pig's intestinal walls to make the skin of sausages; the stirring of pudding in huge black kettles over an open-hearth fire in the butcher house; and the delightful earthy aroma of sausage being smoked in the smokehouse.

Yes, life on a farm can be a lot of fun and hard work, and growing up there brings one in first-hand touch with nature and God's handiwork, with seldom a conscious awareness of it at the time—for it happens so gradual-ly and silently and peacefully and satisfyingly.

ONE-ROOM SCHOOLS

Is there anything more nostalgic than the memory of one-room schools, especially to those who attended them? A reunion call to any one-room school worth its salt will bring out hundreds of its graduates and their spouses to the local fire hall or other noteworthy eating establishment. And why not? It's in a similar category to the almost universal admiration held for old cars, period furniture, baseball cards, and antiques in general.

To those who may never have experienced the heady thrill of attending a one-room school, here are some of the more noteworthy ingredients that made such a place a fascinating memory for millions of Americans across this country of ours—causing some to even say that they were "ahead of their time," and so unique that they have never been adequately replaced since their demise.

• *Togetherness*. Most one-room schools contained all grades 1 to 8, with one teacher, and often had forty or more pupils.

• *Country living*. The schools were often situated along a country road, or at the end of a dirt lane.

• *Exercise*. All pupils walked to school.

• *Fresh water*. A nearby farm provided clean springwater that was carried in buckets to the school by the older boys.

• *Air-conditioning*. There were condominium-type outhouses, with the south side for girls, and the north side for boys—and plenty of fresh air for ventilating both sides.

• *Radiant heat*. A huge, round black stove dominated the room, and provided an abundance of heat through its red-hot coals.

• *Discipline*. There was discipline! The discipline of last resort for the teacher was the switch brought from the nearby woods for whippings.

• *Fun time*. Morning and afternoon recesses.
Fall—Softball, hopscotch, jumping rope, and hide-and-seek.
Winter—Cornerball, fox-and-geese, building snowmen, and hide-and-seek.
Spring—Softball, shooting marbles, jumping rope, and hide-and-seek.

• *Lunch*. Usually a happy hour of fifteen minutes for lunch and forty-five minutes for fun and games.

• *Luncheon dining.* Often done in alfresco style, as in Europe.

• *Luncheon Menu:*
Peanut butter and jelly sandwich (or cheese sandwich)
Apple or orange
Slice of angel's food, devil's food, or coconut cake
Small thermos of milk (sometimes chocolate)

•*School equipment.* Tin lunch box, brightly colored. Book satchel, brown—large enough to hold most textbooks, tablet, pencils, and crayon boxes.

• *Curriculum.* Arithmetic, civics, English, geography, health, history, penmanship, reading, and spelling.

• *Extracurricular activities.* All occurred during school hours, and usually rotated among the bigger pupils throughout the year.
Winding the clock (stretching privilege)
Filling the inkwells (tantalizing privilege)
Bringing buckets of black, shiny, hard coal from the cellar for the fiery furnace (back-breaking privilege)
Washing the blackboard (clowning privilege)
Clapping the blackboard erasers on the porch at the end of the day (honored privilege)
Dusting the alphabet cards and the picture frames of George Washington and Abraham Lincoln hanging on the front wall of classroom (sacred privilege)
Participating in spelling bees held each Friday during the last hour of school (weekly privilege)
Chasing the opposite sex around the outside of the school (daily privilege)

• *Gifted classes.* Gifted pupils could listen in on the learning recitations held at the front of the room for the upper grades, and silently participate in these advanced classes.

• *Library.* None. Was not missed, since any surplus time was used to eagerly look at the history and geography textbook maps and illustrations, and fondly dream of faraway times and places.

• *Learning.* After years of taking daily and weekly teacher-made tests in all subjects, prepared pupils could then apply for taking the comprehensive county examination, which took an entire Saturday to administer. If satisfactorily passed (score of 75 percent or better), the student would then receive the Common School Diploma certifying the honorable completion of the first eight grades, and enabling the recipient to enter the "big city" high school the following year. *(Note:* It has been widely reported over the years that country kids from one-room schools could easily surpass their city counterparts when matched head-to-head in ninth grade in most subjects, but especially in arithmetic, reading, and spelling.)

With all these superlative virtues going for it, is it any wonder that today's living graduates continue to sing the praises of the one-room school, and vigorously defend it against all the onslaughts of modern "progressive" education?

BODY LANGUAGE

I am a firm believer in body language—from an uplifted head to a curled-up toe. I believe that the body sends out many messages and signals that have both conscious and subconscious origins.

As a close observer of the body and its movements, I have no difficulty in detecting certain silent signals being sent out. My big problem is in correctly interpreting what the signals mean (legs crossed at the knees, body leaning backward, piercing eyes), and they sometimes leave me in a quandary as to what the messages are—except in *handwriting*. In analyzing the strokes used in handwriting, the language of personality traits can be deciphered with surprising accuracy. (*Note:* All handwriting readings should be done in a light-hearted manner, being careful not to reveal too much about a person the first time around.)

Here are a few handwriting observations that have stood the test of time:

> *The Slant.* If letters slant to the left, the person is an introvert. If letters slant to the right, the person is an extrovert. If the letters are straight up and down, the person is matter-of-fact and businesslike.
>
> *Letter formations.* If individual letters are large and open, the person is gregarious and sociable. If the formations are small and carefully closed, the person is more tightly structured and secretive. If the letter *d* is widely looped at the top, the person is warm and affectionate.
>
> *Style.* If the style is flamboyant and artistic, the handwriting conveys a similar message about the writer. If the style is totally illegible, the writing must be that of a professional person, an escape artist, or an extreme egotist.

Be careful—your handwriting will reveal far more about yourself than your fingerprints.

P.S. By the way, why has personal letter-writing become almost a lost art in today's computer age?

LOOK-ALIKES

Do you have a look-alike here on earth that causes hundreds and hundreds of people to honestly mistake you for some well-known personage, and maybe even ask for your autograph?

You're fortunate if you do, for it's fun being a famous person's double. It's just as though you've suddenly become well-known, and are living a twin life—like being a live daily impersonator without even trying—it just happens!

So it is that I have been mistaken for Joe Paterno hundreds of times, and been asked for autographs dozens of times, especially during the football season. Most of you know that Joe Paterno is head football coach of the Penn State Nittany Lions football team, rated No. 1 for the 1986 season.

As long as Joe continues his winning ways at Penn State, I'll continue to stay knowledgeable about his philosophy of life and style of coaching football. The way things stand now, I can answer nearly all questions unsuspecting people might fire at me in social gatherings, thinking they're talking to "the real Joe." I tell them about my continual search for outstanding linebackers, intelligent scholar athletes, and a rock-ribbed defense....Who knows—I may someday be asked to fill in for my look-alike at a sports banquet. All I'll need to do to insure complete success is develop more of a Brooklyn accent, and continually remind my audience that "playing football is pure fun."

Joe, I've often wondered...Has anyone, even just once, ever mistaken you for me?

GOLF

Winston Churchill once said of golf that it was such a difficult game because you're trying "to hit a small ball into an even smaller hole with weapons singularly ill-designed for the job."

On some disgusting days golf does seem to be as temper-testing and devilish as any game ever invented. It's true—the ball is small and sometimes difficult to hit straight, and the club heads are not much larger than the ball, leaving little room for error in muscular coordination. To be sure, the cup is small enough, but testy grounds keepers on some courses seem to take a fiendish delight in placing it behind a protruding sand trap, or on a tricky spot on top of a knoll (instead of a flat spot in the middle of the green). To add to the misery, greens are built with wavy, slick surfaces; the sand traps (bunkers) are designed by the course architect to entrap even some of the better shots; trees, some with undergrowth, are planted so as to "catch and knock down" any slightly wayward tee-off and fairway shots; water hazards of various kinds (creeks, ponds, lakes) are there to torment the golfer; rolling hills of all degrees of inclination are there to interfere with a level swing; and high grass and weeds are purposely allowed to grow alongside the narrow fairways to punish "off-center" fairway and approach shots to the green.

With such a scenario, it is easily understandable why otherwise mature and grown-up men give up golf, and why the game is played assigning *handicaps* to remaining players. The use of this term is apt, for it's plain to see that dozens of handicaps have already been built into the courses—enough to put each golfer at such a disadvantage that success is rendered extremely difficult—so why not give handicaps to the players, too.

Now for the good news!

Golf is a beautiful game to play on a bright sunny day with temperatures around eighty degrees, blue skies, and a slight breeze. There is nothing more inviting than to see bright green grass freshly mowed on fairways, with flags waving in the breeze on the greens, and a slight smell of a "musky, grassy perfume" in the air. Golfing is pure fun on such days, even with scores in the high 90s.

It's double fun if you are fortunate enough to be playing on some of the best, most beautiful golf courses in the country—like Merion Golf Club in Ardmore, Pennsylvania; Bay Hill Country Club in Orlando, Florida; and the Pebble Beach Golf Club in Monterey, California. But the National Golf Course in Augusta, Georgia, where the Masters Golf Tournament is played each year, has to be the most beautiful golf course in the world: A neatly manicured course that winds through trees and flowers so stately and luxuriant that it resembles an outdoor cathedral; every hole is named after a plant that grows beside it, like Juniper, Yellow Jasmine, and Tea Olive; Rae's Creek meanders with its alluring, curvaceous, clear-running stream and pond; artistically sculptured white sand bunkers; and the captivating beauty of its featured azaleas, camellias, dogwoods, magnolias, wisteria, rare trees, and tall evergreen groves.

It's triple fun if you think about the many health benefits of playing golf, with all its fresh air and sunshine. Some golfers also enjoy walking the course rather than riding a cart, thus gaining extra beneficial exercise especially good for heart and lungs.

Another nice thing about golf is that you can play it well into your retirement years. Senior citizens have been known to play the game into their eighties, thanks to golf carts. There is no other popular sport that can make such a claim, and it must be one of the reasons why the game is growing so rapidly among both sexes, and why there are now over 12,000 golf courses across America, of which 7,500 are public.

Watching the pros like Sam Snead, Ben Hogan, Arnold Palmer, Jack Nicklaus, and Tom Watson makes playing golf look so easy. And the ladies like Nancy Lopez, Jan Stephenson, Sally Little, and Alice Miller make it look even easier with their natural, easy rhythmic swings. (If one is able to concentrate on the swing and not on their curves.) All you need to do is choose the right club, put the proper grip on it, take your correct stance, and execute a smooth, accurate swing—the ball will be heading straight for the target! The swing is the thing!

Of all things, there should be no excuse for hitting a poor tee-off shot: (1) You're standing on the level; (2) the ball is teed up off the ground and is perfectly level; (3) the ball is resting comfortably still on the tee—no one is throwing you a curved ball out of the strike zone, nor are you hitting at a moving target.

However, if the ball occasionally happens to stray a bit from the fairway because of imperfections in the owner's swing, lack of concentration, or "bad biorhythms"—be a good rationalizer and let your playing partners know that you are a creative golfer, that you like to hit a variety of shots at different angles, and that you tire easily if hitting only monotonously straight shots.

Someone has said that "the enduring allure of the game of golf has always been its utter unpredictability; it may offer abysmal ruin one round and then, for no apparent reason, hold out glorious salvation the next."

I play golf faithfully by that abiding premise and promise.

PRINCETON!

There's something *about that name* that casts a magic spell on its beholder! What is it that attracts people to Princeton, and continues to lure them back for more?

Could it be the geography of the town, the way it is poised on top of a gradually rising hill above Lake Carnegie in central New Jersey? Maybe it's the abundant history of the place? Or could it be the architectural beauty of the buildings in Princeton? Or is it the university itself that is responsible for bringing people back, enticed by the intimate beauty of the campus and its pastoral serenity? (Or as Jimmy Stewart, one of its most illustrious graduates, puts it—"the charm of its atmosphere.")

Perhaps it's the university alumni and their fierce loyalty to "Old Nassau" and the "Princeton Tiger" that propels them back for sporting events—like Saturday football games at historic Palmer Stadium to possibly relive the glory days of number 42, Dick Kazmaier, 1952 (All-American, Heisman Trophy winner).

Or perhaps it's the annual Alumni Reunion Week festivities at commencement time in early June when more than 10,000 alumni descend on campus for class reunions featuring dozens of faculty-alumni forums on vital issues, receptions, luncheons, art shows, music concerts, theater performances—all topped off by a huge fun-loving, carnival-like parade (P-rade) of alumni and their families across campus and down Prospect Street with its alluring array of handsome eating clubs. The parade starts with the oldest class down to the youngest (each class has distinctive costumes, banners, and placards), and features lots of bands, balloons (mostly orange and black), cheers, and wild, spirited applause.

What is there *about that name* that entices people back to Princeton? Could it be a rich combination and happy blending of all the aforementioned factors of geography, history, and the contagious spirit of its people? A recent visitor to Princeton was heard to exclaim, "Princeton is the most beautiful college town in America!"

But come see for yourself—and help determine if there is something *about that name* and *place*—and *people*—and *spirit* that casts its magic spell on *you*!

FINDING PENNIES

Do you think millionaires get as much kick out of finding pennies as I do? Just what is the magic in finding pennies and being thrilled by it? Does it have anything to do with Ben Franklin's adage, "A penny saved (found) is a penny earned"?

And somewhat beside the point, why is it that most coins found are pennies—and not quarters or nickels or dimes (which are even smaller than pennies)?

Maybe millionaires wouldn't ever stop to pick one up if they found it. I hope this is not so. Sometime I must be sure to ask the millionaires I know personally (two of them, to the best of my knowledge) if they do, in fact, pick up pennies—and if they do, are they thrilled by it?

In any event, whether a millionaire or not, I do hope you enjoy finding pennies, and then picking them up unashamedly—even if being watched by a crowd of people. This boldness comes with experience. "Courtesy of the road" rules should apply at all times, however, especially if you are in line at a checkout counter. Pushing and shoving people ahead of you to grab at a penny should be frowned upon and avoided, even at the cost of "a penny lost."

I'm convinced that the real joy to be gained in playing this "finding coins" game is in the discovery of the coin itself—"getting something for nothing." It's psychological. Further, the joy of discovery is heightened if the coins are found in a parking lot because the sun's rays brightly reflected them and pointed them out. If you are especially lucky, you may even find three or four pennies at the same spot—which is really akin to having "pennies from heaven."

I'm also convinced that it's not the accumulation of the pennies that matters, for they are always turned over to my wife, and I don't know what she does with them. We don't even have a penny piggy bank.

Anyone told to "Keep looking up" should never play this wicked game.

A MEDLEY OF FUN TIMES

Since this world is so full of a number of things, it should be easy to list a variety of times and events that cause us to *have fun*—good wholesome fun which radiates from cheerful hearts that are enthusiastically responsive to God and mankind.

It could even happen that we might get so caught up in an activity or event that we lose our sense of identity, and awareness of time and space. Now that's *pure fun!*

Here are some worthy fun times I've experienced:

• Bull Sessions during college days at Shippensburg.

• Parades of all types—with lots of bands, balloons, cheerleaders, flags, and floats—especially the Tournament of Roses Parade on New Year's Day.

• Celebrations of all kinds—births, baptisms, graduations, anniversaries, weddings, housewarmings, homecomings—and the surprises of giving and receiving gifts.

• Birthday parties that feature a birthday cake, balloons, presents, and lots of friends.

• Singing or playing musical instruments in a group that blends self into a larger whole.

• Moments of spontaneity and creativity—especially in the fine arts.

• Spirited contagious conversations that crackle with good humor and laughter.

• Being with people who smile a lot.

• The world of clowns, circuses, magicians—and the zoo, too.

• Spending summer vacations in Ocean City, New Jersey—the beaches, riding bikes on the boardwalk, the Tabernacle with great preaching and singing.

• World Series time, hoping to see another superstar like Willie Mays, who had great fun playing baseball—whether at bat, making circus catches in center field, or running the bases with cap flying.

• County fairs, with the fragrance of fresh grapes and apples in the horticulture hall—and having the total appearance of an abundant harvest of colorful fruits and vegetables.

• Taking photographs and seeing the happy results.

- Hearing the train whistle of an old steam locomotive.
- Playing the devil's advocate at a dull meeting.
- Dating girls on Saturday nights during my youth.
- Eating outdoors—picnics, football tailgating, patio restaurants.
- Getting autographs from baseball players—just like a kid.
- Being taught a new skill by a master craftsman.

CHAPTER V

STRUGGLES WITH OVERCOMING EVIL

Do not be overcome by evil, but overcome evil with good.

—Rom. 12:21 (NIV)

Put on the whole armor of God so that you can successfully resist all the devil's schemes and methods of attack....We are up against the unseen power that controls this dark world, and spiritual agents from the very headquarters of evil.

—Eph. 6:11–12 (RSV, P)

"THE WORLD, THE FLESH, AND THE DEVIL"

What an enticing trio for getting all of us into all kinds of mischief and trouble. But hear this—the religious community would be quick to point out that this unholy trio will not only get us into a peck of trouble if we are lured too much by its attractions, but would also warn us sojourners here on earth that if we want to live lives that are pleasing to God, we are going to face some mighty formidable opposition from this tempting trio.

We are further forewarned by the religious sages that if we earthlings succumb to the multitude of temptations that can dart at us from all directions from these three enemy seducers, we will be headed for a downfall of major proportions.

The warnings go something like this:

The World. By the world, religious sages mean the world system and its rulers, not the earth or its inhabitants as being part of a world globe. In this sense the world is viewed as being our spiritual opponent, as being the embodiment of force, stealing, greed, selfishness, and idol worship. The world is thought of as "looking out for me first," "wanting to be No. 1," "seeking status, position, and wealth," and "getting what you want when you want it no matter what the cost" (often through instilling fears and threats—as done by nations).

It includes the *showy deadly sins* of pride (self-justification), envy, and avarice (desire for wealth and hoarding it).

The Bible says: What shall it profit a man [or woman] if he [she] were to *gain the whole world,* and lose his [her] own soul? (Matt. 16:26, RSV, KJV [my paraphrase].)

The Flesh. The flesh refers to the earthly nature of mankind apart from the spiritual influence of God, not to the skin that covers our physical bodies. In this sense the fleshly nature of our lives is viewed as being very susceptible to temptations for sinning against God. We speak of the "sins of the flesh," and seem to recognize them more easily than we do the "sins of the world" or those that are attributed solely to the devil. The sins of the fleshly nature are thought of as overeating, drunkenness, wild parties, sexual immorality, sensuality, carousing, and even murder.

It involves the *active deadly sins* of gluttony, lust, and anger.

The Bible says: "Walk in the Spirit, and *do not gratify the desires of the flesh.*" Gal. 5:16, KJV, RSV, italics mine.)

The Devil. The devil is usually thought of as the personification of evil, such as in the silent goading of a person's will to have the person think and do something that is contrary to his or her inner conscience, and that will ultimately result in trouble and be in opposition to God. We sometimes refer to this jokingly as "the devil made me do it." The devil is biblically portrayed as being an accuser, deceiver, divider, imitator, liar, pretender, tormentor—and is a clever schemer in organizing jealousy and hatred campaigns that will divide and tear down persons and groups rather than unite them and build them up. The devil subtly desires to fill our minds with ideas that lead to doubt and despair, and often encourages us to be complacent, become inactive, and do nothing to solve the problems of the world. The devil is at his deceptive best when we are sometimes led to believe that "the devil doesn't even exist," that every evil idea we ever entertained was of our own creation.

The devil's domain includes the whole world, but he could be viewed as being a special promoter of the *silent deadly sins* that often seek to steer and stupefy our minds. These are self-doubt, false accusations of others' motives, jealousy, lying (truth cover-ups), and slothfulness (laziness, idleness).

The Bible is very clear and direct in what it has to say about the devil as seen by four varied writers:

Peter: Awake! Be self-controlled and alert! Your enemy the devil prowls around like a roaring lion looking for someone to devour. (1 Pet. 5:8, NEB [my paraphrase].)

Paul: Put on the whole armor of God so that you can successfully resist all the devil's methods of attack. (Eph. 6:11, RSV, P.)

James: Submit yourselves to God. Resist the devil and he will flee from you. (James 4:7, KJV.)

John: He who commits sin is of the devil; for the devil has sinned from the beginning. The reason the Son of God appeared was to destroy the works of the devil. (1 John 3:8, RSV.)

In our daily living, let us not be overcome by "the world, the flesh, and the devil"—but let us be overcome by God's Holy Spirit.

DECEPTIONS AND COUNTERFEITS

Deceptions. As for deceptions, they're all around us—individually and collectively.

In the stock market: "There was so much pessimism around that the only thing the market could do was to go up."

In the political world: "The more nuclear weapons we have, the greater are our chances for world peace."

In the scientific world: "The technological revolution will lift mankind into a new age of lasting peace, and prosperity, and incredible progress."

In the world of religion:

On God: "God is not all-powerful anymore, and is no longer in control of the universe."

On Jesus: "Jesus was okay for helping individuals one-on-one in past centuries, but he is no longer able to reach and help the masses in the late twentieth century."

Counterfeits. We usually think of counterfeits as being false and artificial, imitators of the real thing, and easily detectable. However, the best description heard of a counterfeit concerns money: "The best counterfeit bill is the one that is made to look so nearly like the real bill that it is indistinguishable to the untrained eye."

Counterfeit people may fool us for awhile through their clever imitations and pretensions and falsehoods, intended to deceive and mislead. Counterfeit people are more dangerous than forged checks and counterfeit money.

Beware of counterfeits!

God's messengers? The false apostles [of Christ]? They are counterfeits of the real thing, dishonest practitioners [of Christ]. And no wonder, for even Satan can disguise himself to look like an angel of light! (2 Cor. 11:13–14, P, TEV.)

We are told elsewhere in the Bible (Luke 21:8, NIV) to "watch out and not be deceived" in any way, to shine as God's special beacons of light here on earth, and to be agents of showing the real thing—God's truth and grace.

THE ANTICHRIST

It was at a Main Line Bible class near Philadelphia some thirty-five years ago that I first heard the word *Antichrist*. At that time some of the members of the class thought the coming Antichrist would be a pope from Rome; others thought that the Antichrist would come from the Middle East, possibly out of Jerusalem. I can well remember my dismay at hearing there would be such a person—somebody opposed to Christ. I had always taken a high view of Christ, believing everything the prophets and apostles of the Holy Scriptures had to say about Him, and it was difficult for me to believe that someone would be brazen enough in this world to want to rise up as a kind of egotistical world leader, push Christ aside, and usurp Him. I even cringe to this day when I hear someone in ordinary conversation, more often in a state of disgust and anger, take Christ's name in vain by saying something like: "*Jesus Christ*, I'm mad as *hell* about that."

How naive I must have been, knowing how Christ's name is often kicked about in military and civilian swearing circles today, not to realize that His whole mission in coming to earth some 2,000 years ago might also be upstaged in a most dramatic way someday.

I remember reading about Hitler during and after World War II, and learning that many people believed that Hitler was the Antichrist come into the world. He is said to have been heavily influenced by Nietzsche's writings, including his work, *The Antichrist*. Hitler certainly would fit many of the Antichrist's characteristics as commonly portrayed—a ruthless dictator with immense hypnotic qualities who could rally millions to his evil will and Nazi cause, and, but for a few miscalculations, could conceivably have conquered the world with his "Super Race" beliefs. His followers saluted him with "Heil Hitler," waved their swastika banners feverishly, and worshiped him as God. Suffice it to say, Hitler, who sometimes claimed to be the Messiah, came the closest to being the Antichrist of any other figure in recent history.

More recently I have read that there are literally hundreds of persons living on earth today who claim to be the Messiah. Some of them number their followers in millions. Full-page ads in major newspapers around the world on the weekend of April 24–25, 1982, announced, "The Christ Is Here Now," and confidently predicted that he would make himself known publicly soon—when the consciousness of the human race was ready for him. Even millions who are not Christians or Jews are hoping for a "Messiah" of some kind.

How can one tell the real Antichrist from the other aspiring antichrists?

95

And how can one tell the revealed Antichrist from the true Christ?

It won't be easy, for there will be a lot of deceptions and lies out there.

There are not many Biblical passages directly relating to the Antichrist, but the following four references are to the point, and will help answer the above two questions.

1 John 2:18 (P, TLB)—"You have heard, I expect, the prophecy about the coming of the Antichrist—the one who is against Christ. Believe me, there are antichrists about already, which confirms my belief that we are near the end."

1 John 2:22 (TLB, RSV)—"Who is the greatest liar? The one that denies that Jesus is the Christ, God's anointed one. Such a person is an Antichrist, for he denies God the Father and His Son."

1 John 4:1–3 (TLB, P)—"Don't always believe everything you hear just because someone says it is a message from God, but test it to see whether it comes from God or not. For the world is full of false prophets. You can test them in this simple way: every spirit that acknowledges the fact that Jesus Christ actually became man, comes from God; but the spirit that denies this fact does not come from God. The latter comes from the Antichrist."

2 John, v. 7 (NEB)—"Many deceivers have gone out into the world, who do not acknowledge Jesus Christ as coming in the flesh. These are the persons described as the Antichrist, the arch-deceiver."

Here are a few further thoughts I have gleaned from the prophetic writers:

• There will be no problem in finally determining who the real Antichrist is from among the many other competing antichrists, for peoples from all over the world will "worship" the Antichrist and his image (through television) as the Great World Ruler, the Messiah, the Savior of the World—the only one having the solution to the world's insoluble problems; the one capable of performing wondrous miracles, perhaps even "resurrecting" a famous person from the dead.

• He will have mystical hypnotic qualities similar to those that Hitler had, but he will be a better "deceiver," especially at the beginning of his rule, for he will imitate the true Christ so skillfully that billions will be deceived and think that he truly is the long-awaited Messiah—the one who will at long-last bring peace to the earth and elevate the human race to the highest levels of self-realization it has ever achieved.

• But alas, after a few years of peace and prosperity, things begin to break down. The Antichrist begins to shed his dovelike image of love and peace and assumes a tougher dictatorial role more in keeping with his true character of "the lawless one," and will ultimately be defeated by the true Christ, as foretold in St. Paul's Second Epistle to the Thessalonians:

Concerning the coming of our Lord Jesus Christ and our being gathered to Him, we ask you not to become easily unsettled or alarmed by some prophecy, report or letter saying that the day of the Lord has already come. Don't let anyone deceive you in any way, for that day will not come until the rebellion occurs and the man of lawlessness [the Antichrist] is revealed, the man doomed to destruction. He opposes and exalts himself over everything that is called God or is worshipped, and even sets himself up in God's temple, proclaiming himself to be God. (2:1–4, NIV.)

Then the lawless one will be revealed, whom the Lord Jesus will overthrow with the breath of his mouth and destroy by the splendor of his coming. The coming of the lawless one will be in accordance with the work of Satan displayed in all kinds of counterfeit miracles, signs and wonders. (2:8–9, NIV.)

ARMAGEDDON!

There are few words in the English language that have a greater ring of finality to them than does the word Armageddon. Whether used as a sobering title for a book, or as a striking word in social conversation to make a telling point ("Jane's marrying that no-good guy was her Armageddon")—the word is like dynamite to the irreligious and irreverent as well as to the obediently faithful.

It's impressive to see its arresting effect on hearers. It's just as though the minds and consciences of most people are attuned to the fact of an eventual Armageddon taking place in the history of the world, perhaps in the late 1980s or 1990s.

Countless people may doubt whether there is a God (dead or alive), or may raise all manner of questions about whether Jesus is the Son of God, but rarely will these same people question the reality of a future Armageddon. They apparently sense something of Noah Webster's riveting definition of Armageddon in the fifth edition of *Webster's Collegiate Dictionary*: "The place of a great battle to be fought out on 'the great day of God' between the powers of good and evil." (see also Rev. 16:16.)

With such a view of an ultimate great climactic conflict (warfare), no small wonder that this compelling word has captured the attention of both scoffers and believers, the secular as well as the spiritual world.

THE SIGNS OF THE TIMES

"Can *you* not discern the signs of the times?" (Matt. 16:3, KJV, italics mine.)

The glowing optimism of past generations sounded like the world was getting progressively better year by year, and that mankind could solve all of the world's problems if but given enough time. An unknown orator in 1900 declared that "laws were becoming more just, rulers more humane, music sweeter, and books wiser." Some fifty years later, following World War I, the Great Depression, and World War II, high optimism returned once again. It was generally felt that with the defeat of Nazi Germany, Fascist Italy, and Imperialist Japan, most of the evil forces on earth had been wiped out, and that "war would be no more." Most people felt that the world was getting better and better, especially with the aid of new scientific methods and achievements. America was the most powerful nation on earth, and the unquestioned world leader of nations.

This utopian world outlook for "world peace, prosperity, and the pursuit of happiness" has been somewhat shattered in recent decades by the Korean War, the frustrating war in Vietnam, the Watergate dishonesty disclosures, the Middle East hatred tensions, the Iranian hostage crises, the Latin American Communist infiltration, and countless recessions and inflationary cycles—all these have helped to dampen the optimism for an increasingly better society during recent decades.

During the last twenty years, optimism seems to have been replaced by a more sober realism of the times in which we're living. There are problems such as bankruptcies, child abuse, divorce, drug abuse, federal debt, gambling, hijackings (airline), homosexuality, international terrorism, kidnappings, nuclear weapons, pollution, pornography, racism, trade deficits, unemployment, and world hunger—to which could be added the age-old problems that have defied solutions: adultery, fornication, incest, lying, murder, and stealing. (see Hos. 4:1–2.)

Does that sound like what we read in our newspapers and see on our television screens today?

As disturbingly real as all the above problems are, the most pervasive predicament that seems to be robbing people of all ages and nationalities of much of their optimism for future peace and prosperity in the world is the threat of nuclear warfare and the ultimate annihilation of our spaceship Earth.

As Dr. Carl Sagan has said on numerous occasions, "The United States and Russia have 40,000 nuclear warheads. Only 1,000 nuclear warheads would be needed to trigger a 'nuclear winter catastrophe.' "

The whole world's civilization is at stake in this nuclear weapons buildup, possibly leading us toward World War III and Armageddon.

It's interesting to compare these disturbing problems of the 1980s with a list of "signs of the times" that have been revealed by Biblical prophecy scholars, some of which have been foretold thousands of years ago (see Matt., ch. 24). We are told to study world current events, and to look for trends and signs in our times that show an increase in the following:

Wars and rumors of wars	Peace and prosperity talk
Famines (drought conditions)	Business (corporation) mergers
Pestilences (diseases)	Rapid intercommunication
Earthquakes (natural catastrophes)	(electronics)
Lawlessness (crime, violence)	Space travel
Immorality	Human life-span
Family breakups	Ecumenism
Aggressiveness of women	Church apostasy
Destructive weapons	Cult and idol worship
Military forces	Satanic activity
One-world movements	False prophets

Astrology dependency (horoscopes)

Some scholars would suggest that the most telling prophecy being fulfilled right now, and that has been a reality for nearly the last forty years, is the return of the Jews to their homeland (see Jer. 16:14–15), the State of Israel (1948) and the old city of Jerusalem (1967). Others would point to the relatively recent formation of the European Common Market (the United States of Europe), with Brussels as its headquarters, as another fulfillment of prophecy.

"Now when all these things begin to happen, look up and lift up your heads, for your redemption is drawing near—you will soon be free." (Luke 21:28, NKJV, RSV, P.)

IS THE END NEAR?

Are we moving toward the end of the world? Are we moving toward a cataclysmic end of history as we know it? These questions are haunting people everywhere today. The decade of the 1970s has been called the "Me Decade," and the 1980s the "Decade of Survival."

Surviving the decade of the 1980s usually has special reference to some type of nuclear disaster on the earth. It is reported that many youth of today do not expect to live out their natural lifetimes and grow to old age because of a possible nuclear war intervention, with many of them expecting a holocaust by the year 2000. Certainly there are sufficient stockpiles of nuclear weapons, if used, to destroy all of us many times over. Even the concept of a limited nuclear war is out of the question if most of us are to survive. Short of widespread death and destruction, it has been said that a single nuclear warhead detonated 250 miles above Nebraska would send enough electromagnetic pulses generated by the blast over the entire United States so as to shut down all power and communications—no telephone lines working, no electricity, no computers; only confusion and widespread chaos through failure of solid-state devices that have replaced vacuum tubes.

Apart from a possible "nuclear Armageddon" of some sort, some writers warn of other tribulations to come that could lead to potential world crises that would not respect national boundaries, such as (1) the greenhouse effect created in warming the earth's atmosphere through excess carbon dioxide produced by human activity; (2) water shortages; and (3) a worldwide financial disaster (debt defaults by borrowing countries).

An impending "gloom and doom" scenario has become a prosperous big business for many writers and publishers. "The Doomsday Clock is Ticking" and "One Minute 'Til Midnight" are headlines sometimes used to grab our attention. Some investment advisors have further frightened millions of people with their dire warnings about the "death of the dollar" and the collapse of the world banking system—inviting readers to invest heavily in gold and silver bullion, to flee the cities, and to hoard a year's supply of food and tangible securities out in the country.

Predictions concerning the end of the world often appear in newspapers from time to time, and have been for centuries. Sometimes the followers of a seer are told to flee to the mountains on a certain date to await the end of the world. At times the "religious prophets" are falsely led to predict an exact date for a climaxing event to happen, and are made to look foolish when it doesn't. It is reported, for example, that a "group of the faithful"

101

were told by their leader that a climactic event would occur on *October 22, 1844*. Some of the farmers refused to harvest their crops that summer. Many of them faced a bleak winter with no food in stock and no money to buy other necessities when the predicted day turned out to be a false alarm by midnight of the twenty-second.

In England a local newspaper notice read, "The world is definitely coming to an end on Wednesday, *December 11, 1968* at precisely noon." There was no doomsday to report the next day.

We read about the "Countdown of the 1980s," and are sometimes led to wonder if civilization will survive this dangerous decade envisioned by scientists, religious leaders, and others.

Obviously the end of the world did not come in the first half of the decade, despite such warnings as the following:

1981 Forecast

The world to an end will come,
In nineteen hundred and eighty-one.

Comment: This obviously didn't happen as predicted by an unknown poet almost 2,500 years ago.

1982 Forecast

In 1982 the nine planets will not only be on the same side of the sun, but in perfect alignment, known as the "Jupiter effect." *Newsweek* magazine referred to this situation as "An Apocalyptic Prediction"—when all the planets will come into line and exert a united gravitational pull on the earth that will set off dire consequences such as the earth has never experienced before.

Comment: Although the event in the latter half of 1982 did happen and was unique in our solar system, its effects on the earth were minimal—far less than had been expected by way of a series of devastating events and a possible "end of the world" scenario in the minds of many people.

1984 Forecast

George Orwell's book entitled *1984*, written to warn the Western world of what he thought the future might hold, created enough media attention before and during 1984 to motivate some writers to think that 1984 might be the year when the world nears its end. "Countdown to 1984" was the theme of many articles written before that time, some of which thought that a triggering incident such as terrorists exploding an atomic bomb at some strategic time and place might occur during 1984.

Comment: The year 1984 came and went, and although many of Orwell's predictions for our society did come true, none of his most terrifying forecasts came to fruition during 1984.

1988 Forecast

The Club of Rome, an exclusive association of one hundred policymakers from twenty-five nations, has been warning of a coming disaster for years. At a recent gathering they were told that they had until 1988 for all nations to unite together and achieve international cooperation, or else planet Earth is doomed.

Comment: We'll wait and see what unfolds. Given the recent track record of the "United" Nations, it's difficult to see how all nations will unite by 1988, given their fierce individual national wills, and in some cases rivaling factions warring within nations to exert their own wills to gain more power and control for themselves.

On top of this, there is a growing sense of expectancy in both scientific and religious circles that some apocalyptic event is soon to occur.

Will *1989* contain such a cataclysmic world happening? Or the *1990s*? Will there be a series of worldwide events leading to a climax of history as we know it by the year *2000*?

Is the end near??

CHAPTER VI

INSECURE LIVING—WITHOUT GOD'S SPIRIT

The man [generic] without the Spirit does not accept the things that come from the Spirit of God, for they are foolishness to him, and he cannot understand them, because they are spiritually discerned.

—1 Cor. 2:14 (NIV)

He who conceals his sins does not prosper, but whoever confesses and renounces them finds mercy.

—Prov. 28:13 (NIV)

Do not restrain the Holy Spirit.

—1 Thess. 5:19 (TEV)

ON BEING DIFFICULT

Why is it that some people (often one's closest relatives, friends, or neighbors) can be so difficult to get along with?

And the issues that "bug them," "hang them up," make them "touchy" and irritable—yes, and sometimes red-faced "mad"—are usually little things that are blown way out of proportion and, in fact, seem to contain little substance or truth. Yet, all manner of wrongdoings can be quickly pointed out by the accusing tongue, and one can be blamed for almost anything.

In extreme cases of false, unjustified accusations, a somewhat typical pattern of behavior seems to manifest itself. The difficult persons feel sorry for themselves, and think that you (and the world) are against them (for whatever imagined reasons) and are out to "get them" and "do them in." Often these paranoid-type feelings seem to grow out of stressful situations in their lives that have never been fully resolved psychologically and spiritually—and hence continue to cause a negative, fearful, guilty state of mind within such persons. The behavioral result is to project these unresolved problems onto the shoulders of others, but worse yet, through self-delusion, to accuse those "loved ones" within earshot of somehow being responsible for bringing on their misfortunes and ills.

In such states of mind, it's almost impossible to do or say anything that will please these difficult persons. In attempts at reconciliation, they will eagerly misinterpret what you say, and draw the wrong conclusions. In fact, it is doubtful that even God could please them and make things right when they're having really bad days.

What can we do when encountering such people who seem to pride themselves on being difficult?

Here are some debatable insights that have helped me survive (and on occasion overcome) nasty, and at times vicious, onslaughts—and still retain my sanity:

• Listen politely, with no retorts, and let what is said "go in one ear and out the other."

• If a response is demanded by the difficult person, reply: "This blowup of yours is only the second time I've heard it. I'll give you three more blowups before I plan to make any responses."

• If the accuser resorts to employing the weight of the Almighty against you by saying, "I've prayed about this, and God told me that you were plainly wrong in this matter," respond by saying, "That's odd, but God never told me that."

• Remain as cool and calm under attack as possible, remembering that as yet you have not been spit upon, cursed, given vinegar to drink, nor have you been nailed to a cross and crucified—as Jesus was.

• If all attempts at reconciliation fail, and you are not able to "sit down and reason together"—then do as Jesus did when he told his disciples (in effect): Whoever will not welcome you, or *even listen* to what you have to say, leave that house or town, shake the dust off your feet, and go into the next house or town, where they will gladly welcome you. (see Matt. 10:14.) (Moral: "You can't win them all.")

P.S. In case your accuser is a close personal friend or relative that you do not ever want to give up on, then adopt the stance of a persevering saint and "pray without ceasing," imploring the help of the powerful, invisible mediation of the Holy Spirit to hopefully provide a reconciliation breakthrough.

GAMES PEOPLE PLAY

No, I'm not thinking about checkers, chess, backgammon, Uncle Wiggily (do people still play this game?), Scrabble, Monopoly, Trivial Pursuit, or a whole host of card games that people play. Rather, I'm thinking about the more deadly games of deception and denial some people play, using "white lies" and cover-up attempts to throw onlookers offguard in seeing the real truth in a situation.

Here are a few deceptive, and often tricky, games:

• *Keeping Up with the Joneses* (Pride)—Can be played by any number of families, whatever the last name, but best practiced when least able to afford the showpieces—be it Waterford crystal, a whole stack of Windsor chairs, a bigger home at a more prestigious address, a Mercedes Benz in the driveway and a station wagon (with roof rack for skis) for good measure, plus a bicycle or two (with all the extras) for the children's pleasures.

• *Pointing the Guilty Finger* (Finding Fault)—Most generally played by those folks who unwittingly find serious faults in someone else's behavior—who, upon closer inspection, are found to be projecting their own faults onto others. So it was that Peg continually criticized the custodial staff where she worked for not keeping her office clean of dust and dirt, only to be secretly hiding her own housekeeping shortcomings back home in the form of having a badly cluttered house in need of a long overdue housecleaning.

• *Elevating Oneself at the Expense of Others* (Selfishness)—This game requires only a selfish spirit, and a desire to play it to the hilt at opportune moments. One such timid soul, fearful about driving her own car home from work during a heavy snowstorm, begged a ride with a fellow worker. Upon arriving at the crest of a hill, and seeing buses and cars stalled in crisscross patterns all along the hillside, she exclaimed gleefully while clapping her hands excitedly: "O goody! If there's anything I enjoy seeing, it's people getting stuck in a ditch."

• *Getting the Last Buck* (Greed)—Any rascal desirous of playing this game should observe the rules carefully: Take out all the tax shelters possible, hopefully letting your children pay the accrued taxes upon inheritance; complain about the exorbitant charges for any services rendered, requesting a lower bill; delay paying your bills indefinitely, hoping your bills will eventually be lost or forgotten; give as little to charity as possible, even faking large contributions through the "I gave at the office" routine; figure out a way of having the government owing you large sums of money at tax time; never join a church or service organization where you would be expected to pay your fair share of the community load. Instead, hoard all your money, and if you must use any of the accumulated piles, spend it only on yourself.

Special situations: If you're an owner of a business, use all the tax loopholes conceivable—and exert pressure on legislators to create new ones for your direct tax-advantage benefit. *If you're a salaried person*, pressure your employer to pay you maximum salary ahead of schedule, seek an unlimited travel allowance (no records), ask for an annual housing allowance, and request a lump sum amount toward payment of your federal, state, and local taxes.

The above games that some people play are nauseating, and deserving of more than a burp or two from its tricky players.

"KNOCKING EACH OTHER OFF"

Do you, or other members of your household (perhaps your spouse), ever engage in this wicked game?

No, it's not like warfare between nations, or even warfare between two people that results in physical harm.

Instead, it's the insidious parlor game that involves a series of put-downs, where in a "joking" devilish manner some "friends" seem to enjoy (?) unduly criticizing others, such as their own spouses and other folks who are around, by pointing out their faults, being sarcastic, and making derogatory comments. In short, by taking others apart and supposedly taking them down a peg or two, the gossipers appear to be psychologically elevating their own egos to a superior (albeit false) position.

For those of you who are innocent, or have never been present when this malicious parlor game was played, here are some put-downs that were heard recently.

To a spouse present:

> "You always think you're so smart and know all the
> answers—you're never wrong."
> "—Oh shut up!"

Said about absent "friends":

> "I never did care for her—and I don't like her sister either."
> "I don't know what she sees in him—he's terrible."
> "Did you notice how badly Edna looked on Sunday?"
> "That's one of his biggest faults—you can't trust him."
> "I'll never forgive them for the way they mistreated me."
> "I don't talk to them—they're the scum of the earth."
> "They're interested in knowing about me only if it's bad news."
> "To hell with 'em!"

There is an antidote for all this backbiting and downgrading of others if you're present and can pull it off at the right strategic moment. Just say courageously:

"I would prefer to wish everyone well, even their perfection."

"GOING FOR THE JUGULAR"

There is nothing more descriptive of "finishing off one's opponent" than the phrase, "going for the jugular." Phrases such as, "heading for the eye of a hurricane," "hitting the bull's-eye," or "shooting from the hip" are tame by comparison.

Why would anyone want to "go for the jugular" in a civilized society? After all, we're not like a bunch of tigers out there pursuing animals in the jungle. It's akin to "going for the kill" in a culture that is supposedly advancing toward more maturity with each passing year. Yet...

In the business world, a phrase is often used to describe "the climb to the top" by aspiring corporate officers; it's called "in-house fighting," a subtle form of "going for the jugular," even among supposed friends. Once at the top of a young, rapidly growing company, some executives actually become *ruthless* in their dealings with other competitive companies.

Politically, Watergate gave us many vivid illustrations of what can happen, even at the top echelons of the White House, when men, through lust for power and "saving their own hides," will resort to "bloodletting" of all kinds through blatant accusations of wrongdoing aimed at their peers.

Even presidential campaigners have been known to "sling the mud," to engage in "dirty smears," and to repetitiously belittle their opponents and discredit them.

Nor have the afternoon soap operas, viewed by increasing millions of adults, been asleep in this area. The performers, often jilted in the game of love, set a merry pace of "going for the jugular"—attempting to mortally wound or "finish off" a person (either a close relative or friend) who is conceived to be a living threat to them, and resorting to such "jugular tools" in their episodes as gossip, slander, fear, hatred, greed, anger, or even murder.

The best connotation that might possibly be given this most descriptive phrase is in the legal profession. It is sometimes used to describe a lawyer's skillful success in the courtroom in aggressively attacking his opponent's arguments, using penetrating steel-trap cross-examination techniques that eventually result in the strangulation of the opponent's arguments, thereby winning the case for his client.

It's a tough world we all face at times! We are told to "hang in there," and not to let "the world grind us down."

There are times in life, however, when we do seem to be ground down by outside forces that seem beyond our control. We feel hemmed in...surrounded...squeezed. We, in fact, sometimes feel that other people are

111

"going straight for *our* jugular." At such times, we need the comfort and wisdom that the Scriptures can bring and in Rom. 12:2 (P) we find this gem to guide us:

> Don't let the world around you squeeze you into its own mould, but let God re-make you so that your whole attitude of mind is changed.

WHEN ALL LIFE GOES TO HELL

There are times in life when it seems that "all hell breaks loose," whether at the international, national, local, or personal level. History reminds us of times when this seemed so: terrorist car bombings by the dozens killing hundreds of innocent civilians; a Flight 90 crash during a blinding snowstorm into the icy waters of the Potomac River with few survivors; Pearl Harbor; the first atomic bomb dropped on Hiroshima with widespread destruction of the city and loss of life from the intense fire, heat, and radiation; the Battle of the Bulge; the mass raids on European cities in World War II with thousands of bombs and incendiary devices that set entire cities ablaze (in Dresden it created a firestorm that leveled the city's buildings and killed 135,000 people in one night); the concentration camps; the flame-throwing devices used in the Vietnam War to get at enemy troops in tunnels and fighting like guerillas—all these events were hellish.

Is there anything more hellish than warfare?

One would hardly think so—until faced with personal hells that seem to have no real beginning and no announced end, as most warfare does.

Consider the following booby-trap situations that seem to have no parameters, no containments, no solutions, no hope:

• A married couple of forty years living in separate sections of the country—separated, constantly hating one another, with no desire for reconciliation.

• A teenage girl of fifteen, first living with her father, then told to live with her mother who doesn't want her—going from pillar to post knowing that neither of her divorced parents wants her.

• A mother of four school-age children trying to keep the family together after the father suddenly announces he's leaving them all to marry his twenty-five-year-old secretary.

• The poor who have nothing to live for and to whom life has nothing to offer, who have to exist on the fringe of death—many with little food, naked, no medicine, flies, and no washing, laundry, or elementary sanitation facilities.

• A psychiatric ward of a mental hospital that contains moaning and screaming patients on the prowl in rooms that are padded and devoid of furniture.

• Senior citizens in a nursing home having no relatives or friends to visit them, and dying inch-by-inch from loneliness.

• A cancer victim, after years of chemotherapy treatment, finally learns that the disease is in remission—only to find his wife wants a divorce, his teenage son runs away to get a quickie marriage, his business is entering bankruptcy, and his house is up for sheriff's sale.

• A female having sexual intimacy with a male, after which she learns that he has AIDS.

But even when it seems that everything has gone to hell, there is *always hope*.

In my distress I called to the Lord, and He heard me. Out of the depths of hell I cried for help, and He heard my voice. (Jon. 2:2, NIV, KJV, NAB.)

CHAPTER VII

LIVING BY FAITH

Have faith in God.

—Mark 11:22 (KJV)

This life that I live now, I live by faith in the Son of God, who loved me and gave his life for me.

—Gal. 2:20 (TEV)

To have faith is to be sure of the things we hope for, to be certain of the things we cannot see.

—Heb. 11:1 (TEV)

So we fix our attention not on the visible things but on the invisible; for the visible things are transitory: it is the invisible things that are really permanent [eternal].

—2 Cor. 4:18 (TEV, P)

V-FORMATIONS

V-formations are beautiful sights usually reserved for special occasions. World War II veterans may recall that the convoys of troopships crossing the North Atlantic to England were usually escorted by naval warships (headed by a battleship) in broad V-formations. The Battle of the Bulge in Belgium, also during World War II, was aided immeasurably by scores of B-17 bomber squadrons flying in powerful V-formations, wave after wave, to bomb enemy positions. Nor will history ever forget Prime Minister Churchill's V-sign made by his raised right hand indicating expected victory in the battle for Britain. The Air Force Thunderbird aerial demonstration team often flies in spectacular V-formations. Winning sports teams also like to display the V-for-victory sign.

In nature the most spectacular display of V-formations belongs to the graceful Canada geese. They neither fly in power or military might, nor do they fly to gloat over an athletic victory, but they seem to fly for the love of flying in an orderly and peaceable kingdom. Who among us has not had their faith restored time and again by the orderly procession of the geese going north or south as if by divine Providence?

In the face of the many earthly problems of mankind, isn't it refreshing to feel that "all is right with the world" when the Canada geese are making their appointed rounds each fall and spring—and revealing to us through their seasonal migrations something of the mystery, beauty, and orderliness of God's universe?

CADAVERS

To see a cadaver—dozens of them—lined up in rows on tables in the basement of a medical school, with white damp sheets covering each of them, might seem gruesome to many and something to be avoided at all costs. But for those with an adventuresome inquiring mind, viewing cadavers with the expert help of a knowledgeable senior medical student who also functions as an informative tour guide to answer questions, can be a rare, unforgettable experience—one that will enhance a greater appreciation of our wonderful bodies, and strengthen our faith.

It's the inside of the cadaver that is full of revelations and wonderments. In particular, it's the five vital organs that command the most attention, each of which is essential to staying alive.

The Heart. This most remarkable organ has got to be one of the wonders of the world! It is romanticized in literature, and cited hundreds of times in the Bible, especially in the Psalms: "Create in me a clean heart, O God; and renew a right spirit within me" (Ps. 51:10, KJV). Jesus mentions it in the Beatitudes: "Blessed are the pure in heart: for they shall see God" (Matt. 5:8, KJV). It's a complete surprise to see how small the heart is. It's barely the size of a fist, and can easily be held cup-shaped in the hands; some grapefruit seem larger than it is.

Yet this miraculous muscle beats an average of 70 times a minute, 24 hours a day, for 70 or more years—nonstop, except to slow down while we're sleeping. That equates to over 36 million heartbeats in a year, or over 2-1/2 billion heartbeats in a life span of 70 years. It is said that this amazing pump, aided by the blood vessels, circulates the blood through the body every 23 seconds at an approximate rate of 5 quarts per minute. What a remarkable tiny organ to perform all that heroic work!

The Lungs. The lungs look like we've been led to expect—they are large spongy tissues. Since we have two lungs (left and right), they occupy a lot of space beneath our rib cages. The process of breathing in oxygen and breathing out carbon dioxide goes on automatically throughout life, so that like our heartbeat, we tend to take our lungs for granted. Yet the lungs, too, perform miraculous functions. For example, it's still a mystery (except to the architect of the lungs) how the lungs can take in the oxygen we breathe from the air in a gaseous form, transfer it to the blood system, which transports it in a liquid form, take the impurities from the blood, which are in a liquid form, and expel them as a colorless gas back into the air as carbon dioxide—and all done in one effortless silent breath of several seconds!

117

A pointed health lesson learned from observing the lungs should be noted: Anyone wanting to quit smoking, but not having enough motivation or willpower to do so, would likely quit for good if they ever saw the lungs of a normal nonsmoking cadaver alongside the lungs of a heavy-smoking cadaver. It's a dramatic contrast, like comparing a clean water-sponge with a grimy sponge after washing a dirty car. It also looked as though the lungs' filter system, its air sacs, had been clogged with black soot.

The Liver. The biggest surprise in seeing all the five vital organs had to be the liver. It's huge by comparison with the other organs. Its dark mass weighs about 4 pounds, and is fairly solid and compact. Nevertheless, this special master regulator and purifier of our blood distributes just the right amount of sugar and amino acids to every cell in the body, and stores what is not needed as a reserve for later possible use. An improperly functioning liver can cause us to feel miserable and debilitated.

Another vivid health lesson was learned from observing the liver: The liver needs to be treated with respectful wisdom concerning the foods and liquids we ingest. If the liver becomes overloaded and damaged through excessive alcohol consumption, for example, it will become enlarged, hardened, and diseased (as in cirrhosis of the liver)—and will no longer be able to perform its noble deeds of purifying and regulating the blood's life support system for the body.

The Kidneys. Our two kidneys are by far the smallest of the five vital organs—small, but oh so mighty! They are bean-shaped and delicate look-ing, yet contain 64 miles of filtering pipes to remove liquid wastes, and also purify and regulate, in just the right amount, the blood's mineral con-tent flow throughout the body. The inside of a kidney contains millions of tiny tubes, and looks something like a honeycomb, or the finlike blades of a jet engine. Every day these small kidneys filtrate 180 quarts of blood, sending 178 quarts of the purified liquid back to the bloodstream, and sending the remaining 2 quarts to the bladder as separated urine. Our kid-neys for all their small size are absolutely amazing!

The Brain. Our brain is a miracle of design and function, and would appear to be God's crowning achievement in the intricate design and mys-tery of the human body. This relatively small organ, weighing approxi-mately 3 pounds, and suspended in a liquid to help protect it against sud-den blows, looks something like a small cauliflower in outward appearance. Our brain has to be the most ingeniously contrived, complex mechanism ever made, and which no human engineer can begin to equal.

Our brain has been likened to a gigantic telephone switchboard in which each of 10 billion brain cells can send messages to other brain cells (10 billion cells with more than 100,000 miles of nerve fibers) in billions of different combinations. It has also been compared with an electronic computer—or a supercomputer, (as in the study of cybernetics)—yet it is able to far outshine its mechanical imitators, for it is its own programmer, can think and feel with emotions, and make value judgments.

A listing of the brain's many functions and attributes would read like an encyclopedia. Here are a few main functions: balance, conscience, consciousness, dreams, emotions, imagination, intelligence, knowledge, listening, memory, reading, seeing, speaking, subconscious, thinking, values, willpower, and writing. The brain is also the master-control switchboard (just like an electrical system with a flow of electric currents) for regulating all the other body systems and functions, including circulatory, digestive, glandular, muscular, nervous, reproduction, respiratory, sensory, and skeletal systems. The brain controls and directs the entire body, like an orchestra conductor or a NASA flight director. What a complex marvel of efficiency!

This wondrous human body of ours, when healthy, is like a smoothly running quiet engine of many parts, all working harmoniously together, each part needing, reinforcing, and energizing the other part—and especially is this true of the five vital organs in their continual goal and task of receiving, revitalizing, and preserving life through the blood. If any one of them breaks down and fails to function, the body will soon die.

Even cadavers can reveal to us, to paraphrase the Scriptures, that "we are fearfully and wonderfully made" into this ingenious interconnecting body network by our omniscient Creator, God.

PATRIOTISM

To show love for America should be a daily duty not limited to the two national holiday observances of Memorial Day and Independence Day (always on July 4). Too often the longtime citizens of a country take its virtues for granted; or worse, bad-mouth their country ad nauseam starting with the president. It makes little difference who is president. ("They just don't have any good people running for president anymore.") As popular as President Eisenhower was in the 1950s, with his infectious grin and victorious-waving right arm—and with the further help of all those catchy "I like Ike" buttons—Ike received his share of unkind remarks.

It is often helpful at times when too many hypercritical remarks are made about our country, ofttimes in a highly biased and prejudicial manner, to get in touch with immigrants to this country and hear them speak with sincerity and passion about the America they love. To them America is another word for opportunity, and still represents one of the best hopes remaining among the free democratic nations of the world to pursue "life, liberty and happiness" without the heaviness of an oppressive (often dictatorial) government restricting their basic freedoms of living, speaking, working, and worshiping.

Exhibit One—Patriotic Immigrant

This immigrant I prize so highly for his patriotic passion and zeal heard about America being "the land of opportunity" when he was a young boy in his native Greece, and continually dreamed of someday going to America. So it finally happened in 1906 that as a poor immigrant lad of sixteen from a small village in Greece, he sailed past the Statue of Liberty and landed in New York City—not knowing anyone there. After a few years of wandering from one dollar-a-day job to another, he somehow heard about a shoeshine business that was for sale in downtown Hanover, Pennsylvania (about 200 miles from New York City). He borrowed $200 to buy the shoeshine business in 1912, which included cleaning and blocking hats, as well as the roasting of peanuts, making popcorn, and roasting chestnuts—and, oh yes, shining lots of shoes for a "nickel a shine."

His business career was interrupted six years later when he volunteered to serve in World War I as a private in the front lines of three major battles in France. Following his military decorations and service in World War I, he helped found the American Legion Post back in Hanover, Pennsylvania —and has never missed a year since 1917 marching in the town's traditionally impressive three-division Memorial Day parade (which attracts thousands of flag-waving onlookers even today).

After returning to his shoe-shine business at the end of the war in 1919, George Stratigas really made his "land of opportunity" dream come true, for his business prospered handsomely. At the peak of his business, he maintained a twelve-chair parlor, with no less than nine bootblack boys on duty on Saturdays. He had approximately 1,700 boys work for him during his career, and is reported to have gotten along well with each one.

George's many customers likewise looked forward to having their shoes shined and to be greeted with a smiling, cheery "Hello there, how are you? It's good to see you again." A local reporter, speaking for his many beloved friends in the community, noted at George's retirement that, "He has been blessed with a rare personal trait that enables him to strike up a lifetime friendship with a stranger in a matter of minutes."

George always had full-size photographs of the recent presidents prominently displayed on the walls of his shoe-shine shop for all his patrons to see while getting their shoes shined. One of his three daughters told a reporter that her father was so patriotic that when he sat down to watch a baseball game on television he automatically stood at attention while the national anthem was being played.

Upon retiring in 1978 at the age of 90, after 65 years of prosperity and happiness in the shoe-shine business, George had this to say about the closing of his shoe-shine parlor: "There are now too few men who wear hats, and not many want their shoes cleaned and shined—not like the good old days. So I must retire at 90 even though I don't want to."

What a replica of the Spirit of '76!

Exhibit Two—Historic Times and Words

A variety of patriotic celebrations occurred during the week of July 4, 1976, to commemorate the 200th birthday of our independence, especially along the Eastern Corridor from Boston to Washington. There were imaginative fireworks displays in many cities, evening concerts held in city parks, and tall sailing ships on display in large ports.

In Philadelphia, the birthplace of our nation and the site of Independence Hall and the Liberty Bell, a gigantic parade lasting four hours was held on July 4, 1976, with over a hundred colorful floats and marching bands highlighting the festivities. On July 6 the Queen of England paid a visit to Philadelphia and its historic sites.

Across America then, people remembered the signing of the Declaration of Independence, the framing of our Constitution, and other immortal words spoken by famous Americans some 200 years ago when our people needed to hear them as rallying cries.

In the belief that we all need to hear the courageous voices of brave people of our illustrious past again and again, and to whom we owe an eternal debt of gratitude for their visions, commitments, and sacrifices in laying such a solid foundation for our unique country—here then are some words worthy of our inheritance:

These are the times that try men's souls....Tyranny, like Hell, is not easily conquered; yet we have this consolation with us, that the harder the conflict, the more glorious the triumph....Heaven knows how to put a proper price upon its goods; and it would be strange indeed if so celestial an article as *freedom* should not be highly rated.—Thomas Paine.

Three millions of people, armed in the holy cause of liberty, are invincible by any force which our enemy can send against us. Besides, we shall not fight our battles alone. There is a just God who presides over the destinies of Nations....Is life so dear, or peace so sweet, as to be purchased at the price of chains and slavery? Forbid it, Almighty God! I know not what course others may take, but as for me, *give me liberty, or give me death!*—Patrick Henry.

I only regret that I have but one life to lose for my country.—Nathan Hale.

By the blessing of God, may our country become a vast and splendid monument, not of oppression and terror, but of wisdom, of peace, and of liberty, upon which the world may gaze with admiration forever.—Daniel Webster.

I believe in the United States of America as a government of the people, by the people, for the people; whose just powers are derived from the consent of the governed; a democracy in a republic, a sovereign Nation of many sovereign States; a perfect Union, one and inseparable; established upon those principles of freedom, equality, justice, and humanity for which American patriots sacrificed their lives and fortunes. I therefore believe it is my duty to my country to love it, to support its Constitution, to obey its laws, to respect its flag, and to defend it against all enemies.—William Tyler Page, *The American's Creed.*

Exhibit Three—Patriotic Songs
If all else has failed to arouse your patriotic fervor by now, then let there be a rendition of "America the Beautiful" as played and sung by Ray Charles at the piano, or "The Battle Hymn of the Republic" as recorded by the Philadelphia Orchestra and the Mormon Tabernacle Choir. These two numbers will stir your soul and move you to tears, for the songs are

soulfully and powerfully expressed by the aforementioned artists.

Beyond the artists, however, the hauntingly beautiful words of each song, and how they came to be written, are worth noting briefly.

Katherine Lee Bates was on a trip westward across our country. Her first stop was in Chicago and the great Columbian Exposition with its gleaming white buildings, which inspired her to write in verse 4: "Thine alabaster cities gleam…" She continued westward across the plains to Colorado, and from the summit of Pike's Peak was inspired to write of her lofty view as she looked eastward:

O beautiful for spacious skies,
For amber waves of grain,
For purple mountain majesties
Above the fruited plain!

America! America!
God shed His grace on thee,
And crown thy good with brotherhood
From sea to shining sea.

Thus were the four stanzas to "America the Beautiful" brought forth.

The words to the "The Battle Hymn of the Republic" were written by Julia Ward Howe after she visited some of the wounded servicemen in a hospital during the Civil War—and saw the resulting agony and suffering of soldiers fighting a terrible war. When would it all end? Only when the Lord returns with great power and glory, she thought. Thus was born the inspiration for writing this stirring hymn, which has an abundance of vivid spiritual visions in its five stanzas, such as:

Mine eyes have seen the glory of the coming of the Lord;
He is trampling out the vintage where the grapes of wrath are stored…

He has sounded forth the trumpet that shall never call retreat;
He is sifting out the hearts of men before His judgment seat…

In the beauty of the lilies, Christ was born across the sea,
With a glory in His bosom that transfigures you and me;
As He died to make men holy, let us die to make men free,
While God is marching on.

Glory! glory! Hallelujah!

TAKING RISKS

As children, most of us were admonished not to take risks, for if we did they often led to accidents and pain—like touching the hot stove with our fingers and getting seared flesh; running before we had fully learned to walk and getting bruised lumps on our heads from falling; or climbing trees beyond our skills to get back down and getting spanked after the parental rescue.

But later in life, someone who takes risks is often looked upon as a hero. In fact, preachers sometimes encourage us from the pulpit to take risks in life, to venture out into something new that we've never tried before. This is the age of new discovery. Be adventuresome. "Nothing ventured, nothing gained," we hear it said. "Don't be afraid to fail." We are reminded that faith is the essence of risk taking—to venture into the unseen and unknown.

So there's quite a wide gulf to bridge for most of us between the early stern warnings we received about not taking risks and playing it safe, and the exhortations later in life to take risks, to be adventuresome, to calculate the dangers, and to develop a fearless mind-set.

Most of us have grown up and matured facing normal risks that are part of natural living: driving automobiles on highways, taking occasional flights in planes, being caught outside in a driving thunderstorm, and overindulging in eating.

In the sports world, blitzing linebackers in football take risks by going "all out" in their attempts to throw their opponents off-balance and throw the quarterback for a loss.

In basketball, teams take chances by using the "all-court press" in attempts to rattle the other team and steal the ball from them.

Enos Slaughter, the daring St. Louis Cardinals right fielder and Hall of Famer, personified risk-taking at its best on the baselines: "I always wanted an extra base. If I hit it up through the middle, I left the plate not wanting to stop at first; I wanted two. If I hit it down the right-field line, I didn't want two bases, I wanted three. And I wasn't afraid to take a gamble."

But the risk takers I prize the most highly are the people who know the dangers involved in a risk, think through ways of minimizing the risk, and develop a steel-trap mind to "go for it" in a positive way, overcoming doubts and fears in the manner of a superperson. Two such persons immediately come to mind: Chuck Yeager, whom I've seen and read about, and Jim Irwin, whom I know personally.

Chuck Yeager, born in 1923, was the first man to fly faster than the speed of sound in an X-1 rocket plane. He has taken hundreds of risks as a war fighter pilot and later as a test pilot.

During World War II, after having been shot down by the Germans over France, and later helped by the French underground to make his escape to Spain, Chuck was ordered to return to the United States and not fly any more combat missions over Europe. Yeager stated his case before General Eisenhower for a return to highly risky warfare: "I don't want to leave my buddies after only eight missions. It just isn't right to send me back home. I have a lot of fighting left to do."

Eisenhower agreed, and Yeager returned as a fighter pilot, scoring an ace on one mission by downing five enemy planes over Germany. "Flying combat is deadly serious, life-and-death stuff.... Even today I'm definitely not a rocking-chair type. I can't just sit around, watch television, drink beer, get fat, and fade out."

Jim Irwin, *Apollo 15* astronaut, and one of only a few select men to have ever walked on the moon, must typify the breed of test pilots and astronauts who are risk takers of the highest order. He relishes doing new things for the first time, has an incessant curiosity, and a tenacious drive—yet possesses a cool manner that thoughtfully and thoroughly plans for any contingencies in advance. It's personality traits like these that help make astronauts appear to be superhuman and almost supernatural.

Even though astronauts are in an extremely risky duty situation, Jim gives five reasons why they are able to handle fear:

• We could deal with fear because we had thought through the results of anything that might happen.

• We thought "success" to the point that we never imagined the possibility of defeat.

• Being busy all the time helped us combat useless fear.

• We were totally dedicated. We believed in the mission from the very depths of our beings. We felt it was the most important task we could do with our lives and were willing to give even our lives if necessary.

• We had faith in our resources, in all the research, and in the people and equipment that helped launch us.

Jim continues to fill his life with many earth-circling speaking engagements, and further risk adventures—like searching for Noah's Ark on Mount Ararat, and wanting to go back into space as a civilian on a future flight mission. He continually reminds his audiences that "God's walking on the earth is more important than man's walking on the moon."

Many of us have experienced enough near-death physical risks in our lives—such as in World War II during D day or the Battle of the Bulge, or in Vietnam with no front lines, or being on a battered ship during a fierce Atlantic Ocean storm, or surviving the crash of a jet airliner—that we don't want to take any more risks like them.

However, if we're made of "the right stuff," we might want to try taking spiritual risks—such as trying to help salvage a vulnerable person needing all kinds of support, or attempting to love an unlovely person, or professing faith in a project before it is launched, or projecting hope in the unseen and unknown future.

We may find that the spiritual risks taken in exploring the "inner space" of peoples' lives are just as rewarding as the risks taken in going to outer space in the universe.

We may also find that we will need to be trained in self-discipline just like the astronauts.

PROPELLED INTO OUTER SPACE

There are days when we all must feel that "life's a jungle out there." We hear about grand hotels and favorite department stores closing permanently and causing 1,500 people to lose their jobs; workers striking in an ugly manner with upraised fists and overturning cars; prisoners rioting in jails and some escaping, armed to kill innocent people.

We visit sick friends in hospitals who are in bed with all manner of tubes going in and out of their bodies, unable to move. We see loved relatives in nursing homes confined to their beds or wheelchairs, unable to escape. We experience traffic jams that make us feel hemmed in and completely frustrated.

On such trying days we all somehow yearn for being freed from this earth's gravitational pull and weighty problems, and being hurled into outer space in some fashion.

We're not talking here about emulating the person who can jump straight up over seven and one-half feet, or pole-vault vertically over 18 feet, or long-jump over 28 feet—nor are we thinking about trying balloon rides or parachute jumps when we soon fall back to earth. We want a more lasting escape than that!

Mankind has always had this urge to "fly in the sky like a bird," or to "fly me to the moon" for whatever the reason.

In the early days of flying by machine, near the turn of the twentieth century, it was the airplanes *with propellers* that finally got us off the ground for hours at a time—to be followed by lots of Piper Cubs and Cessnas. It is reported that World War II pilots, despite the jet age, still like to fly planes that have "the lure and romance of that propeller," like the vintage Corsairs and Mustangs.

From another perspective, we're talking about the feelings we sometimes experience at an airport while seeing loved ones depart in a jet plane for an overseas flight of thousands of miles—first seeing those loved forms disappearing into the aircraft, then watching the jet finally take off down the runway and lift off, climbing steeply to its appointed altitude as it curls up its wheels that are no longer needed for its quick escape from earth, and shortly disappearing into the white billowy clouds and "wide blue yonder."

Others of us would prefer more *direct propulsion action*—something akin to the astronauts being propelled by fiery rockets into outer space that eventually is beyond the pull of earth's gravity. It's got to be an exciting thrill at blast-off time to be hurled so quickly into space at such rapid speeds.

Astronauts report that the most exciting parts of space flight are the launch and reentry, and space walks when scheduled.

Once launched, all astronauts seem to be fascinated with the view of earth from space:

• Jack Lousma aboard a Skylab space station (stayed up fifty-nine and one-half days) reported:

In orbit we could see all the beautiful colors of the earth. We could see the blue of the water (75% of earth is water), the white (lacey) clouds, the snow on the mountains, the green-and-brown patchwork of the farmers' fields, and the beautifully painted desert.

• Jim Irwin aboard *Apollo 15* said:

The first time we could see the whole earth, we saw it as a ball in the sky, about the size of a basketball, and the most beautiful thing you could ever want to see in your life. Then, as we got farther and farther away, it diminished in size. We saw it shrink to the size of a baseball, then to the size of a golf ball, and finally to the size of a marble... the earth looked like a beautiful, fragile Christmas tree ornament hanging against the blackness of space.

Thoughts about outer space should include some references to *UFOs* (unidentified flying objects). Millions of Americans believe that UFOs are real and not imaginary. Many people believe that flying saucers are also real—so real that they contain aliens who are visiting us from another planet or solar system.

The UFO literature tells us that the true UFOs (usually flying saucers) operate with total disregard for the laws of physics, having been clocked by radar at speeds well in excess of 15,000 m.p.h. They are able to accelerate from a hovering dead stop to several thousand m.p.h. in mere seconds without sonic booms, and frequently execute 90-degree turns while traveling at several times the speed of sound.

The flying saucers reported are usually seen at night, and are described as luminous spheres or cylinders—usually displaying a flashing light or probing searchlight, colored halos, luminous tails, and a lingering cloud trail. They occasionally make a humming noise, although most are silent.

The official government posture has been that UFOs are attributable to normal causes, although the air force has at times admitted that a small percentage of UFOs (flying saucers) defy a natural-cause explanation.

It is only natural that after so many supposed sightings have been reported in the news media, and after having seen science-fiction films such as *Star Wars* and *Close Encounters of the Third Kind,* millions of Americans believe in UFOs more than they believe in angels or devils.

Furthermore, the staunch UFO followers believe that the flying saucers are from another world in outer space that is more advanced than ours, or that they are from a parallel world like ours but operate in a different realm while occupying the same space as we do.

Whether we believe UFOs (and especially flying saucers) are from other worlds other than our own solar system or not, the whole UFO phenomenon raises interesting thought parallels between what is physical reality and spiritual reality.

Is there life in outer space that is capable of thought and action beyond that on our own earth? If so, does it possess human intelligence that is superior to ours?

Many people like to feel that somewhere out there in space other human beings are living a life that is happier than ours and are having fewer problems—a sort of Paradise regained. Such people had hoped that a better life might be found on other planets within our solar system. However, close-encounter probes of Mars, Saturn, Jupiter, and Uranus suggest otherwise. Spacecraft launched by NASA (the National Aeronautics and Space Administration), such as the Viking probes of a lifeless Mars, and the more recent discoveries of Uranus by Voyager II (built by the Jet Propulsion Laboratory), offer no new hope that human life as we know it might exist elsewhere in our solar system.

Others would see the UFO craze as a sign of the times, as a longing for an escape from the world and its many problems, either by going to another world where a better civilization exists with fewer problems, or else by having those other-world citizens enter our world and help us solve our problems.

For the more devoutly religious, UFOs are seen as a prelude to the main extraterrestrial event to occur soon from space—for many Jews, the long-awaited coming of the Messiah to earth, and for many Christians, the Second Coming of Christ to reenter this terrestrial ball. Then, it is believed, the world will be brought to its senses, problems will be solved instantly and fairly, and the new age of love for the Creator and his redeemed creatures will have begun.

Returning to the original thesis that began this article, namely that most of us, especially on miserable days, yearn to be propelled into outer space for an indefinite period of time—and if space stations ever get to be more plentiful and accessible, perhaps change addresses and make a blast-off move to live on them for years.

However, a recent NASA test study done on twenty-four white rats in space for seven days suggests living in space in zero gravity entails a definite health risk. The rats were chosen for the flight tests because they have physiological and biochemical similarities to man, and they use their muscles in comparable ways. NASA scientists confirmed that the rats suffered extensive muscle and bone deterioration in space that could have far-reaching implications for long-term space travel. They also suggest that astronauts possibly also experience irreversible muscle and bone damage during prolonged stays in zero gravity. The question now is whether future missions involving long periods of weightlessness—such as living aboard a space station—could inflict permanent bone and muscle damage.

So what's left that is risk free?

What other avenues of escape into outer space are there?

God has the vertical perspective of altitude in respect to space. We earthlings are limited by having physical bodies that are built for the pull of the earth's gravity; our bodies do not relish zero gravity. We need to see ourselves as God sees us from space—not as the centers of the universe, but as objects of His love on an earth that is "whole and round and small and beautiful"—a little lovely floating blue ball encircled by white swirling strands that are part of the earth's protective atmosphere (that look like guardian angels), and that are symbolic of God's loving protection and care over us.

Could it be that in our desire to escape from this earth and be propelled into outer space to get rid of our earthly problems God is telling us to stay put, and look within the *inner spaces* of our lives to find all the peace, comfort, and security we need for our earthly journey?

Could it also be that someday, after our physical bodies have run their course and have done their appointed work on earth, at death we will be miraculously transformed into a spiritual being that will instantly fly away from its dead body on earth, and be propelled into outer space—custom designed for zero gravity?

We can imagine a completely freed spiritual body that will enable us to have a new clarity of thought that will be from above—and a loving spirit that will be forever free from differences of tongue, and color, and creed, and property lines, and boundary lines. We will be living "the life of the Spirit" in that gloriously free outer space. We will be finally *free forever!*

The length of our days is seventy years—or eighty, if we have the strength; yet their span is but trouble and sorrow, for they quickly pass, and we *fly away*. (Ps. 90:10, NIV.)

For our earthly bodies must be *transformed* into heavenly bodies that cannot perish but will live forever. (1 Cor. 15:53, TLB.)

TRAGEDIES THAT MAKE US "ONE EARTHLY FAMILY"

It's been some time now since the *Challenger* space shuttle exploded in a massive fireball some ten miles up in space while traveling at 1,977 miles an hour—disintegrating the spacecraft and all seven astronauts aboard.

There will be continuing inquiries on why *Challenger*, which lifted off from Cape Canaveral on Tuesday, January 28, 1986, at ll:38 A.M., blew up into many fiery bits and pieces after being only one minute and fourteen seconds into its flight mission.

Was it an act of God? Hardly.

Was it sabotage? Unlikely.

Was it a computer malfunction? Probably not.

Was it mechanical failure? Probably so—perhaps in one of the booster rockets that appeared to leak some fuel that within seconds ignited the gigantic 500,000 gallon external fuel tank like a blowtorch, causing a massive celestial fireball explosion that was the equivalent of one million pounds of TNT.

Scientists and engineers are trained in their calm, cautious, cool, and collected manner to look thoroughly into the probable causes of accidents, and to correct the problems once found so that future spaceflights will not repeat the same malfunctions.

However, for the hundreds of millions of people across America and many parts of the world who saw the television replays of this catastrophic event, the shock of that one-second explosion has been sending trailing emotional shock waves into our numbed bodies that will be etched into our minds forever.

There hasn't been a singular event since the assassination of President John F. Kennedy on November 22, 1963, that has so shocked us with horror, and that has saddened and grieved the soul of our nation.

It isn't as though our nation has not been exposed to tragedy, grief, and death in its previous history. In October 1983 there was the terrorist bombing of a U.S. Marine barracks in Beirut that killed 241 Americans. In 1985, terrorist attacks and bombings of United States civilian and military personnel abroad continued; and with the increasing severity of airplane disasters worldwide, the death toll mounted to almost 2,000 Americans killed in dozens of airplane accidents. The December 12, 1985, crash of a chartered DC-8 in the snowy woods of Gander, Newfoundland, shortly after takeoff—killing all 248 U.S. 101st Airborne troops coming home for

Christmas with their families—was a shocking disaster.

Furthermore, most of us knew people personally who have been killed in accidents of one kind or another—whether airline crashes, train wrecks, or fiery automobile accidents. Perhaps we've even known people who were highly adventuresome and enjoyed doing things that most of us would consider too dangerous and risky—like mountain climbing, parachute jumping or deep-sea diving—and lost their lives doing it.

But was the NASA space program considered dangerous and risky?

Most of us were lulled into believing that flights into space were safer than traveling on our highways. When the crew members of *Challenger* boarded the space shuttle on Tuesday morning, it appeared to be just another routine spaceflight. During twenty-four previous shuttle missions, space shuttles had performed without a major mishap. Furthermore, with no major accidents on any of the fifty-five manned spaceflights over a twenty-five-year span, NASA's record of excellence caused us to become complacent.

Thus, many of us were doing different things on Tuesday, January 28, at 11:38 A.M., so that we were not even thinking about the shuttle's launch. The three major networks did not even televise the event live.

Then the word spread quickly: *Did you hear that the shuttle exploded?*

This was followed by a quick rush to the television sets to see and hear the shocking news that Tom Brokaw, Peter Jennings, and Dan Rather had to report.

First there was the horror and disbelief of it all. In the early minutes one wanted to believe that it wasn't true, that it was some make-believe science fiction episode.

Others responded by saying, "Oh my God!" "Oh my God, no!"

Still others reported that they couldn't believe they were so ecstatic and proud during the first minute of lift-off, and so downcast and disbelieving the next minute.

Questions quickly flashed to mind:

Could *Challenger* somehow have survived the fiery blast and have blown free somewhere among the white puffy clouds, with its passengers still whole?

Could the parachute seen descending toward the ocean somehow contain some of the crew?

Could the cabin compartment, with the *Challenger* crew, still be found intact by ships or planes, even though the orbiter had exploded?

Would any of the crew ever be found alive?

As reports of the totality of the explosion began slowly to register, leaving no further hope for any human survival, other emotional shock waves of the horrible tragedy began to flood the mind, including waves of sadness and bereavement for the astronauts, their families, the NASA support team, and our nation.

How cruel that fate should deal such a devastating blow and obliterate the lives of seven astronauts who deeply believed in space exploration, who trusted the NASA space program implicitly, who were totally committed through self-discipline and training to this twenty-fifth space shuttle voyage, and who expected to come back to earth safely after the successful completion of their six-day mission.

Yet, others reported that the space crew knew all about the dangers of their work, and the possible nearness of death as they ventured forth—especially during the early minutes of the flight when the highly explosive fuel rockets and fuel tank were still attached to the orbiter—but they were not possessed by the fear of it. Once they had worked out in their minds that they might die in space, then everything else in the program was fairly easy, including weightlessness.

Other emotional waves kept bombarding our thoughts:

• The swift departure of seven gifted astronauts who all had "the right stuff": daring courage, very good physical reflexes, high intelligence, and pleasing personalities—what a loss!

• All seven astronauts were in "the prime of their lives"—ages 35, 36, 37, 39, 40, 41, 46—what a loss to their families and our nation!

• The *Challenger* crew left eleven surviving children who ranged in age from one to twenty-five, with the oldest being a student at the Air Force Academy—what a parental loss!

As the emotional shock waves began to subside, and as memorial services were being held at various places all across our land—the United States Naval Academy; Akron, Ohio; Concord, New Hampshire; Lake City, South Carolina; Houston, Texas; and Washington, D.C.—and as children in thousands of classrooms tried to understand what had happened; as flags flew at half-staff; as President Reagan spoke movingly to the families and the nation at Houston on Friday; as President (acting appropriately as "the father of our country") and Nancy Reagan tried to comfort the grief-stricken families with consoling words and personal touches—some softer spiritual waves began to flood the soul.

These waves will be beamed to the seven brave men and women of the

Challenger space shuttle—thus helping all of us to remember forever their excellence in living while on earth, and their supreme sacrifices made high in the heavens.

Dick Scobee, Mike Smith, Judy Resnik, Ron McNair, El Onizuka, Greg Jarvis, and *Christa McAuliffe*: Through a space tragedy, you have all been emblazoned into our history books, and through death you have been enshrined in our souls in a more far-reaching and meaningful way than had you returned from a completed six-day mission successfully, with praise and parades in your honor.

You seven *Challenger* crew members (most of you were trained as astronauts for eight or more years) were destined to be a kaleidoscopic cross-section of the best all-American team that could be mustered. You collectively embodied the best ideals of America and its aspirations. You inspired our national imagination. You were special.

You represented all of us proudly in many ways. You flew for all of us, and you died for all of us—and a part of each of us died with you.

You were such a diverse American adventure team: single, married; black, white, Asian-American; Catholic, Jew, Protestant.

You were such a gifted team: air force pilot, navy pilot, aerospace engineer, aircraft engineer, electrical engineer, research scientist, social studies teacher.

You had so many varied talents and interests: Eagle Scout, classical pianist, jazz saxophonist, singer, painter, bicyclist, church-school teacher, community worker.

You had received many earthly honors and awards: perfect 800 scores on Scholastic Aptitude Tests, most outstanding senior, Presidential Scholar, magna cum laude graduate, six master's degrees, doctorate in electrical engineering, doctorate in physics, many medals for flying 225 combat missions in Vietnam, star athletes.

Christa, you were selected to be the first private American citizen to fly in space. In ceremonies at the White House last July, you were chosen as the winner among more than 11,000 applicants to become the first teacher to teach lessons from space. In your acceptance speech, honoring you and the other nine finalists, you said amid sobbing tears as you held your trophy aloft: "When I go up on that space shuttle, there will be nine other souls that will be going up there with me."

Christa (even your name has a spiritual ring to it), your perky personality, winsome smile, and blithe spirit will never be forgotten or destroyed by a one-second blast. Nor were there just nine other souls who went up with you on the twenty-fifth space shuttle mission—there were millions of other souls up there with you and your fellow crew members.

As Dan Rather, CBS anchorman, said in signing off that first day of the tragedy: "You seven astronauts are now *one in the sky.*"

But because of the heroic sacrifice of your lives in space, you have helped to bring us painfully together as *one sorrowful people*, and thereby helped mold us (at least for a time) into *one earthly family*—bound together as one in soul and spirit.

Someday, we hope to *join you in the sky* when our soul-spirits take their quick flight from our mortal bodies at death. We too will "slip the surly bonds of earth to touch the face of God."* We too will escape to soar into the blue heavens like you did when you vanished, to reach for the stars, fly with the angels, and go to a pure Heaven that is safe from explosions and mechanical errors.

You will become space pioneers all over again, and serve as our advance agents for searching out new frontiers, as we belatedly join you in exploring more fully the whole of God's magnificent creation—for all eternity. We will then become as *one heavenly family* for endless space explorations.

*From the poem, "High Flight" by John Gillespie Magee, Jr., a World War II RAF pilot.

TRIUMPH BORN OF TRAGEDY

Andre Thornton, the thirty-six-year-old Cleveland Indian first base-man/designated hitter, was named the American League's 1982 Comeback Player of the Year after slugging thirty-two home runs and driving in 116 runs in 1982. He was also named the 1982 Most Courageous Athlete by the Philadelphia Sports Writers Association.

These two awards came following a knee injury that almost ended his baseball career in 1980, and another year of injuries in 1981. However, they were minor in comparison to the healing that needed to be done earlier following the tragic accident that claimed the lives of his wife and young daughter in October 1977, on the icy western section of the Pennsylvania Turnpike. Andre was driving the family's van and miraculously survived the crash along with his preschool son.

During the ceremonies honoring Andre Thornton as the "Most Courageous Athlete" of 1982 for the way he picked up the pieces of his life and dealt with the overwhelming sadness and guilt following the tragic loss of his wife and daughter, Andre said devoutly, "The Lord gave me the strength to uphold me and gave me inner peace after the accident. My Christian beliefs have been the strength of my life. It was sorrowful for me as a man, but the Lord gave me the strength to go on."

In the fall of 1977 I was privileged to attend the funeral services held for Andre's wife Gertrude and daughter Theresa in the Bethel A.M.E. Church in West Chester, Pennsylvania. I shall *never, never, never* forget the most soul-piercing part of the service. At the conclusion of the service, as the closed casket was rolled down the center aisle toward the back of the church, the procession stopped. Andre, with one hand holding his four-year-old son's hand and the other hand clutching a photograph of his wife and two-year-old daughter that stood atop the closed casket, spoke in a halting but clear voice amid tears rolling down his cheeks. He spoke meaningfully about his faith in the Lord, how the Lord had upheld him during his grief even though he didn't fully understand the reasons for the double tragedy, and how this loss could turn out to be more meaningful if it led to someone there turning to the Lord and accepting Him.

It was as though one were caught up in a most unforgettable drama, intensely involved with this giant frame of a man (6 feet 2 inches, 210 pounds), witnessing him reveal his innermost soul before relatives, friends, and the moguls of the Cleveland Indians baseball organization—crying with him, trying to control emotions and realizing the frailties of our earthly lives—and all the while knowing that you were standing on

137

holy ground, feeling the presence and comfort of the Lord Himself, sensing invisible angels hovering over Andre and his broken family, not wanting to leave the place and have temporal time begin again.

It is from such unforgettable hallowed moments of tragedy that triumph does occur, and six years later this reality was detailed in Andre Thornton's 1983 book titled, *Triumph Born of Tragedy.*

THE CRUCIFIXION—IS IT NOTHING TO YOU?

There was a time, decades ago, when the observance of Good Friday was a solemn and dutiful event attended by many churchgoers in thousands of communities throughout the land.

I can recall living in a fair-sized town of 15,000 people some forty years ago that the observance of Good Friday through holding community-wide church services from 12:00 noon to 3 P.M. was a sacred time. All downtown stores were closed (no malls then), the sidewalks were empty, and few cars were seen moving on the streets. Many industries even permitted their employees time off from work during those three hours.

Times have changed. It seems as though the world at large is rapidly forgetting the observance of Good Friday and hence the meaning and reality of the Crucifixion. It's business as usual, with stores in most communities remaining open, and with community church services during the three early afternoon hours having fewer and fewer worshipers.

It's just as though most people nowadays want to avoid the Crucifixion observance and go right into the celebration of Easter.

But there must be a meaningful remnant for whom the Crucifixion of Christ and His Seven Last Words have a profound and lasting impact from the standpoint of pain, suffering, and the ultimate sacrifice—the giving of one's life for another. Such a remnant would most likely be found among the following crossbearers:

• Anyone who has lost an arm or leg.

• Someone who is a quadriplegic, such as Joni Eareckson—who after a diving accident in a pool at age 17 became a paralyzed wheelchair quadriplegic (well documented in the best-selling book and movie titled *Joni*)—going through years of pain and suffering, bitterness and despair—and finally arriving at a place of trust and thankfulness to God, thus being able to help others who are suffering.

• Anyone suffering through a prolonged illness with no earthly hope of cure, yet retaining a smile and gracious sense of humor through it all.

• Persons who have been "crucified" in the world through untruths spoken about them—who have suffered wrong when no wrong was committed or—who have been accused falsely when no guilt was found.

• Any innocent person who has been cursed and "spit upon"—and took it, without answering a word or talking back to get even.

• The shooting or bombing death of an innocent victim.

• The tragic loss of a young child or adolescent, or the untimely death of a spouse or parent.

• The willful giving of one's life for another person—as in the case of an airline stewardess losing her life in rescuing passengers from a burning plane, or in a fireman or policeman sacrificing his life to save others.

While none of these examples are meant to say that they are as excruciating in pain or as degrading to selfhood as a crucifixion, nor are they meant to be compared with the Ultimate Sacrifice of God's Innocent Son in Jesus Christ on the Cross—with nails driven into His hands and feet, and a spear thrust into His body—yet they do contain some of the very essence of what Jesus experienced while hanging on the Cross between two thieves, and as expressed in some of his Last Words on earth:

"My God, my God, why have You forsaken Me?" (Matt. 27:46, NKJV.)

"Father, forgive them, for they do not know what they are doing." (Luke 23:34, NIV.)

"Father, into your hands I commit my Spirit. " (Luke 23:46, NIV.)

"Today you shall be with me in Paradise. " (Luke 23:43, NEB.)

The Crucifixion of Christ was sharply noticed almost 2,000 years ago—for the Bible says that at midafternoon the dark clouds rolled in, the sun stopped shining, the earth shook, the rocks split, and the tombs of the dead broke open, and many of God's people who had died were raised to life.

If such an earthshaking event were to occur today, the whole world would pay more rapt attention—and some might even fall to their knees and yield to professing a faith in God.

GREAT SERMONS

There's nothing on earth to equal the hearing of a great sermon delivered by a great preacher! (Unless it be the hearing of great music performed by a great ensemble of voices and instruments.)

Depending on the title and thrust of the sermon, it can either prick the conscience, stir the imagination, comfort the soul, lift the spirit heavenward, renew confidence, help us appreciate the "true, beautiful, and good," inwardly commit us to some kind of Christian action, or otherwise send us joyfully "out into the world" better equipped to be a more loving family member and a more caring person to whomever we may meet during the week.

A great sermon involves the recipient's body (emotions), mind (thinking), and spirit (God-consciousness)—all three. Even the Super Bowl of pro football is hard-pressed to match this total involvement.

Throughout the centuries countless great sermons have been preached. Some memorable titles spring to mind:

- "The Gift of God" (the greatest) by Martin Luther
- "The Scripture Way of Salvation" by John Wesley
- "Sinners in the Hands of an Angry God" by Jonathan Edwards
- "Heaven" by Billy Sunday
- "Love and Forgiveness" by Alexander MacLaren
- "Honor Thy Father and Thy Mother" by J. B. Baker
- "Thanks Be unto God for His Unspeakable Gift" by Walter Maier
- "Come before Winter" by Clarence Macartney
- "The Child and the Cross" by Reinhold Niebuhr
- "The Secret of Inner Security" by Andrew Blackwood
- "The Authority of the Holy Spirit" by Martin Lloyd-Jones
- "To God Be the Glory" by Donald Grey Barnhouse
- "The Church Is Precious" by Elmer G. Homrighausen
- "Angels Innumerable" by Billy Graham
- "A Religion that Sings" by Bryant Kirkland
- "The Costliness of Discipleship" by D. Reginald Thomas
- "One Nation under God" by D. James Kennedy
- "The Second Coming of Christ" by Robert Lamont
- "Variations on the Resurrection Theme" by Robert D. Young
- "Living the Abundant Life" by Lloyd J. Ogilvie

Sermons like these (and thousands more)—whether received through printed pages, radio, TV, or in person—can send us forth as soaring eagles on this earth, better equipped to face each day in tune with God and His universe.

THE SILENCE OF GOD

Silence is sometimes better than sound. It can also be better than pictures and words. Silence can be golden, as in these examples:

• A 30-inch snowfall when nothing moves.

• Being alone in God's Great Outdoors on a summer day with miles of beauty to see and silence everywhere.

• Gazing in awe and reverence at the stars on a clear night amid complete stillness.

• The hushed beauty of a rose, daffodil, or carnation.

• A newborn baby sleeping so calmly.

• The quiet recesses of an art museum or library.

• Times of quiet meditation, prayer, and reflection with one's eyes closed.

• Peaceful moments of inspiration and comfort provided by the silent Spirit of God.

Yes, God is often a God of Silence—and yet how paradoxical: He seems to speak to us most clearly when we are silent before Him.

The Lord is in His holy temple: let all the earth keep silence before Him.—Hab. 2:20 (KJV.)

THE INVISIBLE WORLD

So we fix our attention not on the visible things but on the invisible; for the visible things are transitory: it is the invisible things that are really permanent [eternal]. —2 Cor. 4:18 (TEV, P.)

We are encouraged by the Scriptures to look not only at the things we can see now on the earth—beautiful as they might be—but at the more permanent unseen things. The temporal things of earth will soon be over; it is the invisible things that will endure, that are eternal, and that will last forever in Heaven.

However, we are expected by God to get some practice in living in the invisible world while still here on earth. Here is a brief list of some invisible realities that are a precious part of our present world, and most worthy of our appreciation, attention, contemplation, and cultivation:

Air	Jesus Christ	Space
Angels	Joy	Spirit
Dreams	Love	Time
Eternity	Meditation	Truth
Faith	Mind	Visions
Fragrance	Peace	Will
God	Prayer	Wind
Heaven	Resurrection	Wisdom
Holy Spirit	Soul	Wonder
Hope	Sound	Zeal

INSPIRATIONAL ONE-LINERS*

Do you have a collection of memorable quotes from your favorite writers that you keep nearby and reread occasionally? Quotes that are clear, concise, and compelling? Here are some of my favorite quotations that energize my faith.

Christmas has a beauty lovelier than the world can show.—Christina Rossetti.

Appreciation is a wonderful thing: it makes what is excellent in others belong to us as well.—Voltaire.

A *great teacher* is one whose spirit enters the soul of his pupils.—John Milton.

My accountability to God is the greatest thought that ever crossed my mind.—Daniel Webster.

The only theme in history worth mentioning, the only theme besides which all themes pale into insignificance, is the theme of *faith versus unbelief.*—H. G. Wells.

Human nature cannot bear prosperity. It invariably intoxicates individuals and nations. Adversity is the great reformer. Affliction is the purifying furnace.—John Adams.

Unbroken and unbruised men and women are of little value in life, for we can never truly "dry another's tears" or share their sorrows unless we have wept ourselves and experienced our own Gethsemane.—Helen Steiner Rice.

Only those who suffer greatly will have the opportunity to demonstrate great faith.—Robert Schuller.

Apart from Jesus Christ we do not know the meaning of our life or of our death, or of God or of ourselves.—Blaise Pascal.

This Gospel (The Gift of God's Love as found in John 3:16) is one of the most precious passages in the whole New Testament, and fully deserves, if it could be done, to be written with golden letters into our hearts.—Martin Luther.

O God, Thou hast made us for Thyself; our hearts are restless until they find their rest in Thee.—Saint Augustine.

*Italics occurring in quotes are mine.

If I had my life to live over, I would just believe God more.—Henrietta Mears.

The *Holy Spirit* not only originates faith, but increases it by degrees, till He conducts us by it all the way to the heavenly kingdom...For illuminated by the Spirit, the soul receives, as it were, new eyes for the contemplation of heavenly mysteries.—John Calvin.

For a *happy life* three things are necessary: something to hope for, something to do, and someone to love.—William Barclay.

The most profound theological discovery I've ever made is that "Jesus Loves Me, This I Know..."—Karl Barth.

Rejoice means "to shine, to gleam, to give forth light, to be bright." In the context of knowing Jesus as Messiah and Lord, it means to be radiant with the joy of God's peace, to beam with the warmth and glow of His love.—Moishe Rosen.

Many times I have led a volunteer crusade choir of 5,000 voices in "The Lord's Prayer" or a great hymn of praise, and thought: "Lord, when you take me to Heaven, I'd like to go at the height of a chorus like this!"—Cliff Barrows.

If we love Jesus above everything else in life, He will give us power to master our problems, overcome our fears, and rise above every temptation and every sin...and then we shall be granted a foretaste of life eternal even in this mortal life.—Charles H. Malik.

Treat people you meet each day as though it were their last day on earth.—Percy Ross.

The following one-liners are my own reflections:

One of the most telling qualities of spiritual maturity is laughter—especially when directed at self.

One of the hardest things to learn in life—be it in the business and professional world, or on the golf course—is to wish the best for your fellow competitors as much as you wish it for yourself.

Be grateful for joys found in victories, and for loyalties deepened by defeats.

God is especially close to those who are brokenhearted.

There's much to learn about living by reading the obituary pages in newspapers and the gravestone epitaphs in cemeteries—for at such times we are all brought face to face with our own mortality—and immortality.

The Holy Spirit is a courteous Spirit.

The beauty, color, harmony, and order found in God's universe should be reflected in my attire, home, and life-style as well—if I am to be God's special agent here on earth.

God wants us to retain our childlike faith and innocence right through adulthood.

It is God's Spirit that inspires all the clairvoyant, spontaneous, and joyous moments of our lives.

We should plan our lives as though we will be here our full life-expectancy, but live as though Christ may come today.

CHAPTER VIII

CONFIDENT LIVING—IN THE SPIRIT*

If our lives are centered *in the Spirit*, let us be guided by the Spirit.

—Gal. 5:25 (P)

This is the *confidence* that we have in Him, that if we ask *anything* according to His will, He hears us.

—1 John 5:14 (NKJV)

We know that *in all things* God works for the good of those who love him...

—Rom. 8:28 (NIV)

In *every thing* give thanks...

—1 Thess. 5:18 (KJV)

God is able to make all grace abound to you [believers], so that *in all things at all times*, having all that you need, you will abound in every good work [to help others].

—2 Cor. 9:8 (NIV)

*Italics appearing in quotes are mine.

THE JET STREAM

Have you ever dreamed of flying high in the clear blue sky on a cushion of air—sort of like Aladdin riding carefree on a magic carpet way above the clouds, or like flying in a colorful magic balloon? And traveling at speeds between 100 and 300 miles per hour at a height of 30,000 to 40,000 feet—usually in a west to east direction around the world? What a thrill that would be! All you need to do is get there, like the jet pilots do, and ride its currents.

Years ago pilots of jet aircraft learned about the wonderful jet stream, and knew if they got high enough (30,000 feet or more) on eastbound flights, they could "hitch a ride" on the jet stream and thereby cut their travel time in half, thus saving significant time, energy, and cost.

This *invisible*, yet powerful, current is often depicted on TV weather maps of the United States as meandering in its travel patterns from west to east, and is given credit by weathermen for being the chief determiner of weather conditions in various parts of the country.

The jet stream is the main reason why we may end up having sunny, clear blue skies or dark, damp, and dreary weather. It's a powerful force, far beyond the weatherman's control for giving us good or bad weather. There is nothing we humans on earth can do to change the jet stream's direction or location and its resulting weather effects on us.

How like the jet stream are the days of our lives. There are days when we meander in irregular patterns of behavior, with lots of ups and downs, sometimes moving in circles, encountering stormy weather on all sides, and the days ending without any worthwhile accomplishments. In fact, we sometimes feel as though we retrogressed during the day—children misbehaved, neighbors gossiped, electricity failed, accidents happened—all seemingly beyond our control, just like the jet stream.

Ah, but glory be! There are other days in our lives when everything seems to clear up and go right. The day's events just seem to fall in line at the right time, in the proper place, and with the desired results—all for our good. Telephone calls bring good news from loved ones; making telephone calls never brings a busy signal; a long-awaited letter arrives in the noon mail as though an answer to prayer; conversations with neighbors are sprinkled with joy; serendipities happen—like bumping into an old friend on the street whom you haven't seen in years; and the day's agenda is more than realized—just as though there had been an invisible advance agent going ahead of you to prepare the way for an abundance of good things to happen to you at just the right time and place.

On such "jet stream" days, burdens are lifted, gravity seems to have lost its pull, the body seems lighter, brisk walking reappears, talking becomes animated, the right word appears at the right time, clear thinking prevails, silences become golden, and loving deeds return.

How like the jet stream is the Holy Spirit. It is *invisible*, powerful, beyond human control; it blows where and when it wills—yet how it affects all the sunny and stormy days of our lives.

Like jet pilots "hitching a ride" on the jet stream at 30,000 feet, we need to "hitch a ride" on the jet stream of the Holy Spirit and let its currents flow through us at ground level—and experience its abundant, spontaneous, uplifting power in our daily lives.

THE ART OF LISTENING

Being a good listener in our fast-paced, instant-gratification society is becoming a lost art. How many people do you know who are good listeners? Barely a handful—you're fortunate if even your spouse is.

Most of us prefer talking to listening—we like to "get things off our chest," to tell others where we've been and what we've done, to "tell all" to our close friends, and perchance to tell God what's on our minds, especially when we need a quick, favorable response.

Furthermore, it has been noted by researchers that 70 to 80 percent of what we generally talk about is negative stuff anyway, and not worth listening to in the first place.

There are also fewer opportunities afforded in our society to listen intently in natural situations. Old radio shows allowed us to listen and become seriously involved with our own imaginations. The radio listener saw nothing;...he had to use his imagination.

But there are still opportunities around to practice the art of listening. Reading to young children at an early age (when they can sit on your lap before bedtime) encourages careful listening to pleasant sounds, imaginative words, and floating thoughts.

More recently, audiotape cassettes are providing us abundant opportunities to listen to great music, inspiring sermons, and entire book readings—including the Bible. This translation of the printed page for easy listening is a boon to the elderly with vision problems, and to those who never learned to read very well.

But the primary responsibility for being a good listener rests with each one of us as we engage in daily conversations with those we meet. If we learn to cultivate this lost art, others will flock to us for comfort and understanding. They will see us as caring, loving persons and will think of us as "visible angels."

To be a good listener is to tune in to what others are saying, to get on their wavelength, and to put our own desires for talking into the background.

As it says in James 1:19 (NIV), "Everyone should be quick to listen, but slow to speak..."

It's difficult to see how a close friendship or relationship will ever develop into a lasting one unless one or both of the persons has practiced the art of being a good listener along the way.

Once we've learned to listen naturally to people, it should become just as natural and important to listen to God and the promptings of the Holy

Spirit—first in our quiet times of prayer and meditation, and later in the company of people, starting with one's own immediate family. Such listening will inspire us with inner confidence that we are being guided in making future decisions by God's Holy Spirit.

The best listeners are the ones who possess a great deal of inner peace and security—and no longer need to inflate their own egos, prove themselves, or justify themselves to others. This frees them up for attentive listening.

Happy listening!

PRAYER

> More things are wrought by prayer
> Than this world dreams of.
>
> —Lord Tennyson

Do you pray?

If so, what condition is your prayer life in right now?

Most of us were taught at an early age to say our bedtime prayers ("Now I lay me down to sleep..."), and to say grace at the table ("God is great, God is good, and we thank Him for our food. Amen"). Yet, our prayer life requires a tremendous amount of self-discipline along the way if we are to advance beyond our childhood utterances. Even the praying of the Lord's Prayer later on is often done in a meaningless, monotonous, rapid fashion.

Do You Believe in Prayer?

Jesus said to his disciples: *"If you believe*, you will receive whatever you ask for in prayer." (Matt. 21:22, NIV, italics mine.)

The apostle John said: "This is the confidence that we have in Him that if we ask anything *according to His will*, He hears us; and if we know that He hears us, whatsoever we ask, then we know that we have the petitions that we desired of Him." (1 John 5:14–15, NKJV, KJV.)

What bold, positive statements of faith to be made on behalf of the value of prayer! Here are some others.

Cornelius Vanderbreggen, Christian World Missionary, believes that "prayer is the most costly and most precious investment that someone can make in the life of another."

Bill Bright, founder of Campus Crusade for Christ in 1951, began this ministry by organizing a twenty-four hour prayer chain. He believes "prevailing prayer is hard work in one sense, but there is another sense in which you can *pray without ceasing* as a life-style....If a person is not filled with the Spirit, he can't pray effectively....Apart from the Holy Spirit, we have no power with God or with man. Prayer is simply developing a relationship with God. Practicing the presence of God can be a joyful reality all day long."

Helen Smith Shoemaker, prominent American churchwoman, says, "I try to *listen* to the promptings, leading and guidance of God's Spirit...without such listening, creative prayer is impossible."

Many radio and TV ministries have organized extensive telephone hookups and counseling center booths whereby prayer requests can be made known to a listening, caring person. Other prayer requests concerning health, job, or marriage problems are sent in on cards, enough to fill a huge cylindrical bin over a period of time.

Breakfast prayer groups have sprung up all over our country in recent years among business and professional people. In our nation's capital, members of the House, the Senate, and other government officials have organized prayer groups that meet weekly.

Other citizens believe that prayer is "the soul's sincere desire," and is the most direct way to get "in tune with the universe." Kathleen Norris says, "I base my whole life on prayer." "Prayer is as necessary as breathing," wrote Albert B. Chandler.

To Whom Do You Pray?

Our historic forebears were fond of using such terms for Deity as Creator, Divine Providence, Supreme Judge of the World. These sounded most reverential, but somewhat distant.

In the Lord's Prayer, Jesus used more intimate words: "Our Father, Who art in Heaven"—which is paraphrased by many today as, "Our Heavenly Father...."

I like the intimate simplicity of this thought: "O God, Thou who art nearer to us than breathing and closer than hands and feet...."

Many Christians believe that true prayers should be made only to "the God and Father of our Lord Jesus Christ."

What Do You Pray For?

Most prayers are naturally selfish (even sometimes downright materialistic—praying for a new car, a pay raise, a better boat); so we pray for ourselves, our families, friends, neighbors, all the people we know best. Yet it is at this point that growth should take place over a period of years. Our prayers should become increasingly less selfish and contain more yearnings for improving the lot and welfare of others—even people in other countries who are in dire straits (lacking food, shelter, clothing) and who we do not know by name.

President Abraham Lincoln had a deep yearning to improve the lot of a divided people from North and South during the Civil War when he issued a proclamation for a day of Humiliation, Fasting and Prayer on Thursday, April 30, 1863, to "humble ourselves before Almighty God, confess our national sins, and pray for clemency and forgiveness for our divided and suffering country."

Beyond our many necessary petitions to God for ourselves (prayers for health, peace of mind, a forgiving spirit) and for seeking divine guidance for our lives, there is the added dimension attained by some veteran creative prayer persons who set aside a period of prayer time *to listen* to what

155

God may have to say to them through the leading and guiding of His Spirit—prompting thoughts and ideas to be followed up later by obedience and action out in the world. For such spiritual people, prayer is a two-way conversation with God.

Some churches have organized prayer chains (usually it's the sensitized women who organize such meaningful efforts) whereby the prayer requests of the parishioners are made known by telephone to some sixty women who earnestly pray daily for the listed persons and their problems. My dear wife Jeanne, for example, has been known to pray for forty to fifty people on her daily prayer list (which is periodically changed as prayers are answered), which necessitates a definite block of time for her daily devotional period.

In passing, it should be noted that while women generally are far more faithful in their prayer pursuits and beliefs than men (their very nature seems to allow for a more natural and very real dependence upon God—could it be the "mother instinct"?)—in all fairness I must report that I know a man (single like St. Paul) who has about 900 friends and acquaintances on his prayer list. So, men, if you have the right competitive spirit within you, there's a worthy mark to emulate.

Also, some churches develop small prayer and study groups for fellowship purposes, and for sharing with one another on a personal, caring basis their innermost thoughts, feelings, and desires. It's better to be in a prayer group than in a pressure group.

The world's biggest church, the Full Gospel Central Church in Seoul, Korea, with more than 300,000 worshipers, is a fervently praying church—and would not have prospered as it has without the faithful constant prayers of the people (according to its pastor, Paul Cho).

Jesus says in John 14:13 (NKJV, RSV, italics mine): "Whatever you ask *in My name*, I will do it."

How Often Do You Pray, and When?

Experience tells me that the frequency of prayer is extremely wide among people—from barely praying once a day (usually upon retiring at night), to those who say grace before a meal, to the dear saints who have almost convinced me that they pray throughout each minute of the day (and they're not in convents), asking God to find a parking space for them downtown and other such minute details. I salute such continuously praying persons, for they must be obeying the spiritual admonition to *pray without ceasing.*

It has been reported that President Lincoln arose at four o'clock every morning to spend an hour in Bible reading and prayer.

George Müller, who operated a series of homes for orphans in England

156

over a century ago solely through amazing faith and prayer power, followed a formula of "one hour of prayer for every four hours of work."

As a discipline that most of us could follow, Martin Luther said this: "It is a good thing to let prayer be the first business in the morning, and the last in the evening."

How Long Do You Pray?

Answers here could vary from spontaneous one-second "Praise God!" exclamations to a more carefully planned time of reading, meditation, and prayer that could easily last one-half hour or more—depending primarily on how long a period you allow for listening to God's Spirit, or how extensive your prayer list is.

Most people pray longest—whether Christian or not—when in the midst of anxious difficulties, like being in a foxhole during warfare, facing serious surgery in a hospital, or experiencing the loss of a loved one through divorce or death.

On other occasions, such as saying grace at the family table, the person praying aloud is often admonished for "letting the food get cold" if the prayer is longer than a minute.

The length of most of our private prayers will be determined largely by the promptings of the Holy Spirit from within us, and the degree to which we may have been taught that a good, balanced prayer contains four essential elements (ACTS): *adoration* (praising God)—this could take minutes, or considerably longer if you're a charismatic-type person filled with the Spirit; *confession* (confessing our sins—this is open-ended, according to the workings of the Holy Spirit within us; *thanksgiving* (for blessings received); and *supplications* (petitions and requests for ourselves and others)—this could take many minutes if you're a detailed, well-organized person who is especially sensitive about the needs of other sojourners.

"Prayer is a boon to the soul whether it is prolonged, of short duration, or a single thought prayer flashed spontaneously to God many times during the busiest and most tense moments of the day."—Harvey M. King.

Jesus said: "Don't rattle off long prayers like the pagans do. Do not be like them, for your Father knows what you need before you ask Him." (Matt. 6:7–8, P, RSV.)

Where Do You Pray?

The simple answer could be—anywhere: standing up, sitting down, on your knees (a fading habit); in your upper room, your study, your favorite spot under a tree; amid the traffic noises of a busy world (less likely); or on the golf course (least likely).

Jesus said: "When you pray, you must not be like the hypocrites; for they love to stand and pray in synagogues and on street corners, that they

157

may be seen by men....But when you pray, go into your room and shut the door and pray to your Father who is in secret; and your Father who sees all private things will reward you." (Matt. 6:5–6, RSV, P.)

Are Prayers Ever Answered? Does Prayer Work?

While untold millions could answer these questions in the affirmative, others still experience a divine mystery in prayer that defies earthly understanding.

Richard J. Foster, well-known writer and professor of theology, believes that because the church has abrogated the teaching of solitude and meditation, prayer is often diluted and ineffective. (Meditation upon Scripture, he believes, is the foundation of the inner life.)

One should never expect much from prayer if there is the feeling of being rushed, or pushed for time. Prayer time should be a time of solitude, meditation, relaxation, and waiting. On occasions when the mind is prone to wander, try praying aloud to improve concentration.

Chaplain Fred Henry, of the Devereaux Schools, tells about the many times he had prayed for his special education child to be made whole again, but to no avail. However, on another occasion while holding a deliriously high-fevered neighbor's child in his arms, he prayed for the child's fever to leave—and immediately felt an electriclike current passing from his body into the child's body, and by the time the child arrived at the hospital, the fever was miraculously gone.

While many folks can report miraculous healings, with or without the aid of the medical profession, other persons do not experience physical miracles of healing, but sometimes experience an inner spiritual healing of the mind and soul as recorded by an unknown handicapped person. The piece is titled, "The Prayer of the Handicapped":

I asked God for strength that I might achieve
I was made weak, that I might learn humbly to obey...

I asked for health, that I might do greater things
I was given infirmity, that I might do better things...

I asked for riches, that I might be happy
I was given poverty, that I might be wise...

I asked for power, that I might have the praise of men
I was given weakness, that I might feel the need of God...

I asked for all things, that I might enjoy life
I was given life, that I might enjoy all things...

I got nothing that I asked for—but everything I had hoped for.

Almost despite myself, my unspoken prayers were answered.
I am among all men most richly blessed!

The Spirit helps us in our weakness. We do not always know how we ought to pray, but the Spirit Himself intercedes for us with groans that words cannot express. (see Rom. 8:26, NIV.)

But there is the opposite side of the coin to report.

"In every crisis I turned to God for help and I never called for help in vain."—Harold R. Medina.

"I know from experience that prayers bring actual and immediate relief from worries."—Wernher von Braun.

A recent Gallup poll reports that seven and a half million people in America have experienced miracles in answer to prayer—most of them healings.

God answers all prayers in some way in His own good season. Sometimes the answers may come through your spouse, your brother or sister, or a close friend—without their awareness of being the prayer's channel.

Prayers are more likely to be answered if we can learn the secret of becoming more fully surrendered to God, and say with conviction, "Not my will, but Thine be done."

Prayer does help relieve tensions and fears, and helps give us an inner peace of mind and body. The Holy Spirit has a way of transforming us.

George Müller of England preached on answered prayer at age 75. He told of keeping a diary on everything he had ever asked for in prayer over a fifty-four-year period, and putting a check mark after each when it was answered. His results were amazing. He received 30,000 answers to prayer on the same day they were made. Some took a week; others took a month. One prayer was brought to God about 20,000 times over a period of eleven and a half years before it was answered.

The Bible says: "Pray in the Spirit on all occasions with all kinds of prayers and requests." (Eph. 6:18, NIV.)

This means that prayer is to be a natural and consistent part of our lives. We are to be people of prayer—holding up before God our lives, families, friends, and other matters so that He can honor our prayers and shower abundant blessings upon us.

Jesus said: "Whatever you ask for in prayer, believe that you have received it, and it will be yours." (Mark 11:24, NIV.)

A well-known hymn, "What a Friend We Have in Jesus," says it all: *Take everything to God in prayer!*

PURSUED BY EXCELLENCE

How many books and magazine articles have you read or heard about lately that are urging you to pursue excellence? "In Search of Excellence," "A Commitment to Excellence," *The Pursuit of Excellence*. Excellence! Excellence!! Excellence!!! Everybody seems to be searching for or pursuing excellence—whether in the business world, education, or the sports world. (Is there any college or university anywhere in America nowadays that recruits anybody other than the best *scholar*-athletes??)

I don't know about you, but I'm about "excellenced out." We seem to need at least a one year's reprieve on anymore new books on excellence and how to achieve it, so we can avoid getting a permanent guilt complex for never having achieved this elusive state of perfection.

Yet, there is a haunting counterpoint melody to what has just been said. On many days in many ways we do crave for more excellence in ourselves, in others, in government and public officials, in world leaders.

And has not God been glorified throughout His whole creation for being excellent?

O Lord, our Lord, how excellent is your name in all the earth. (Ps. 8:1, NKJV.)

And have we not been urged in Scriptures to achieve excellence?

Earnestly desire the best gifts, and I will show you a still more excellent way [the way of love]. (1 Cor. 12:31, NKJV, NASB.)

Some of us have even been challenged to emulate Paul the Apostle when he wrote in Phil. 3:12–14 (P, NIV):

I do not consider myself to have "arrived" spiritually, nor do I consider myself already perfect....But one thing I do...I press on toward the goal to win the prize for which God has called me heavenward in Christ Jesus.

THE BEST PREACHERS

To identify "the best" of anything is a "high risk" adventure of the highest order, whether it is baseball players, movie stars, teachers, lawyers, senators, or U.S. presidents. Likewise, attempting to identify "the best preachers" could be thought of as a foolhardy exercise, for there are so many thousands of them to be heard and evaluated, with so many styles, so many personalities, so many motivations.

Then, too, how many preachers is it possible to hear in a lifetime —either in person, on radio, or on TV? And which ones do we choose to hear more than once? What special qualities do our favorite preachers have?

Here is an attempt to identify some of those special qualities found in the best preachers, for they are the ones who:

• Reveal to us the heart of God.

• Become channels for letting God's Holy Spirit flow through them to us.

• Help us to see God's Kingdom on earth, and in Heaven, as being from everlasting to everlasting.

• Continually help us to understand who we are, why we are here, and where we are going (what we might become).

• Give practical illustrations to help us better understand Biblical truths.

• Stir us to loving concern and action out in the world.

• Speak extemporaneously, seldom using notes, and look directly at us. Upon entering the pulpit to preach, are guided by this silent entreaty: "We would see Jesus."

Even though fellowship, intimacy, and personal involvement are lacking in the passive watching of television, TV preachers have become quite popular in the United States in recent years, as witnessed by the lineup of TV personalities and programs on weekends, and some by satellite during the week. A dozen or more TV preachers or personalities could easily be identified, with such varying emphases as evangelism, healing, prophecy, missions, Bible study, worship services, charismatic meetings, talk shows, and variety shows. Their styles range from the dramatic throwing away of crutches and wheelchairs onto the auditorium stage by the preacher-healer (just like a javelin thrower) after having effected a "miracle healing cure" on some lame person—to the less dramatic, but nevertheless impressive format of an entire church worship service, including organ and choir music, Scripture reading and prayer, and a sermon.

Whenever possible, however, most of us would prefer seeing and hearing our favorite preachers (whatever their specialties) in person. So it is that from among approximately 300 preachers I've heard in person over a period of more than fifty years (as well as scores more seen on TV or heard on radio and tape), and some 5,000 sermons—think of it!—five have been chosen for brief elaboration. Each of the five has a distinctive brand of uniqueness, yet they collectively epitomize what I believe most of us are looking for when we use the term "best preacher."

• *Dr. Donald Grey Barnhouse* (1895–1960). "Bible Study Hour," Philadelphia, PA

Dr. Barnhouse had many excellent qualities as a preacher and teacher: A deep resonant voice that rang with authority! ("Thus saith the Lord!") A pleasing rugged physique! A brilliant mind! But his best quality was his humaneness—his abundant, warm, everyday examples used to illustrate spiritual truths, to make the Bible live, whether from the pulpit or in his weekly "Bible Study Hour" radio messages. He also possessed the ability to bare his soul, and to expose his love for Christ. He was an internationally known Bible expositor, and minced no words. If his words at times, especially on controversial topics, seemed foreboding, he would gently chide his listeners: "These are not my words; they are the words of God." He began a voluminous study of Romans that took twelve years to finish, and produced 455 lessons. The last message on Romans, "To God Be All the Glory" (Rom. 16:27), was completed just months before his death in the fall of 1960. Dr. Barnhouse was the best Bible preacher/teacher I've ever known!

• *Dr. Elmer G. Homrighausen* (1900–1982). Princeton Theological Seminary, Princeton, NJ

Dr. Homrighausen was a preacher filled with the Spirit of Jesus Christ! His love for Christ and the Church Triumphant rang through many of his sermons. He read the Scriptures with wonder, awe, reverence, and lots of rhythmic inflections in his voice. His sermons were masterpieces that were faithful to the Word of God, and were filled with comfort and hope—often beginning with the realities at hand that day, and then gradually lifting the listener heavenward by their close. His vibrant personality radiated the fruits of the Spirit—love, joy, peace, gentleness, goodness, faith. "Homey" (as his friends affectionately called him) had many therapeutic soul qualities worth emulating: his enthusiasm (he lived each day to the fullest right up until his death at age 81), his brilliant insights, his innocence (it is said that he never made a cynical remark about anybody or anything), his childlike faith (he liked to be around children), his "twinkling-eye" smiles and occasional catchy afterthought chuckles, his capacity to praise his Creator and Redeemer. Dr. Homrighausen was the best preacher/theologian I've ever known!

• *Billy Graham* (1918–   ). Billy Graham Evangelistic Association, Minneapolis, MN

Billy Graham is one of the most famous and dynamic preachers of all time. He has spoken in person to more people than any other man in history, more than 100 million people. He has traveled on every continent, attracting huge crowds wherever he has taken his evangelistic crusades—usually to large sports stadiums in big cities of the world. His more than thirty-five years of large-scale evangelism have stood the test of time with heads of state as well as common people. He has survived all manner of criticism from his would-be detractors, primarily because of his singular aim to preach the Gospel of Christ in sincere simplicity, using his open Bible as the sure foundation for his sensitive messages. His sermons are hard-hitting, straightforward, full of Bible verse quotes, and often deal with the evil problems of our society and the sins that so easily beset us as individuals (the world, the flesh, and the devil)—with the only perfect remedy for sin being "making a Decision for Christ." In addition to his crusades, other ministries include films, TV, radio, magazines, and numerous books. Billy Graham is the best TV preacher/evangelist I've ever seen!

• *Dr. Lloyd John Ogilvie* (1930–   ). First Presbyterian Church, Hollywood, CA

Dr. Ogilvie is blessed with an abundance of excellent qualities as a preacher. Outwardly, one immediately notices (particularly the females) that he is handsome, dark-haired, deeply tanned, smartly dressed—just the right image for a big Hollywood church. Inwardly, he is even more winsome. He has a rich, deep-baritone voice that grabs one's attention immediately. He appears completely relaxed as he surveys his audience, speaks in unhurried, well-modulated tones, never uses a script, possesses a rich vocabulary that emits just the right descriptive word to dramatize a situation, and tells some of the most intimate, heartwarming, self-revealing stories in a way that is penetrating, real, and almost supernatural. At such times, the presence of God's Holy Spirit is felt, and it's just as though Dr. Ogilvie is being used as a channel to communicate the heart of God. He is noted for his ability to relate Scriptures and the principles of Christian faith to aspects of daily life, at the deep personal level of dealing with the sensitive emotional and spiritual needs of people—somewhat in the fashion of being like a wise counselor and loving friend. He is a prolific writer of books. Dr. Ogilvie is the best preacher/sensitizer I've ever known!

• *Dr. Robert D. Young* (1928–   ). Westminster Presbyterian Church, West Chester, PA

Bob Young is one of the most creative preachers in the pulpit. He uses innovative ideas to illustrate his sermons, speaks in a deep, resonant, clear voice, never uses notes except for occasional literature quotes, and has a keen mind that produces gifted insights. His inviting sermon titles usually stir the imagination even before the sermon begins, and give a clue to his spontaneous versatility, such as: "Return to Central Station," "Resurrection with One Less Trumpet," "Ready for Greater Things," and "Sing Out with Praise!" Some of Bob's sermons have a rhythmic cadence—a musical quality to them (perhaps because he's a skilled singer and trumpeter)—with lots of crescendos. "Well, Glory Be!" was such a sermon, with some picturesque illustrations of the earth's beauty, and other vignettes of noble Christian character in people—each punctuated with lots of "Well, Glory Be's...to God!" The whole sermon gave the feeling that one was listening to another version of Handel's "Hallelujah Chorus." With other sermons, he will sometimes leave the pulpit, step into the center of the chancel, and dramatize his message. Whatever his style, his sermons are rooted in Scripture, and related to practical daily problems of living. Bob Young is one of the best preachers I've ever known, and has been my present pastor for over twenty years!

From a different perspective, I would have thoroughly enjoyed hearing such historical spiritual giants preach as St. Augustine, John Wycliffe, Martin Luther, John Wesley, Jonathan Edwards, Karl Barth, and Dietrich

Bonhoffer. They undoubtedly would have made the "Best Preachers List."

In my imagination, I often wonder how some of the Biblical "giants of the Faith" would have looked preaching on TV, or what they would have sounded like in person. Whether they would have made the "Best Preachers'" list I do not know. In any case, I would have loved to hear, close-up: Abraham, David, Elijah, Isaiah, Luke, John, Peter, Paul—and of course Jesus. I have the distinct feeling that Jesus might have been a captivating charismatic-type preacher—but more significantly, I believe he would have been even more captivating in a one-to-one situation, for I believe that if he had looked me straight in the eye, he could have told me exactly what I was thinking, and revealed my innermost thoughts and feelings, even before I spoke a word.

THE SIMPLICITY OF THE GOSPEL

Temptations are all around us daily to make things more difficult than they are. We're being tempted to try out some new religious philosophy, a different political system, a new theory of economics. We are continually being encouraged with messages to "go it on our own," pull ourselves up by our own bootstraps, and justify ourselves to the world—and in the process piling up brownie points for all our accomplishments and works, hoping our good deeds outweigh our bad actions.

Most of the world's religions and cults would have us climb higher and higher ladders to achieve success, ever climbing to reach the top, yet seemingly never quite getting there to achieve perfection and total self-fulfillment. It becomes a matter of self-will. We desire to achieve our salvation the hard way—by earning it.

It many times becomes a never-ending game of reading an approved list of books, taking higher-level and more difficult courses, reciting the proper chants and creeds, bowing the required number of times in the right direction....

But there really is a *simplicity* to the Gospel story. It's the opposite of earning your way. It's a free gift. For the good news of the Scriptures can be said in all *simplicity*:

> For by grace you have been saved through faith; and this is not your own doing, but it is a gift from God—not by anything you have done, so that no one may boast about it. (Eph. 2:8–9, RSV, JB, TEV.)
>
> For no one can lay any foundation other than the one already laid, which is Jesus Christ. (1 Cor. 3:11, NIV.)
>
> I determined to know nothing but Jesus Christ and Him crucified. (1 Cor. 2:2, NASB.)
>
> All I want is to know Christ and to experience the power of His resurrection, to share in His sufferings, and become like Him in His death, in the hope that I myself will be raised from death to life. (Phil. 3:10–11, TEV.)

ONE OF A KIND

This comment is usually made about valued possessions, such as rare antiques, coins, or stamps. It is also made in reference to a person with a unique personality and character. Winston Churchill and Abraham Lincoln could easily have been called "one of a kind." Each of us is "one of a kind" as envisioned by our Creator. We should thank God for our designed uniqueness—it's just that some people are more unique than others. And Jesus Christ was the crowning achievement, the zenith of "one of a kind" creation and development. We read in the Bible:

He was revealed in the flesh,
vindicated by the Spirit,
seen by angels,
proclaimed among the nations,
believed in throughout the world,
taken up into glory.
              —1 Tim. 3:16 (MLB, NEB, NAB)

WORDS OF WISDOM (Selected from Proverbs)

The Proverbs collected by Solomon represent divine wisdom as applied to earthly living. The wisdom of God's Spirit can be clearly sensed in these sayings. The following selections seem to be as pertinent to confident, commonsense living today as they were many centuries ago.

Trust in the Lord with all your heart
   and lean not on your own understanding;
In all your ways acknowledge him,
   and he will direct your paths.

Wisdom is the principal thing; therefore get wisdom,
   and with all your getting, get understanding.
Hold on to instruction, do not let it go;
   guard it well, for it is your life.

Wisdom is more precious than rubies,
   and nothing you desire can compare to her.
The blessing of the Lord brings wealth,
   and he adds no trouble to it.

The path of the righteous is like the first gleam of dawn,
   shining ever brighter till the full light of day.
The fruit of the righteous is a tree of life,
   and all who win souls are wise.

Above all else, guard your heart,
   for it is the wellspring of life.
A soft answer turns away wrath,
   but a harsh word stirs up anger.

The eyes of the Lord are everywhere,
   keeping watch on the evil and the good.
All a man's ways seem innocent to him,
   but motives are weighed by the Lord.

A cheerful heart is good medicine,
   but a crushed spirit dries up the bones.
Pleasant words are a honeycomb,
   sweet to the soul and healing to the bones.

A man of knowledge uses words with restraint,
  and a man of understanding is even-tempered.
A word aptly spoken
  is like apples of gold in settings of silver.

Train up a child in the way he should go,
  and when he is old he will not depart from it.
He who spares the rod hates his son,
  but he who loves him is careful to discipline him.

Pride goes before destruction,
  a haughty spirit before a fall.
Let another praise you, and not your own mouth;
  someone else, and not your own lips.

Anger is cruel and fury overwhelming,
  but it is nothing compared to jealousy.
If you want people to like you,
  forgive them when they wrong you.

Wine is a mocker and beer a brawler;
  whoever is led astray by them is not wise.
Do not wear yourself out to get rich;
  have the wisdom to show restraint.

Righteousness exalts a nation,
  but sin is a disgrace to any people.
He who conceals his sins does not prosper,
  but whoever confesses and renounces them finds mercy.

The lamp of the Lord searches the spirit of a man;
  it searches out his inmost being.
As a man thinks in his heart, so is he;
  a faithful man will be richly blessed.

The glory of young men is their strength,
  grey hair the splendor of the old.
A good name is more desirable than great riches;
  To be esteemed is better than silver or gold.

All the aforementioned quotations are from Proverbs—3:5,6; 4:7,13,18,23; 8:11; 10:22; 11:30; 13:24; 14:34; 15:1,3; 16:2,18,24; 17:9, 22, 27; 20:1,27,29; 22:1,6; 23:4,7; 25:11; 27:2,4; 28:13,20. All selections are taken from the NIV, with the exception of 4:7 (KJV), 17:9 and 27:4b (TEV).

THE LAST WILL AND TESTAMENT

Seeing a lawyer about making or updating a will should not be looked upon as something to put off as long as possible (many times until it's too late)—but as a golden opportunity to "do things decently and in order" (1 Cor. 14:40, KJV), and make a *bottom-line statement* on the fair and worthy distribution of our earthly goods should death occur.

The procrastination experienced by so many otherwise well-intentioned folks might have something to do with our unwillingness to face the reality of death, or perhaps a real fear of it, or just plain procrastination and poor planning.

But seen from another perspective, making a will should be viewed as a glorious opportunity to think through in advance how you want your personal and real property to be allocated to loved ones, special friends, or favorite charities—and not left to chance, or to someone who cannot read your innermost thoughts once you are gone.

Some rare individuals still practice the custom of including a statement of their beliefs—a testament of their faith—alongside a copy of the will. This sounds like a creative, soul-satisfying thing to do.

Thus, wills are a neat way to have your intentions known and carried out after your death. They carry a lot of power, and could be the biggest, all-inclusive document you'll ever attest to with your signature. The will can be so powerful that it has been known to send its message loud and clear long after death—sometimes to the dismay of close relatives who may have taken for granted that they were going to inherit the whole estate, despite their cantankerous ways and lack of attentive care shown during the last years of your life. Many such people have been chagrined to find out at the reading of the will that it had been rewritten, with their names removed, and the names of other persons and/or organizations substituted instead.

"He [or she] being dead, still speaks" (Heb. 11:4, NKJV) with powerful authority through an updated will—and its message is final, authoritative, irrevocable, and lasting.

GROWING OLD GRACEFULLY

> Grow old along with me!
> The best is yet to be,
> The last of life, for which the first was made.

This wise optimism expressed by the poet Robert Browning is worth repeating daily, especially if you're in your golden retirement years.

Arthur Reed, a black man from Oakland, California, and believed to be the oldest person in the United States, died two months short of his 124th birthday. He was born the year Abraham Lincoln was elected president (1860), and died in 1984. "They made me out of good dirt. They took time, and they made me good," he said of his longevity.

The genetic stock of our ancestry is one of the determinants of our eventual age on earth, as well as our own personality type, mental attitude, and spiritual outlook. "Eat the right foods, get some daily exercise, and have a positive, optimistic outlook on life" is a refrain worthy of emulation.

Persons entering their sixties, seventies, and eighties are admonished to "keep busy." Said one person who was having a love affair with life, "I just want to live and do as much as I can. If it were possible, I would like to have done everything and known everybody. Times goes so fast."

Perhaps the most telling quality of "growing old gracefully" is the cultivation and retention of a sense of humor—particularly the grace to tell jokes about oneself, even in illness, and let others join in holy laughter. What a precious gift to lift burdens and thoughts of despair, and to clear the heavy air of complaining and worrying that often accompanies those who are *not* growing old gracefully.

One often yearns for a breakthrough of God's holy laughter when visiting folks in retirement villages and nursing homes. Apart from the physical difficulties many patients have in nursing homes, there is even the more excruciating mental and emotional anguish shown on the distraught faces of many, and heard through the wailing, piercing cries of: "Get me out of here" and "I want to go home."

The greater proportion of older people seem to prefer spending most of their time with people of all ages, and thus will not enter retirement villages or nursing homes until health conditions and other family circumstances finally dictate it.

One of the pleasing signs of change in our society recently is the increasing number of senior citizens who are eager to engage in volunteer work of some kind, such as knitting for charitable groups, or assisting in the work of such worthy organizations as the American Red Cross, the Salvation Army, the Gideons, and local church activities. It is reported that nearly 25 percent of older people participate in one or more volunteer endeavors.

Age should be worn as a mantle of glory. One should not hide it, but rather be proud of it. Telling one's exact age at 65, 70, 75, 80...should be like wearing a badge of honor, a kind of Phi Beta Kappa key. People who dye their hair to look younger only delude themselves about showing their age. Gray hair can be thought of as beautiful, as having "the distinguished look," and is properly representative of a person filled with golden memories, valuable insights, and an accumulation of wisdom.

Every age has its joys, sorrows, pains, glories, and wonders. A balanced society needs the delights and innocence of childhood, the forward-looking exuberance of youth, the advancing productivity of middle years, and the growing wisdom and peacefulness of old age.

General Douglas MacArthur made this observation about growing old on his seventy-fifth birthday: "In the central place of every heart is a recording chamber. So long as it receives a message of beauty, hope, cheer and courage—so long are you young. When the wires are all down and your heart is covered with the snow of pessimism and the ice of cynicism, then, and only then, are you grown old."

In a related manner, people of all ages have memorized verses from the Bible that have abundant meaning for them, and bring them thoughts and visions of beauty, life, cheer, courage, and comfort—to face whatever life may bring. And if, for example, blindness happens to be the lot of a 90-year-old who is no longer able to read, then recalling these Scripture passages memorized years ago and stored in the "recording chamber of the heart" will bring countless blessings of inner peace and joyful hope, and serve as reservoirs of spiritual strength. Here is a sample reservoir of Bible verses for storage in the memory bank:

It is the Lord who goes before you. He will be with you. He will not fail you or forsake you; fear not, neither be dismayed. (Deut. 31:8, RSV, KJV.)

This is the day the Lord has made. We will rejoice and be glad in it. (Ps. 118:24, TLB.)

Thy word have I hid in mine heart, that I might not sin against Thee. (Ps. 119:11, KJV.)

Trust in the Lord with all thine heart; and lean not unto thine own understanding. In all thy ways acknowledge Him, and He shall direct thy paths. (Prov. 3:5–6, KJV.)

Thou wilt keep him in perfect peace, whose mind is stayed on Thee. (Isa. 26:3, KJV.)

They who wait upon the Lord shall renew their strength; they shall mount up with wings as eagles; they shall run, and not be weary; and they shall walk, and not faint. (Isa. 40:31, KJV.)

The steadfast love of the Lord never ceases, His mercies never come to an end; they are new every morning. (Lam. 3:22–23, RSV.)

We know that all things work together for good to them that love God. (Rom. 8:28, KJV.)

I can do all things through Christ who strengthens me. (Phil. 4:13, NKJV.)

In everything give thanks. (1 Thess. 5:18, NKJV.)

I will never leave you or forsake you. (Heb. 13:5, NKJV.)

Cast all your worries upon the Lord because He cares about you. (1 Pet. 5:7, NAB, NASB [my paraphrase].)

We love Him, because He first loved us. (1 John 4:19, NKJV.)

I have fought a good fight, I have finished my course, I have kept the faith. In Heaven a crown is waiting for me which the Lord will give me. (2 Tim. 4:7–8, KJV, TLB.)

This is the promise that He Himself gave us, the promise of eternal life. (1 John 2:25, NEB.)

Rejoice that your names are written in Heaven. (Luke 10:20, RSV.)

Memorizing Scriptures at any age is a smart thing to do, but doubly smart to do at an early age—for the earlier the memorization takes place (be it Bible verses, poetry, or songs), the better the words will be remembered in later sunset years when the physical powers begin to fail.

Growing old gracefully will mean less hurrying and scurrying about from place to place, less caring about who made the annual "ten best-dressed" list, who was "Man of the Year" or "Woman of the Year," or who will run for president in 1988—but more time will be given to having our minds filled with God and his past blessings to us, to the ever-present need of having our spirits quickened by the ageless power of God's Holy Spirit to help uplift our weakening physical bodies, so that each passing day becomes more precious as a prelude to that ultimate dream of entering into the full glorious light of eternity.

As a golden white-haired great-grandmother of ninety-four said repeatedly as she rested in her rocking chair, "I'm satisfied!" She was stating in simple terms what the end result of a loving relationship to God can be over the years—and since nearly all of her peer relatives and friends had gone "to the other side," she was perfectly content to die in peace and join them too.

Let us earnestly pray that we will have enough wisdom as we grow older to let God build in us the fruits of His Spirit (love, joy, peace), and use us as models of growing old gracefully, so that we will become a source of blessing, and not misery, to those we know and meet in our later years—and perchance to those who may need to take care of us before we exit this earth and are promoted to glory!

> So teach us to number our days aright, that we may gain a heart of wisdom...before we are cut off and fly away. (Ps. 90:12,10, NIV, KJV.)

THE YEAR 2000 A.D.!

If the world holds together by then...and if I hold together by then (I will be eighty-one)...and if the Messiah has not appeared...and if Armageddon has not happened...and if the Biblical millennium has not begun...in short, if a climax in history has not been reached by then—I'll eagerly look forward in childlike anticipation to helping celebrate the year 2000. (Sort of sounds like the end of time, doesn't it?)

Can you visualize New Year's Eve in 1999? There are bound to be giant fireworks set off and pealing church bells at midnight to usher in such an illustrious year. Can you see the calendars, the checkbooks, the diary books? No more 1900s, no more twentieth century dreams and goals and predictions—only talk of the new golden age of the twenty-first century. (By the way, will the year 2000 be called two thousand, or twenty hundred?)

It will be a rare earthly privilege to begin a new year, a new decade, a new century, and a new millennium—all rolled into one at the stroke of midnight in 2000 A.D. This pulsating event should usher in a most unique happening worthy of many special celebrations throughout the year. (How old will you be then?)

There should be lots of parades, concerts in the park, outdoor art shows, balloons, balloon ascensions, six-mile runs, world fairs, and space rides to the moon. (Doesn't this begin to vibrate your cosmic chords?)

Let's start planning now for this most thrilling New Year, and get to work for this rare momentous occasion. (Do you have any special project ideas?)

Let's go, earthlings! It's only twelve years away!

CHAPTER IX

LOVE...JOY...PEACE...AND BEAUTY TOO

The fruit of the Spirit is love, joy, peace...
—Gal. 5:22 (RSV)

Love bears *all* things, believes *all* things, hopes *all* things, endures *all* things.
—1 Cor. 13:7 (RSV, italics mine)

O come, let us sing unto the Lord: let us make a joyful noise to the rock of our salvation.
—Ps. 95:1 (KJV)

You, Lord, give perfect peace to those who keep their purpose firm and put their trust in you.
—Isa. 26:3 (TEV)

All that is true, all that is noble, and all that is just and pure, all that is lovely and gracious, whatever is excellent and admirable—fill your thoughts with these things.
—Phil. 4:8 (NEB)

ROMANCE ON THE ALASKA HIGHWAY

As a former teacher of social studies, one of the most exciting units to teach kids was The Westward Movement—the period of time in our country's past (nineteenth century) when pioneers moved West over long wagon trails, such as the Santa Fe and Oregon Trails, to explore new territories and settle homesteads. It was also the exciting times of the discovery of gold in California and the Gold Rush days that followed, the cowboy days of rounding up cattle on the ranches, the colorful Pony Express, and the driving of the final golden spike to complete the linkup of the first transcontinental railroad near Ogden, Utah.

Little did I realize then that I would have the great opportunity of reliving something akin to the adventuresome, rugged frontier days approximately a century later—not in "going West" across America, but in "going North" across northwestern Canada and Alaska during the early days of World War II as a member of the U.S. Army Corps of Engineers, 341st Regiment, to help build the Alaska (Military) Highway. (It was thought that after Pearl Harbor, the Japanese might invade Alaska and capture it, thus there was the quick need for the Alaska Highway to transport men and supplies inland to Alaska to meet such a possibility.)

The 1500-mile pioneer road had to be surveyed, mapped, and built through virgin forests, past lakes and across streams, through muskeg and swamps, over hills and plains, through valleys and mountains. The Long Trail began near Dawson Creek, British Columbia (the end of the Canadian Pacific Railway North) and ended in Fairbanks, Alaska; no roads had ever existed in this rugged country before, nor had the wilderness ever been mapped.

Even the names of outposts and small villages along the road had frontierlike names: Dawson Creek, Fort St. John, Fort Nelson (several log cabins), Watson Lake and Whitehorse in Yukon Territory, and Tanana Crossing in Alaska.

Indeed, the resemblances to America's westward expansion were many:

• The wealth of wide-open spaces where no one but isolated trappers and hunters had ever been before.

• The abundance of clear-running streams and rivers that needed to be crossed by the initial single-track trail—with such enchanting wilderness names as the Prophet, the Sikanni Chief, the Buckinghorse, the Jackfish, and Muncho Lake.

• The building of dozens of bridges using timbers from the virgin forests that were cut and hewn right at the spot, as were culverts by the hundreds.

• The Long Trail that turned into a muddy quagmire throughout the month of June when it rained almost continually (men and equipment were mired in hip-deep muck), the clouds of dust in the drier months of July and August, and the snowy, icy treacherous traveling conditions over the frozen two-lane dirt roadway during winter months.

• The presence of pesky flies and swarms of mosquitoes during the rainy season.

• The hunting of game with slingshot, bow-and-arrow, and rifles.

• The packing and moving to new campsites almost daily.

• The presence of Indians in the few, sparsely-populated outposts.

But there were also some interesting differences:

• Powerful D-7 and D-8 "cats" (bulldozers), road graders, carryalls, and army tents replaced the horses, hand tools, and covered wagons of a century earlier.

• Many more trees and underbrush were in the path of the Alaskan Trail (the Long Trail) than were encountered going west across the plains and desert plateaus of the various Western trails.

• The more extreme subzero temperatures experienced during the short days of winter when the temperatures reached 60 degrees below zero. (It was 35 degrees below zero on Christmas Day.)

• The wearing of arctic clothing that prevented wholesale frostbites, and the running of truck engines most of the night so that they could be started in the mornings.

• The long days of summer when it was possible to read at midnight without lights.

And oh yes, there was this wonderful romance while on the Alaska Highway. First of all, you need to know that there were well over 1,100 men in the 341st Engineer Regiment who were on the highway for fifteen months—always looking for a pinup girl or two to somehow miraculously show up on Saturday nights. The truth is that in all that time, all we ever saw was a total of three females—three mid-aged Indian squaws who were very shy and, furthermore, were closely guarded by their husband Indian chiefs. So why all this talk about romance on the Alaska Highway?

The romance this time around was not to be found in the scarcity of females, but was found instead in natural wonders:

• Being in an unspoiled country full of scenic grandeur and lush beauty.

• Viewing the brilliant displays of the northern lights dancing on pale gold, violet, and blue-green streamers on perfectly clear nights when it seemed almost possible to reach up and touch the stars.

• Fishing for black trout, grayling, great northern pike, and thirty-six-inch Dolly Varden trout in streams and turquoise-colored lakes overflowing with fish.

• Seeing all kinds of beautiful animals in their natural habitat: partridge, prairie chicken, otter, mink, beaver, black bear, caribou, moose, timber wolf, and mountain goat.

• Watching a five-acre block of ice that was seven feet thick break loose during a spring thaw and majestically make its slow way down the river in cataclysmic fashion.

• Sniffing the aroma of the prolific virgin forests of jack pine, poplar, spruce, and hemlock.

• Standing all alone in perfect silence beneath a bright, warm afternoon sun on a clear-blue-sky day at the edge of towering spruces, whiffing the fragrance of the trees and wildflowers, looking over a glass-clear, sparkling stream rushing nearby to see tall snow-capped mountain peaks in the distant horizon, and feeling "at one with the universe"—perfect peace and joy, and *romance* with God and His Creation!

By the summer of 1943, the pioneer trail had been transformed into a hard, smooth, all-weather road and the army guys were to be shipped back to the States for another assignment—to be replaced by civilians for further refining of the highway's rough edges.

The majority of the soldiers regretted leaving this arctic paradise, for most of us realized what a privilege it was to be romanticized by this Long Trail as it meandered through God's Country of Beauty, Quiet, and Peace—especially at a time when other parts of the world were actively engaged in the disquieting and ugly business of warfare.

If North you may run to the rime-ringed sun...
Or West to the Golden Gate—
Where the wildest tales are true,
And the men bulk big on the old trail, our own trail, the out trail,
And life runs large on the Long Trail—the trail that is always new.

—Rudyard Kipling

(From "The Long Trail")

TRUCK CONVOYS

Sometimes a fairly common occurrence can serve as an apt illustration of spiritual insights that have real meaning. Such was the case on a recent automobile trip I took to Florida while I was traveling south on I-95.

A military truck convoy was observed passing north on I-95. There were dozens of various-sized trucks in the convoy, with the lead vehicle flashing a warning light, and the end vehicle being a derrick. The derrick brought up the rear in case any of the other trucks in the convoy got into any serious trouble and broke down—thus necessitating that it be lifted up by the derrick and towed along the roadway to its destination.

Two spiritual insights came to mind:

• The military trucks traveled in convoy so as to provide a safety net for one another, and give help and strength to all in case of trouble. How like the church and its body of believers this is—providing a safety net for all its members, and utilizing their various individual talents in a combined way (church convoy) to help one another when in need, and to give comfort.

• The derrick is there to lift the heavy load of a truck if it breaks down, and to tow it along the way and escort it safely home. How like the Holy Spirit this is—He is there to help us at all times, and especially when we get into serious trouble and break down, and need to be picked up and helped to reach our destination.

As the convoy of trucks and the derrick go together, so do the body of believers of the church (universal) and the Holy Spirit go together.

S.O.S.'s

S.O.S. is usually thought of as a distress signal sent from a ship in need of rescue at sea—*Save Our Ship*.

But S.O.S. signals can also be identified in the air—such as seen in an airplane mechanic's daring rescue of a plane in flight with a stuck landing gear. The pilot of the plane would have had to crash-land his small plane at the airport in St. Augustine, Florida, with possible risk of death, but instead he radioed to the airfield for help (S.O.S.). A stuntman volunteered to drive a car traveling at 90 miles per hour underneath the airplane traveling at the same speed, and this enabled the auto mechanic who stood up through the sunroof of the car to reach up and free the stuck landing gear of the overhead airplane so it could land safely.

On land, there are the many S.O.S.'s sent out by police radio cars along busy highways and interstates to bring help to stranded motorists with car trouble. Personal experiences in many such traveling situations across the United States indicate that auto mechanics and other associated townspeople in such scattered places as West Jefferson (Ohio), Sioux Falls (South Dakota), Butte (Montana), Augusta (Georgia), and Orlando (Florida) will go "out of their way" to help rescue people distraught with car problems, and will genuinely exhibit a friendly and helpful spirit that can best be described as "angels of mercy."

One such angel was Roy, an owner-mechanic of a modest, unpretentious cinder-block auto shop employing three others in Orlando. Roy was thin, small, wiry, in his mid-forties—with a friendly, easygoing, smiling manner. (He had been highly recommended by the motel manager as a mechanic who was a good diagnostician, could fix anything, and really "knew his stuff"—and would be very reasonable in his charges.) Roy diagnosed the difficulties, took time to explain what repairs would be needed, the approximate time it would take for the repairs (two and a half hours), and the approximate cost (which was modest).

While waiting for the repairs, Roy invited me to have a cup of coffee around a "neighborhood" table (near the office end of the garage) that included some retired men who dropped in each day to have a cup of coffee with Roy. Roy, knowing I was on a tight travel schedule, gave my car top priority, and by 5:30 P.M. had the car finished on schedule. He took time to tell me exactly what he had done, presented a "minimum" bill in relation to his skills, and told me to be sure and stop in again if I ever passed his way—just to say "hello" and have a cup of coffee.

Someday I do hope to return and find out a bit more about this genuine fellow and what makes him tick with such a loving, unselfish heart. Long may his tribe increase. What a 100 percent S.O.S. guy this Roy is! He'll never be rich by monetary standards, but he's already rich in displaying the fruits of the Spirit.

We sometimes hear it said that so-and-so is an S.O.B. Let us firmly believe that there are more S.O.S. people (like Roy) in the world than there are S.O.B.'s. They somehow just don't quite make the news headlines like the S.O.B.'s do.

A final thought: There are countless "angels of mercy" offering food, shelter, and clothing and spiritual help to people who have lost their way and need rescuing. The City Union Mission in Kansas City, Missouri is one such agency that answers such S.O.S. calls hourly. The director of this mission, Rev. Maurice Vanderberg, has this to say about their place for "pilgrims and strangers": "You see them often, moving across the country, without resources, direction, or purpose. The search is for the means of survival, not progress or socio-economic advantages. Life has moved too far beyond them for that. They have been reduced to life at its most primitive level—the level of sheer existence....God has a special compassion for what he calls 'pilgrims and strangers,' and for those who respond by faith to the invitation to be 'born again.'" (In such cases. S.O.S. could well mean "*Save Our Souls.*")

> Is it not to share your food with the hungry and to provide the poor wanderer with shelter—when you see the naked, to clothe him, and not to turn away from your own flesh and blood? (Isa. 58:7, NIV.)

HUDDLING AND CUDDLING

Is there anything more symbolic of the way we should hang together as a human race than when a football team huddles to be informed by its quarterback of the next offensive play? Or when the defensive team, often seen holding hands as though in a prayer circle with heads bowed, are told in the cozy huddle what their defensive alignment will be to meet the next play?

To be sure, there are other delightful huddle-type arrangements in life: litters of newly born animals huddling together around their mother; kindergarten children sitting Indian-style on a circular rug to hear a story read; children sitting in a snug reading circle huddled around a teacher; a closely-knit family group holding hands around the table at Thanksgiving, Christmas, or other special occasions; a small-group committee of adults, "one in the Spirit," planning strategy for its next forward movement; string quartets; various social conversation huddles.

But as great as huddles are, cuddles are even better. For cuddling is more intimate, touching, usually one-on-one, and often involves hugging and kissing. Cuddling at its best involves standing, sitting, or lying close to someone so that you feel body heat, a stirring of the emotions—an affectionate warmth and comfort that only a cuddle can give: a nestle, a snuggle, a squeeze, a fond embrace. Cuddling up to someone has got to be the ultimate essence of expressing real love—akin physically and emotionally to the way God's Spirit "strangely warms" our bodies when we are cuddled (comforted) by His love, and gives us a warm inner spiritual glow of combined peace, and joy, and accepted belonging.

THE NETWORK OF GOD'S NEWS

God's network functions on all wavelengths and frequencies. It broadcasts twenty-four hours a day in every nation around the world. It is heard occasionally on all major and independent networks—but it has a permanent, round-the-clock, invisible network of its own.

This invisible network is available for tuning in day or night, even without the help of a laser beam, radar system, or satellite—and seems especially adapted for tuning in by those experiencing the dark nights of despair and frustration. It operates in all kinds of emotional climates—but seems especially geared to comforting those that are lonely, afraid, and forsaken. It will never give anyone the busy signal if called upon.

God's communications network involves millions of visible people (agents) around the world in helping heal those with "broken and contrite hearts" (Ps. 51:17)—by loving the unlovely, by listening to those who are hurting, by comforting and encouraging the lonely and rejected and bereaved with the spoken word, and by using hands and feet to touch and offer strength to those with special practical needs.

God's silent network also dispatches millions of invisible spiritual agents (angels) all around the world. There are myriad of angels doing God's work, to show mercy and to be like guardian angels to those who believe, and to indicate to them: "Fear not—all is well." There are also countless passages of Scripture to guide and strengthen searching souls. This comprehensive counseling and guidance network is master-controlled by God's omnipotent Holy Spirit.

If we do get into trouble on earth, or foolishly lose our way, and do not know which way to turn, this invisible network provides a mediator here on earth on our behalf, the all-knowing Holy Spirit of God—always present—to intercede for us and point us in the right direction.

This intercession and mediation aspect of God's network is further enhanced by the decentralized infusion of His Spirit into all believers, giving them a variety of spiritual gifts, and involving them in a diverse ministry to people everywhere—in sickness and in health, in hospitals and in vacation spots, in joy and in sorrow, in rich and in poor, in workplaces and in homes, in prayer cells and in prayer chains, in support groups of caring and sharing and in task forces of working and building, in schools and in houses of worship.

The spiritual signals sent to our antenna systems by God's Spirit come in many ways, some natural and some supernatural, such as in:

• Waves of warm compassion for one another.

• Direct clairvoyant thoughts for saying just the right word at the right time.

• Sharp thunderbolt ideas that jolt consciences into the way of truth.

• Spontaneous insights for helping shape confident knowledge and uncommon wisdom.

• Inspired quiet moments that heighten the beauty and joy of peaceful living.

• Healing miracles that bring forth a relaxed mind and songs of praise.

• Spiritual visions and dreams that give a bright, glorious hope for the future.

The network of God's News contains good news and potential for bad news. The good news is that God loves us, forgives us, and will never leave us no matter what gross sins we may have committed or how miserable and God-forsaken we may feel. The bad news is that if we do not ever accept God's offer of love and forgiveness (for our sins), we will remain in a lost condition to continue wallowing around in our own muck and mire—and never experience His gift of grace.

The network of God's News is essentially an invisible network sent from Heaven to earth to announce Good News—news of God's love for us—as at Christmas and Easter. Yet each day is likely to be punctuated with lots of Good News Briefs—items that are inspired by the eternal Spirit of God, but seldom reported on the visible news networks. These items grow out of thoughts and deeds that reflect the presence of the Spirit and His resulting fruits of love, joy, peace, patience, kindness, goodness, faithfulness, gentleness, and self-control.

Here's a closing News Brief from God's Network:

If you do not have God's love, you are nothing.
But if you have His love, you are precious in His sight...
You will always be looking for a way of being constructive.
Your love will not be jealous or boastful, but have good manners.

Such love is not touchy or possessive.
It will not pursue selfish advantage, nor gloat over the sins of other people.
Such love is patient, and is glad when truth prevails.
It can outlast anything—and still stand when all else has fallen.

Such LOVE never fails!
It pursues us to the end!

THE JOY OF LIVING (Selected Psalms)

The Psalms, many of them written by King David, and set to music for worship, are the best-known of all the sixty-six books of the Bible. Some spiritually minded people have memorized their favorite passages. I have combined uplifting portions of the Psalms to form a litany of praise and thanksgiving to God for the joy of daily living.

O Lord our Lord, how excellent is thy name in all the earth!
Blessed be the Lord, who daily loadeth us with benefits.
Thou, O Lord, art a God full of compassion, and gracious, longsuf-
    fering, and plenteous in mercy and truth.
O satisfy us early with thy mercy, that we may rejoice and be glad all
    our days.
It is a good thing to give thanks unto the Lord, and to sing praises
    unto thy name, O most High.

Bless the Lord, O my soul; and all that is within me, bless his holy
    name.
Praise the Lord, O my soul; and forget not all his benefits.
He forgives all my sins, and heals all my diseases.
O give thanks unto the Lord, for he is good; for his mercy endureth
    forever.

Great is the Lord, and greatly to be praised; and his greatness is
    unsearchable.
All thy works shall praise thee, O Lord; and thy saints shall bless
    thee.
Great is our Lord, and of great power: his understanding is infinite.
Let [all the nations] praise the name of the Lord,
    for his name alone is excellent; his splendor is above
    the earth and the heavens.

I love the Lord because he hears my prayers and answers them.
O Lord my God, I will give thanks unto thee forever.
I will bless the Lord at all times; his praise shall continually be in my
    mouth.
At midnight I will rise to give thanks unto thee, O Lord.

My soul thirsteth for God, for the living God.

I will lift up mine eyes unto the hills, from whence cometh my help.
My help cometh from the Lord, who made heaven and earth.
Into thy hand I commit my Spirit.

I was glad when they said unto me, let us go into the house of the
    Lord.
How sweet are thy words unto my taste!
    Yea, sweeter than honey to my mouth!
Let the words of my mouth, and the meditation of my heart
    be acceptable in thy sight, O Lord,
    my strength, and my redeemer.

Make a joyful noise unto the Lord, all ye lands.
Serve the Lord with gladness: come before his presence with
    singing.
Know ye that the Lord he is God:
    it is he that hath made us, and not we ourselves;
    we are his people, and the sheep of his pasture.
Enter into his gates with thanksgiving, and into his courts with praise:
    be thankful unto him, and bless his name.
For the Lord is good; his mercy is everlasting;
    and his truth endureth to all generations.

O come let us sing unto the Lord: let us make a joyful noise to the
    rock of our salvation.
Let us come before his presence with thanksgiving, and make a joy-
    ful noise unto him with psalms.
For the Lord is a great God, and a great King above all gods.
In his hand are the deep places of the earth:
    the strength of the hills is his also.
The sea is his, and he made it: and his hands formed the dry land.
O come let us worship and bow down:
    let us kneel before the Lord our maker.

Delight thyself in the Lord; and he shall give thee the desires of thine
    heart.
Wait on the Lord: be of good courage, and he shall strengthen thine
    heart.
Rest in the Lord, and wait patiently for him.
Be still and know that I am God.

Let the beauty of the Lord our God rest upon us.

God is our refuge and strength, a very present help in trouble.
God be merciful unto us, and bless us;
    and cause his face to shine upon us.
The Lord will give grace and glory: no good thing will he withhold
    from them that walk uprightly.
The Lord is nigh unto all that call upon him, to all that call upon him
    in truth.
Remember, O Lord thy tender mercies and thy loving kindnesses;
    for they have been ever of old.

Out of the depths have I cried unto thee, O Lord.
Out of my distress I called on the Lord; the Lord answered me and
    set me free.
They that sow in tears shall reap in joy.
Weeping may endure for a night, but joy cometh in the morning.
Like as a father pitieth his children,
    so the Lord pitieth them that fear him.
Keep me as the apple of the eye, hide me under the shadow of thy
    wings.
Create in me a clean heart, O God; and renew a right spirit within
    me.

The fear of the Lord is the beginning of wisdom; a good understand-
    ing have all they that do his commandments.
It is better to trust in the Lord than to put confidence in man.
Behold how good and how pleasant it is for brethren to dwell togeth-
    er in unity!
Teach us to number our days, that we may apply our hearts to wisdom.
Thy word have I hid in mine heart, that I might not sin against thee.
The Lord shall give his angels charge over thee, to keep thee in all
    thy ways.
Precious in the sight of the Lord is the death of his saints.

The Lord is my rock, and my fortress, and my deliverer.
He maketh my feet like hinds' feet, and setteth me upon my high
    places.
The Lord is my shepherd, I shall not want.
He restoreth my soul...my cup runneth over.

The Lord is my light and my salvation; whom shall I fear?
The Lord is the strength of my life; of whom shall I be afraid?

I will sing unto the Lord, because he hath dealt bountifully with me.
I will hope continually, and will yet praise thee more and more.
I will extol thee, my God, O king; and I will praise thy name forever
  and ever.
Praise ye the Lord: for it is good to sing praises unto our God, for it
  is pleasant; and praise is comely.

Praise ye the Lord. Praise God in his sanctuary:
  praise him in the firmament of his power.
Praise him for his mighty acts:
  praise him according to his excellent greatness.
Praise him with the sound of the trumpet:
  praise him with the psaltery and harp.
Praise him with the timbrel and dance:
  praise him with stringed instruments and organs.
Praise him upon the loud cymbals:
  praise him upon the high sounding cymbals.
Let everything that hath breath praise the Lord.
  Praise ye the Lord.

All the aforementioned quotations are from the Psalms—8:1; 13:6;
17:8; 18:2,33; 19:14; 23:1,3,5; 25:6; 27:1,14; 30:5,12; 31:5; 34:1; 37:4,7;
42:2; 46:1,10; 51:10; 67:1; 68:19; 71:14; 84:11; 86:15; 90:12,14,17; 91:11;
92:1; 95:1–6; 100:1–5; 103:1–3,13; 107:1; 111:10; 116:1,15; 118:5,8;
119:11,62,103; 121:1–2; 122:1; 126:5; 130:1; 133:1; 145:1,3,10,18;
147:1,5; 148:13; 150:1–6. All selections are taken from the KJV, with the
exception of 103:2–3 and 148:13b (NIV), 116:1 (TLB), and 118:5 (RSV).

MUSIC

Music is the universal language of mankind.—Henry Wadsworth Longfellow.

My credentials in the field of music are checkered: four years of piano lessons—enough to play "Falling Waters" at piano recitals with a soft, caressing touch of most notes; one year of trumpet in junior high school; three years of slide trombone in the front row of the high school marching band; four years of baritone horn in college; and one year of alto horn in an army service force band at the conclusion of World War II in Europe. (Our band helped celebrate the liberation of Paris by getting innumerable hugs and kisses from deliriously happy and grateful French madames and mademoiselles pressing all over our jeeps. Happily, we couldn't even play our instruments that day because of the ecstatic crowds of people lined six-deep along each side of the avenue. Oh joy!)

In addition, I sang bass in a church choir for four years, and sang baritone in the college glee club for another four—so as to give some balance to my love for "bold brass."

These early amateur experiences certainly helped shape my intense interest in the world of music. Over the years I've become increasingly interested in all kinds of sounds (except hard rock)—from the popular dance band music of the 1930s to marching bands; from classical music to sacred hymns; from organ recitals to country and western music; from opera to spirituals; from drum and bugle corps to soul gospel; from bold brass and percussion to softer reeds, harps, and flutes.

In appreciation of all the thousands and thousands of times I've been thrilled and uplifted by hearing infinite varieties of music played and sung—while going to and from work, listening to stereo records in our home, singing in church, and attending musical shows and concerts—here then is my expression of sincere gratitude to the world of music and its countless gifted amateur and professional performers that I have joyfully come to know over the last half-century.

Here's my hearty applause, and an appreciative salute to:

• The relatively few FM stereo stations that still continue to play good relaxing music for "easy listening."

• The Big Band sounds of the 1930s and 1940s, especially Glenn Miller, Tommy Dorsey, and Harry James.

192

- Country and western vocals that express the true feelings of the broken-heart love story.
- Willie Nelson for his recording of "On the Road Again."
- Frank Sinatra singing "New York, New York" with a terrific back-up orchestra.
- Radio City Music Hall Rockettes and their precision dancing numbers.
- The delightful Broadway musicals, such as *Hello Dolly* with incomparable entertainer Pearl Bailey, *Bubbling Brown Sugar*, *Sound of Music*, *South Pacific*, *Oklahoma*, and *A Chorus Line*.
- The equally delightful London musical, *Charlie Girl*.
- Fred Waring and the Pennsylvanians—one of the first one-hour musical variety shows on TV, featuring all manner of vocalists and instrumentalists.
- Lawrence Welk and his Champagne Orchestra—for the many years they provided easy listening enjoyment on TV to the older citizens.
- Ringling Bros. Barnum and Bailey Circus Band.
- The exciting world of drum and bugle corps competition (mostly college students) across America during warm summer evenings with such appealing performances as "Sweet Georgia Brown" and "Marianne."
- College marching bands with their elaborate halftime shows—particularly the West Chester University "Golden Ram" marching band of 250 strong playing "His Honor" march on parade, and such special arrangements as "Prelude to Lohengrin" and "Tenderly" at half-time shows.
- John Philip Sousa's terrific "Stars and Stripes Forever."
- The Philadelphia Orchestra and the Mormon Tabernacle Choir's stirring arrangement of "The Battle Hymn of the Republic."
- Ray Charles's emotionally moving piano arrangement (with orchestra) of "America the Beautiful."
- The Boston Pops, with Arthur Fiedler conducting, playing "The 1812 Overture" on a Fourth of July evening in the park amid firing cannons and colorful fireworks.
- The Philadelphia Orchestra and its outstanding concerts in the Academy of Music.
- Debussy's pastoral, amorous *Prelude to the Afternoon of a Fawn*.

- "Outbursts of Joy" from the *Ascension Suite* by Messiaen.

- Mozart's *The Magic Flute* and Wagner's *Tristan and Isolde* performed in the glittering Munich Opera House.

- The grand pipe organs heard in John Wanamaker's Grand Court in Philadelphia and at Riverside Church in New York City—with Virgil Fox playing Louis Verne's "Carillon de Westminster" and Bach's "Fantasy in G Major" (fantastic endings in both).

- Romantic organ music with ethereal variations on "Weinen, Klagen, Sorgen, and Zagen" by Franz Liszt in the Princeton University Chapel.

- Anita Greenlee Mello, organist at Westminster Presbyterian Church in West Chester, Pennsylvania, playing Bach's "Toccata and Fugue in D Minor," which contains massive grand chords, fast runs, and crescendos—it has everything. (Some devotees of Bach believe that what Jesus was spiritually, by way of completeness and perfection, is what Bach was musically. They think his music is a prelude to transcending glory—like heavenly music.)

- Joseph Haydn's *The Creation.*

- The *Nutcracker* ballet by Tchaikovsky at Christmas—for its childhood fantasies involving the world of imagination and make-believe.

- The Christmas performances of the Meistersingers of Coatesville (Pennsylvania) Area Senior High School, and the volunteer Forty-Niners Chorus of the West Chester (Pennsylvania) community—combining popular secular numbers ("White Christmas," "Silver Bells," "Hurry Home for Christmas") with religious carol favorites ("Hark! The Herald Angels Sing," "Away In a Manger," and "Silent Night").

- George Shearing's beautiful piano rendition (with orchestra) of "Christmas in Three-Quarter Time."

- The "Magnificat" ("My soul doth magnify the Lord...") by Marcel Dupré.

- Mario Lanza singing "O Holy Night."

- Handel's sublime *Messiah*, including the "Hallelujah Chorus," of which Handel said while writing it: "I think that today all of Heaven has opened before me and I have seen the face of the Great God Himself."

- The strong music department of West Chester University and the excellent choral and orchestral concerts given, such as Bach's *The*

Passion according to St. Matthew and Mendelssohn's *Elijah.*

• The soul-piercing spirituals of America, like "Ezekiel Saw de Wheel" and "Ridin' in de Chariot in de Mornin'."

• Ocean City Tabernacle Mixed Vocal Quartet, with soprano soloist Winifred Dettore singing "O Divine Redeemer" (electrifying).

• "Amazing Grace" as sung by Judy Collins.

• George Beverly Shea's rendition of "How Great Thou Art."

• Billy Graham's Crusade Choir of 4,000 voices in Philadelphia singing "Spirit of God, Descend upon My Heart" and "Burdens Are Lifted at Calvary."

• Phil Driscoll playing his crystal-clear trumpet, and singing "Everlasting Life."

• Contemporary gospel songs, such as "He Touched Me" and "It Took a Miracle"—as well as soul gospel.

• The United States Navy Band playing the navy hymn, "Eternal Father, Strong to Save."

• The New York Staff Band of the Salvation Army playing a special arrangement of "What a Friend We Have in Jesus," with a soul-riveting cornet solo.

• The New York Staff Band Male Chorus of the Salvation Army singing an arresting arrangement of "The Old Rugged Cross."

• Great hymns of the Faith, such as Martin Luther's "A Mighty Fortress Is Our God" and Charles Wesley's "O For a Thousand Tongues to Sing"—and Alfred B. Smith's *Treasury of Hymn Histories* with heartfelt stories telling why and how certain gospel hymns came to be written.

In passing, it should be noted that some dear folks have so much inner joy and peace that they go around the house humming a tuneful hymn—as my younger brother Clyde does—or inwardly singing a song of praise while mowing the lawn or doing the dishes.

You may recall the Summer Olympics in 1984 when Greg Louganis of the United States set swimming records in the diving events with near-perfect performances. What was his secret? It is reported that "Greg puts on a headset during practice that plays musical tunes—a different tune for each kind of dive. He thus hears each tune hundreds of times while practicing his dives. This gives him his perfect timing and rhythm. Then, during his Olympic dives, he hears the music playing in his head—without the headset."

What a spiritual parallel lesson this is for us! If we like a spiritual hymn or song so well that we would like to have it remain with us forever—then let's do what Greg did. Buy a record or tape and listen to it every day for at least twenty days. Only by repetition will the beautiful piece of music become an inner part of us (similar to the way commercials become part of us through repetition).

By the way, whatever happened to old-fashioned group singing by friends around the home piano? We need a revival of spontaneously performed music, to help lighten the heavy burdens of the world—like some of us do when singing carols around the piano at Christmastime.

> Sing the words and tunes of the psalms and hymns when you are together [perhaps around a piano], and go on singing and chanting [humming] to the Lord in your hearts, so that always and everywhere you are giving thanks to God.
>
> —Eph. 5:19–20 (JB)

> Teach and help one another along the right road with your psalms and hymns, and Christian songs, singing God's praises with joyful hearts.
>
> —Col. 3:16 (P)

Lord, make my heart a place where angels sing!
For serenely thoughts low-breathed by Thee
Are angels gliding near on noiseless wing...

—John Keble

RING 'DEM BELLS AT CHRISTMASTIME

Christmastime seems to cast a magic spell over most people each year! The beautiful Christmas music emanating everywhere from a myriad of streets, stores, and homes; the nostalgic Christmas cards hinting of memorable bygone years spent in snowy outdoors, or around warm family fireplaces and dinner tables indoors; the inspiring Christmas Eve church services featuring heavenly Christmas carols performed with angelic voices, crisp clear trumpet calls in "Joy to the World" and majestic organ sounds in the rising finale of Handel's "Hallelujah Chorus."

No, I haven't forgotten the gaily decorated Christmas tree with its woodsy aroma; the warm glow of lights in windows, and on doorways and evergreens at night; the enchantment of beautifully wrapped Christmas gifts in all shapes, sizes, and weights under the tree; the scent of burning candles and kitchen delights; the graceful beauty of poinsettias, holly, mistletoe, and fruited wreaths. It's a most wonderful, joyful time of the year!

But have you ever thought about a totally different kind of thing to do during the Christmas season? Like "Ringing 'dem Bells" by the Christmas kettles of the Salvation Army. For those thousands of volunteers who have participated, it's a humbling but joyful experience, bringing its own inner rewards. The rules are simple: Dress warmly for cold weather; ring lustily for two hours with a congenial partner of either sex; and be prepared to vocalize a cheerful "Merry Christmas" to hundreds of people. The result: You will receive abundant choruses of "Merry Christmas" in return, and have a spirited opportunity to watch hundreds of people put money into the kettles—from the wide-eyed tiny tots who expect the "chimes to ring" when they drop their coins; to the teenagers who often empty their pockets for the unadulterated joy of it; to the former servicemen who give bills, remembering gratefully the way the Salvation Army treated them in wartime; to the thoughtful retired widows who give willingly from their Social Security checks, remembering other times of "caring and sharing" when they were on the receiving end.

"Ring 'dem Bells" cheerfully at Christmastime!

WEDDINGS

It is often said that "marriages are made in Heaven." The successful, happy ones usually are. To be married to a spouse "till death do us part" has an enduring quality to it. To be "in love" with someone, to become engaged, and then to be married is a special, sacred time for a couple, and one always to be cherished and remembered.

The church wedding has become more favored since World War II, and is by far the most natural and appropriate setting for a marriage to be performed. In marriage a man and woman become a union physically. They are also to achieve a "oneness of Spirit." A church wedding should be a spiritual service that reflects a holiness and ordination that is of God— enhanced by sacred music, Scripture readings (1 Cor., ch. 13 on love is a natural), and a pastoral meditation.

Is there anything more beautiful on God's earth than to see a lovely bride, dressed in an elegant white gown, coming down the church aisle with a radiantly beaming face that tells all the world: "Look at me! I'm beautiful on the outside, and full of joy on the inside. I'm about to be married to the most wonderful guy in the world."

Is it any wonder that the groom, after seeing such a moving display of grace and beauty coming toward him at the altar, will want to quickly and confidently reaffirm these vows in the ceremony: "I will take thee to be my wedded wife...for better or worse, for richer or poorer, in sickness and in health...to love and to cherish...till death do us part..."

GOD IN NATURE

One of the most beautiful, peaceful, satisfying ways God reveals Himself to us is through Nature—the created world around us—and that reality alone should leave us without any excuses for not wanting to acknowledge God and His wondrous works.

Let's join Psalmist David in his joyous Prayer of Thanks:

Let the heavens rejoice, let the earth be glad;
    let them say among the nations, "The Lord reigns!"
Let the sea resound, and all that is in it;
    let the fields be jubilant, and everything in them!
Then the trees of the forest will sing,
    they will sing for joy before the Lord.
Give thanks to the Lord, for he is good;
    his love endures forever.

—1 Chron. 16:31–34 (NIV)

The heavens declare the glory of God;
    the skies proclaim the work of his hands.

—Ps. 19:1 (NIV)

Thou, Great God, hast provided us
    a world full of wonders and beauty.
Crashing oceans, silent mountains,
    rolling hills and winding rivers.
Fields of flowers on earth
    and fields of stars in the heavens.
For all of nature,
    we are truly grateful, O God!

—David F. Bortner

There is no unbelief;
Whoever plants a seed beneath the sod
And waits to see it push away the clod,
He trusts in God.

—Lizzie York Case

This is my Father's world,
And to my listening ears
All nature sings, and round me rings,
The music of the spheres.

—Maltbie D. Babcock

Each little flower that opens,
Each little bird that sings,
God made their glowing colors,
He made their tiny wings.

Yes, all things bright and beautiful,
All creatures great and small,
And all things wise and wonderful,
The Lord God made them all.

—Cecil Frances Alexander

From Linda, a fifth-grade student, a story about *White Lacey Treetops*:

White lacey treetops. The snow has come again! It floats through the
air so gracefully, then lands on the majestic evergreens. The wind,
which is a cat, prowls around to see what this mysterious white thing
is. I cannot find the answer, but the trees know. They know that the
white lace that trims them is a fairy-like ballet, sent by God to make
the world beautiful.

Great, wide, beautiful, wonderful world,
With the wonderful water around you curled,
And the wonderful grass upon your breast,
World, you are beautifully drest.

—William Brighty Rands

To me every hour of the light and dark is a miracle,
Every cubic inch of space is a miracle,
Every square yard of the surface of the earth
    is spread with the same,
Every part of the interior swarms with the same.

To me the sea is a continual miracle,
The fish that swim—the rocks—the motion
    of the waves, the ships with men in them,
What stranger miracles are there?

—Walt Whitman

Some may think the foregoing passages too sentimental and simplistic
in exalting God's world of Nature. So, for such people, I am posing a few
deep cosmic questions to stretch the mind when contemplating the continuing mysteries of creation:

- What creative forces brought the universe into being in the very beginning?
- How did logic, order, and dependability arise from chaos in the universe?
- How were the billions of galaxies made and arranged in space?
- What law of astrophysics controls quasars and black holes?
- How were the sun, the moon, and the stars designed, and then placed in such perfect harmony in space?
- The earth seems unique among the other planets in our solar system for supporting human life as we know it—with just the right balance between oxygen and carbon dioxide, and a gracious atmospheric layer to screen the sun's rays and give us just the right amount for warmth and good health.

   How is life on earth regulated so that a constancy of 21% oxygen is maintained on the earth?
- Does life exist on any of the 300 billion stars of our Milky Way galaxy? If so, what kind of life? Does it have superior or inferior intelligence to ours?
- How vast is space—in millions of light years?

Teachers in schools can help develop an awareness of the wonders of Nature that inspire and foster a feeling of awe and reverence for life.

Nearly all primary grade children know (and believe) that we are dependent upon God for the sun, rain, soil, and air needed to make flowers and trees grow. It was Froebel's belief that there is a mystical character in Nature that evolves a spiritual response from the child.

In the intermediate grades, the pupils are fascinated (and humbled) by such topics as the vastness of space and the splendor of the heavens; the great size and number of galaxies in the universe as revealed by telescopes; the mysteries of life in the sea; the amazing revelations of the microscopic world; the beauty and form of common crystals; the invisible miracle of the snowflake; the beauty and marvels of backyard flowers and garden plants; the mystery of photosynthesis; the wonder of metamorphosis; the almost unbelievable navigational ability of migrating birds; and the wonder of the human body.

Children are aided in developing a spiritual sensitivity to living by artists who paint the beauty of nature, such as Rosa Bonheur and her paintings of animals; Alfred Parson's peaceful *Bredon-on-the-Avon*; Jean Millet and the simplicity of his paintings (*The Rainbow*); Andrew Wyeth and his earthy tones of the uncluttered outdoors; and the magnificent paintings of John James Audubon, featuring hundreds of colorful birds in their native nesting habitats, like the red-headed woodpecker, black-eyed chickadee, ruby-throated hummingbird, tufted titmouse, beautiful bluebird, orange and black Baltimore oriole, flashy red cardinal (male) and graceful blue-jay, fluted wood thrush, and the amazing, musically talented, fun-loving mockingbird.

Then there is the miracle of the changing seasons witnessed annually by those living in the four-season regions of the earth.

Clarence Edward Macartney (1879–1957), one of the first American ministers to preach on the radio, might well speak for many of us when he wrote:

> I like all the seasons. I like winter with its clear, cold nights and the stars like silver-headed nails driven into the vault of heaven. I like spring with its green growth, its flowing streams, its reviviscent hope. I like summer with the litany of gentle winds in the tops of the trees, its long evenings and the songs of its birds. But best of all I like autumn. I like its mist and haze, its cool morning air, its field strewn with the blue aster and the goldenrod; the radiant livery of the forests—yellow, and orange, and black, and pale, and hectic red.

My personal favorite seasons are spring and fall.

In spring, the sights of the slowly appearing flowers and leaves inspire me to walk more leisurely; the smell of the fresh grass causes me to breathe more deeply; and the sounds of the singing birds remind me to think on things less mundane. I welcome the newness of spring and its refreshment. It's just as though I'm young again, and earthly life could go on forever. It uplifts my spirit and quickens my walk on the first warm days of May, when all my five senses are born anew. Spring gives me renewed hope of eternal life, and a greater desire to get to know this Great Creator God in other revelations of His Spirit beyond His clearly revealed natural world.

In fall, when the world turns golden, October becomes the perfect month of the entire year—the time in Pennsylvania (and many other parts of the world) when the five senses are filled to overflowing. Cool nights are touched with satisfying smells of wood smoke and burning leaves. Sunny warm October days spill long beams of sunlight across the golden leaves just beginning to fall in the woods—creating a soft, ethereal atmosphere usually reserved for vaulted cathedrals with stained glass windows. One glimpse of a flaming yellow-orange-red sugar maple tree, or a sculptured golden aspen, or a deep-red white oak against October's deep blue sky can last in the memory for a lifetime. It's a real joy to see billions of turning leaves against a hillside in a broad spectrum of many-hued yellows, oranges, reds, browns, pale greens, and deep purples. Aided by the vivid colors of varied pumpkins, apples, and other fruits at roadside stands, life seems to reach its full harvest of maturity then, sensing all the while the preciousness of life's opportunities—its beauty, and, like the falling leaves, also its brevity. (For things must be done soon, before winter comes, and it's too late.)

October is so intensely beautiful that it might be regarded as a heavenly foretaste of life in the hereafter.

Since we began this piece with a prayer, we'll also close with one by James Muilenburg:

We praise Thee, Oh God, for the world of nature about us; for the glories of the heavens at nighttime with the myriad stars each of which Thou dost know and callest by intimate name, for the verdure and freshness of the blooming earth; for the majesty of mountain heights and the silent flowing of the great rivers to the sea. We thank Thee for the clouds at sunset; for the fields of waving grain, and for beauty everywhere we rejoice this day. So in all things, may Thy name be praised, for Thine is the Kingdom and Thine is the glory and Thine is the power forever and ever. Amen.

SAY IT WITH FLOWERS!

What would this world be like without flowers?

No flowers at weddings; no flowers at funerals; no flowers at church services.
No flower gardens; no flower borders; no flower shows.
No flowers in fields, meadows, or woods; no flowers by roadsides, paths, or brooks; no flowers dangling from hanging baskets or window boxes.
No botanical gardens; no florist shops; no flower markets.
No floral bouquets; no floral corsages; no floral arrangements.
No flower catalogs; no flower books; no flower photos.

The world would be dull and drab without the beauty and adornment of flowers—with their array of colors, their scents of fragrance, and their variety of shapes, sizes, and habits.
But praise God!
We do have floral abundance everywhere!

We have wildflowers on the mountains, in the deserts, in the marshes and fields, alongside streams and ponds.
We have cultivated flowers around our houses, inside our homes, in hospitals; in the city and in the country.
We have flowers in large pottery urns and glass containers that stand on floors and patios; in driftwood, in tiny glass vases, and small ceramic pieces on mantels and tables.

Each season of the year has its special favorites!

• We have the welcoming flowers of *early spring*: the white snow-drops, the eager crocuses, the yellow eranthis.

• We have the mellow flowers of *later spring*: the golden-yellow daffodils that want to talk, the tulips dressed in so many bright colors, the softer hyacinths, the willowy forsythia, the flamboyant azaleas, the tranquil dogwoods—and in the fields and meadows, the exciting red Indian paintbrush, the conversational jack-in-the-pulpit, the three-sided trillium, and the golden marsh marigolds.

• We have the luxuriant flowers of *summer*: the pastel-shaded snapdragons, the refined carnations, the wispy wisteria, the apricot-colored California poppies, the relaxed petunias, the erect gladiolas, the shade-loving impatiens, the delicate asters, the brilliant marigolds, the multicolored zinnias, the stately foxgloves and delphiniums— and among wildflowers, the artists' delights of Queen Anne's lace, black-eyed Susans, pastel blue cornflowers—all mixed with the pretty orange blossoms of the tiger lily.

• We have the mature flowers of *fall*: the brilliant mums, the puffy pompons, and the sculptured daisy mums. Are there any other fall flowers that can compete with their perfect earthy fall colors—the yellows, the apricots, the bronzes, the browns?

• The flowers of *winter*? If we're gardeners and without a greenhouse, we'll just have to buy our traditional poinsettias at Christmas—and then in January, look forward with eager anticipation to receiving our annual seed catalogs in the mail (Burpee's or equal) and spend the cold winter evenings drooling over its gorgeous photographs of spring, summer, and fall flowers—and dream about how our flower gardens are going to grow and blossom forth...

> Once the winter is past;
> And the flowers appear on the earth;
> And the fig tree forms its early fruit;
> And the blossoming vines spread their fragrance.
> —Song of Sol. 2:11–13 (NIV.)

P.S. I haven't forgotten about you rose lovers out there. It's just that the rose, with its thousands of varieties, has had so many poetic tributes paid it, and has become *the loving symbol* of *fragrance* and *beauty* among all the flowers that I thought it deserved a mention all by itself.

A BEAUTIFUL WOMAN!

God never made a more beautiful creature than a woman—a female! A true work of art and beauty!

How much thought God gave to His creation of a woman has apparently never been recorded. The end result, however, has never been equaled—albeit countless artists through the many centuries since Eve have attempted to put on canvas aspects of this beauty. Da Vinci (*Mona Lisa*), Titian, Rubens, Velasquez (*Venus with Cupid*), Degas, Renoir (*The Bathers*) and Sargent (*Madam X*) have had their moments in history with the woman figure—whether facial or full-bodied, clothed or nude.

The consummate beautiful woman is difficult to find all embodied in one perfect masterpiece. However, there do seem to be some distinctive features that most beautiful women possess:

- Radiant, sparkling eyes (often blue, green, or violet)
- Lustrous, bouncy hair
- Smooth "peaches and cream" complexion
- Angular, pear-shaped face (often high cheekbones)
- Narrow, small nose (pleasing profile)
- Wide, full, soft lips
- Well-proportioned, curvy body (usually tall and trim)
- Long, tapered legs (no protruding knee bones)
- Graceful, well-manicured hands
- Vibrant, warm voice

And clothes that enhance the feminine mystique—free-flowing silky dresses, snugly-fit sweaters and skirts, and coordinated color and line creations that harmonize the clothes worn with the eyes, hair, and skin.

Here is an attempt to identify some beautiful women:

- June Allyson—"The girl next door" look. Movie favorite with World War II GIs. Petite. Blond.

- Jacqueline Bissett—Bronzed, classic face. Tall, shapely figure. British.

- Princess Diana—Elegant clothes on a classic body frame. Shy smile.

• Linda Evans—Healthy look. Simplicity of lines and features. High cheekbones. Willowy.

• Peggy Fleming—Chiseled face, deep blue eyes—both framed by long straight strands of brown hair. Trim, ethereal figure, especially when skating on ice in a white, airy chiffon piece.

• Phyllis George—An "all-American girl" look. Deep dimples. Radiant hair. Fleshy. Bright red clothes.

• Mary Hart—Appears to have it all. Exciting voice. Effervescent.

• Grace Kelly—The epitome of grace and elegance in a woman. Wholesome, refreshing. Radiant beauty.

• Jayne Kennedy—A natural black beauty. Intelligent. Sports-minded.

• Cheryl Ladd—Long, blonde hair. Petite. Lithe body. A natural, healthy glow. Angelic look.

• Sophia Loren—Almond-shaped, violet eyes. Sculptured lips. Chiseled face. Fascinating accent. Italian.

• Marilyn Monroe—37"–23"–37". Enough said!—especially when molded into a one-piece white bathing suit. Alluring glamour. Vulnerable.

• Helen O'Connell—Green eyes. Sexy voice. Still retains her trim youthful figure and bouncy singing voice, even though well into her sixties.

• Juliet Prowse—All-around features. "A great pair of legs." Daring.

• Diane Sawyer—Exudes warmth, personality, intelligence. Wears an array of bright, fashionable clothes.

• Brooke Shields—Beautiful face, especially eyes and lips. Childlike innocence.

• Dinah Shore—Sexy voice. Warm, relaxed personality. Likes to help others. Aging gracefully. Looks better than thirty years ago.

• Leslie Stahl—Cool manner. Intelligent face. Doesn't need to smile to look beautiful.

• Marilyn Van Derbur—Another "all-American girl" look with dimples. Tall, statuesque. Pleasant voice.

Note: Those in the above list range in age from twenty into the sixties. Some women may protest that this list of beautiful women is too narrowly selective—representing only women who are either in movies, modeling, television, news media, or public life exposure, and selecting women who are noted for their outward beauty. What about women who are not as attractive outwardly, not in the public eye, but who possess *inner beauty*? Isn't that just as important?

The Bible indicates a number of women who were just that—beautiful on the inside, and some who were also beautiful on the outside. Consider the following:

• Sarah (Abraham to Sarah: "You are a beautiful woman." Gen. 12:11, TEV.)

• Rebecca (Rebecca was a beautiful young girl and still a virgin. Gen. 24:16.)

• Rachel (Rachel was shapely and beautiful. Gen. 29:17.)

• Leah (Leah had lovely eyes. Gen. 29:17.)

• Deborah (A prophetess and a judge. Judg. 4:4–5.)

• Naomi (Naomi to Ruth on finding a husband: "Wash yourself, put on some perfume, and get dressed in your best clothes." Ruth 3:3, TEV.)

• Ruth (Boaz to Ruth: "You are a fine woman." Ruth 3:11, TEV.)

• Hannah (Hannah prayed for a son, Samuel, and the Lord granted her request. 1 Sam. 1:27.)

• Bathsheba (David saw Bathsheba taking a bath in her house. She was very beautiful. 2 Sam. 11:2.)

• Tamar (David's son, Absalom, had a beautiful unmarried sister named Tamar. 2 Sam. 13:1.)

• Abishag (A search was made all over Israel for a beautiful young woman, and in Shunem they found such a girl named Abishag and brought her to very old King David to lie close to him and keep him warm. She was very beautiful and waited on the king and took care of him, but he did not have intercourse with her. 1 Kings 1:1–4.)

• Jezebel (Jezebel put on eye shadow and arranged her hair. 2 Kings 9:30.)

• Esther (Esther was a beautiful girl, and had a good figure—lovely in form and features. Esther 2:7.)

• Elizabeth (Elizabeth was filled with the Holy Spirit. Luke 1:41.)

• Mary (Elizabeth to Mary: "You are the most blessed of all women, and blessed is the child [Jesus] you will bear!" Luke 1:42, TEV). (See also Mary's Song of Praise. Luke 1:46–55.)

• Mary Magdalene (Followed Jesus, was present at His crucifixion, went to His tomb on Easter morning, and was the first person Jesus appeared to after His resurrection. Mark 15:40–41, 47; Mark 16:1–2, 9–11.)

• Mary of Bethany (Mary took a whole pint of very expensive perfume made out of pure nard, poured it on Jesus' feet, and wiped His feet with her hair. The sweet smell of the perfume filled the whole house. John 12:3.)

• Lydia (A saleswoman of purple cloth who worshiped God. Acts 16:14.)

It's a double blessing to be beautiful on the outside and the inside, as some of the Bible women were, and as some of the aforementioned list of women are.

However, take heart! If you happen to be a woman who is not a No. 10 in matters of shimmering outward physical beauty, you might be a No. 10 when it comes to serene inner soul beauty—and in the eyes of God this is of far greater value. (Those meeting Mother Teresa report this sense of serenity and saintliness.)

1 Sam. 16:7 (KJV) says: "Man looketh on the outward appearance, but the Lord looketh on the heart."

1 Pet. 3:3–4 (TLB, JB) says it clearly: "Don't be concerned about the outward beauty that depends on jewelry, or beautiful clothes, or hair arrangements. *Be beautiful inside*, in your hearts, with the lasting charm of a sweet and gentle disposition—this is what is so precious in the sight of God."

AMEN!

BEAUTIFUL BIBLICAL PASSAGES

In the Old Testament:

Abraham willing to sacrifice his only son Isaac. (Gen. 22:1–18.)

God gives the Ten Commandments to Moses. (Exod. 20:1–17.)

"The Lord bless you and keep you; the Lord make his face to shine upon you and be gracious to you; the Lord turn his face toward you and give you peace." (Num. 6:24–26, NIV.)

"Love the Lord your God with all your heart and with all your soul and with all your strength." (Deut. 6:5, NIV.)

Hannah dedicates her son Samuel in the House of the Lord: *"I prayed for this child, and the Lord granted me what I asked of him. So now I will give him to the Lord. For his whole life he will be given over to the Lord."* (1 Sam. 1:27–28, NIV.)

David's prayer of thanks: *"Yours, O Lord, is the greatness and the power and the glory and the majesty and the splendor, for everything in heaven and earth is yours...Now, our God, we give you thanks, and praise your glorious name."* (1 Chron. 29:11,13, NIV.)

"The heavens declare the glory of God; and the skies proclaim the work of His hands." (Ps. 19:1, NIV.)

"How precious to me are your thoughts, O God! How vast is the sum of them!" (Ps. 139:17, NIV.)

"There is a time for everything, and a season for every activity under heaven:
  a time to be born and a time to die,
  a time to plant and a time to uproot...
  a time to weep and a time to laugh,
  a time to mourn and a time to dance...
  a time to be silent and a time to speak,
  a time to love and a time to hate,
  a time for war and a time for peace."

(Eccles. 3:1,2,4,7,8, NIV.)

"For unto us a child is born, to us a son is given, and the government will be on his shoulders. And he will be called Wonderful Counselor, Mighty God, Everlasting Father, Prince of Peace." (Isa. 9:6, NIV.)

"He was despised and rejected by men, a man of sorrows, and familiar with suffering....Surely he took up our infirmities and carried our sorrows....the punishment that brought us peace was upon him, and by his wounds we are healed....he poured out his life unto death...he bore the sin of many, and made intercession for the transgressors." (Isa. 53:3–5,12, NIV.)

Hosea buys back his adulterous wife, Gomer, at a public auction and restores her in forgiving love. (Hos., chs. 1–3.)

In the New Testament:

The birth of Jesus (Matt. 2:1–12; Luke 2:1–20.)

"Consider the lilies, how they grow; they neither toil nor spin; yet I tell you, even Solomon in all his glory was not arrayed like one of these." (Luke 12:27, RSV.)

The Parable of the Lost Sheep. (Luke 15:3–7)

The Parable of the Lost Son. (Luke 15:11–32)

"God so loved the world that he gave his one and only Son, that whoever believes in Him shall not perish but have eternal life." (John 3:16, NIV.)

"God is Spirit, and those who worship Him must worship in Spirit and in truth." (John 4:24, NAB.)

Jesus said: *"A new commandment I give you: Love one another. As I have loved you, so you must love one another."* (John 13:34, NIV.)

Jesus said: *"I am the way and the truth and the life. No one comes to the Father except through me."* (John 14:6, NIV.)

"But the Counselor, the Holy Spirit, whom the Father will send in My name, will teach you all things and will remind you of everything I [Jesus] have said to you." (John 14:26, NIV.)

The resurrection of Jesus (John 20:1–29; Luke 24:1–45.)

Peter's miraculous escape from prison (Acts 12:1–17.)

"O the depth of the riches both of the wisdom and knowledge of God! How unsearchable are His judgments and how untraceable are His ways!" (Rom. 11:33, NKJV, NEB.)

The *Love* chapter (1 Cor. 13:1–13; see the Phillips translation.)

"First, we have these physical, human bodies, and later on God gives us spiritual, heavenly bodies. The first man Adam was made from the dust of the earth, but the second Man came from Heaven and was the Lord himself. For the life of this world men are made like the material man, made of dust; but for the life that is to come they are made like the One from Heaven. Just as each of us now has a body like Adam's, so we shall some day have a body like Christ's...For it is utterly impossible for flesh and blood to possess the Kingdom of God. These perishable bodies of ours are not the right kind to live forever." (1 Cor. 15:46–50, TLB, NEB, P.)

"Where the Spirit of the Lord is, there is liberty." (2 Cor. 3:17, KJV.)

"All of us who are Christians have no veils on our faces, but reflect like mirrors the brightness and glory of our Lord. We grow brighter and brighter as we are transfigured in ever-increasing splendor into His own image, becoming more and more like Him; this transformation comes from the Spirit of the Lord working within us." (2 Cor. 3:18, P, JB, TLB.)

"God is able to make all grace abound to you, so that in all things at all times, having all that you need, you will abound in every good work [to help others]." (2 Cor. 9:8, NIV.)

"But the fruit of the Spirit is love, joy, peace, patience, kindness, goodness, faithfulness, gentleness, and self-control. Against such things there is no law." (Gal. 5:22–23, NIV.)

"I pray that God, the God of our Lord Jesus Christ, the all-glorious Father, will give you spiritual wisdom and the insight to know more of him: that you may receive the inner illumination of the Spirit which will make you realize how great is the hope to which He is calling you—the magnificence and splendor of the inheritance promised to Christians—and how tremendous is the power available to us who believe in God. That power is the same divine energy which was demonstrated in Christ when He raised Him from the dead and gave Him the place of supreme honor in Heaven—a place that is infinitely superior to any conceivable command, authority, power or control, and which carries with it a name far beyond any name that could ever be named in this world or the world to come." (Eph. 1:17–21, P.)

"We are God's work of art, created in Christ Jesus to live the good life as from the beginning he had meant us to live it." (Eph. 2:10, JB.)

May you be filled through all your being with God Himself!" (Eph. 3:19, P.)

"Be kind and compassionate to one another, *forgiving* each other, just as in Christ God forgave you." (Eph. 4:32, NIV.)

Having Christ's attitude and mind—a humble servant. (Phil. 2:5–11.)

"Let your conversation be always full of grace, seasoned with salt, so that you may know how to answer everyone." (Col. 4:6, NIV.)

May the God of peace make you perfect in holiness, and may your whole spirit, soul, and body be preserved blameless at the coming of the Lord Jesus Christ." (1 Thess. 5:23, NAB, NKJV.)

"The Day when our Lord Jesus Christ will appear will be brought about at the right time by God, the blessed and only Ruler, the King of kings and the Lord of lords." (1 Tim. 6:14–16, TEV.)

The *Faith* chapter (Heb. 11:1–40; 12:1–2.)

"Do not forget to show hospitality to strangers, for in so doing some have entertained angels unawares." (Heb. 13:2, NIV, RSV.)

"Praise be to the God and Father of our Lord Jesus Christ! By his great mercy we have been born anew to a living hope through the resurrection of Jesus Christ from the dead. You can now look forward to possessing a perfect inheritance that can never perish, spoil or fade—reserved in Heaven for you." (1 Pet. 1:3–4, NIV, RSV, TEV.)

"The proving of your faith, which is infinitely more valuable than gold, is planned to result in praise and honor and glory in the day when Jesus Christ reveals Himself....At present you trust Him without being able to see Him, and even now He brings you a joy that words cannot express and which has in it a hint of the glories of Heaven; and all the time you are receiving the result of your faith in Him—the salvation of your souls." (1 Pet. 1:7–9, P.)

"But you [believers] are a chosen people, a royal priesthood, a holy nation, a people set apart to sing the praises of God who called you out of the darkness into His wonderful light." (1 Pet. 2:9, NIV, JB.)

"You should all be of one mind living like one big happy family, full of sympathy toward each other, loving one another with tender hearts, generous and courteous at all times." (1 Pet. 3:8, P, TLB.)

Faith in the Son of God. (1 John 5:1–21.)

"And now unto Him who is able to keep you from falling, and to present you faultless before the presence of His glory with exceeding great joy, to the only wise God our Savior, be glory and majesty, dominion and power, both now and forever. Amen." (Jude 1:24–25, KJV.)

A new Heaven and Earth. (Rev. 21:1–27.)

Note: It may be that some of your favorite Beautiful Biblical Passages have already been found in the more than 150 Biblical references found in over half the other articles. Those verses have not been repeated here.

CHAPTER X

A BRIGHT, GLORIOUS FUTURE!*

Remain faithful even when facing death, and I will give you the crown of life—*an unending glorious future!*

—Rev. 2:10 (TLB)

I consider that our present sufferings [on this earth] are less than nothing compared with the glory that will be revealed to us, and the *magnificent future* God has planned for us.

—Rom. 8:18 (NIV, P)

Now we know that when we die and leave our earthly bodies, we have a building from God, an *eternal house in Heaven.*

—2 Cor. 5:1 (TLB, NIV)

For our earthly bodies...must be transformed into heavenly bodies that cannot perish but will *live forever.*

—1 Cor. 15:53 (TLB)

*Italics occuring in quotes are mine.

VAPOR TRAILS

Vapor trails against a clear blue sky can set my mind to wondering and wandering...What kind of plane is that? Is it a Boeing 727 or 747? Who are the passengers on the plane? What do they do for a living? Why are they taking this flight? (Aren't they lucky to be flying on such a clear day—they'll be able to see forever!) Where are they going? To what cities: Chicago, Denver, San Francisco?

Back to the trails. There are all types of trails: short, wispy ones that soon disappear; puffy ones that quickly meander when buffeted about by the winds; still others drift slowly off course as though not sure of their purpose in life.

But the vapor trails that leave me completely enthralled are the clear, long white trails that are like straight railroad tracks, and seem to last forever. Planes that produce such trails must have pilots who are clear thinkers and chart direct paths; the airline stewardesses must display clear skins and parade shimmering beauty; and the passengers must all possess a noble purpose for living, and know where they are going.

Alas, however, even the best of vapor trails finally vanish—to join, as we all must, the larger invisible spiritual realm.

WHEN EARTHLY LIVING LOSES ITS LUSTRE

There are times and days and seasons when the things of earth pale before us and we inwardly yearn for a better condition and place. This awareness is felt especially at times of pain, suffering, illness, tribulation, and sorrow. By contrast, we are comforted when we read about the new heavenly life in Rev. 21:4 (TLB): "God shall wipe away all tears from their eyes, and there shall be no more death—nor sorrow, nor crying, nor pain."

While living on earth contains far more joyful days than miserable ones, for the record it should be reported that there are enough situations happening on earth to make living far less desirable than living in Heaven would appear to be. For in Heaven, we believe there will be none of the following *disruptions to perfection* found in earthly living:

• Sadness, loneliness, separation, sickness—angers, fears, worries, regrets.

• Accidents, ambulances, hospitals, nursing homes—blind, deaf, lame, retarded, disturbed.

• Lying, stealing, burglaries, robberies, prisons—abortion, adultery, rape, drunkenness, drug abuse.

• Bombs, riots, terrorism, murders—raging fires, wars, funeral processions, cemeteries.

• Floods, hurricanes, tornadoes, volcanic eruptions—drought, dust, dirt, mud.

• Blizzards, avalanches, hot and humid weather—dark, damp, dreary, and dismal days.

• Beetles, bugs, flies, mosquitoes, worms—rats, mice, snakes, skunks, vultures.

• Thorns, weeds, crabgrass, trash, junk, garbage, sewers—shaving, menstruation, taxes, unemployment, tiredness.

And of course, night, sin, and death will be no more.

What blessed relief to have all this unwanted baggage of imperfections left on earth upon our departure for the perfections and splendors of Heaven!

A LETTER TO EVELYN—A CHRISTMAS ANGEL!

December 21, 1983

Dear Evelyn,

You are truly a blessed inspiration to us earthlings! You have been unable to move about physically as you would have liked these past nine months, but your contagious, positive soul-spirit is alive and well, and moving about freely.

In the dozens of times I have visited you during the last six months—in the hospital, and more recently in your home—you have never complained or questioned your lack of body mobility or strength. Instead, you display a lively sense of humor and touch of grace, and seemingly press on, "reaching toward the goal to win the prize which is God's heavenly call to the life above in Christ Jesus." (Phil. 3:14, NEB.)

I know that many days your life is like having one foot on earth and one foot in Heaven. You have shared many of your earthly joys of happy family life while growing up with your sister in Oxford (Pa.); and of your family living joys later in West Chester (Pa.) with your husband and son. You also shared your dreams and visions of what the heavenly life will be like in the future for you and your loved ones. But do you know that you shared an experience you had that serves as a powerful foretaste to me of what spiritual fellowship will be like in Heaven?

Here is that spiritual lesson: For nine months you have not eaten any foods or had liquids. All your intake and output has been through tubes. But on Thanksgiving Day when dinnertime arrived, you sat at the table with the rest of your family, passed the food along as it came to you, and thoroughly participated (except for food) in the spirit of true fellowship and loving thanksgiving at the table. *What a beautiful foretaste of what spiritual fellowship will be like in Heaven*—we will all be seated around a table, feeling fellowship in our spiritual bodies, symbolically partaking of food (although it will really not be needed for nourishment since we will no longer be a physical body with a digestive system but a spiritual body with nourishment from the Spirit of God)—and being thankful for one another, and being *one in the Spirit.*

"But our citizenship is in Heaven. [We are sojourners and pilgrims here on earth.] It is from Heaven that we eagerly await the coming of our Saviour, the Lord Jesus Christ. He will give a new form to this lowly body of ours and remake it according to the pattern of his glorified body, by the same power with which he can subdue the whole universe." (Phil. 3:20–21, NIV, NAB, JB.)

Merry Christmas, Evelyn!

In Christian Love,

Ron

P.S. Evelyn, who was suffering from inoperable cancer of the digestive system, died on January 15, 1984, in her fifty-fifth year.

FORETASTES OF HEAVEN

Some spiritually minded people seem to have learned the secret of living the heavenly life right here in their present lives on earth. They experience many days when it seems as though "they have one foot on earth and one foot in Heaven." It's just as though the heavenly life of the Spirit has come down and entered their physical bodies.

We sometimes say of such people that "God shows in their face"—their faces radiate love and joy, their eyes become a continual smile, and even their skin seems to reflect the shining glow of the Spirit.

Apart from such rare "angelic" examples, however, many of us must have experienced moments that were foretastes of Heaven here on earth, however brief and fleeting they may have been. Consider the following possibilities:

• *"Being at one with the universe."* This feeling is most apt to occur while communing with nature—a stroll through a wooded path; a bird watch; a walk through floral gardens; an awed stance by a stream, lake, or mountain; a rare June-type day when the weather is perfect, with outdoor and indoor temperatures the same.

• *"Not wanting to leave this place."* Usually felt after a moving emotional/spiritual experience—a thrilling church service with inspiring music and uplifting sermon, wanting to stay and talk with others about shared feelings held in common; a Thanksgiving dinner around the harvest table with loved family members, with no one wanting to leave the table after the meal because of spirited conversations, sweet fellowship, and bonded love; a cozy time of amiable chatting among close friends around a warm fireplace; a visit to the Grand Canyon, wanting to see this marvel of creation at each hour of the day.

• *"Wanting temporal time to stop and not begin again."* Realized at rare moments of ecstatic joy—a "once in a lifetime" family visit to a corresponding family overseas where the noontime six-course meal goes on for four hours, with extended time between each course to allow for appropriate toasts, and the translations (often hilarious) of the conversations going on in four languages; attending a convention, family or class reunion, or fiftieth wedding anniversary or graduation celebration—knowing that the same group of people will never be brought back together again; a time of parting from someone you deeply love; during sexual intercourse.

• *Pleasant surprises (serendipities).* Occur unexpectedly and without advance notice—a surprise letter from a long-lost friend; the turnaround behavior of a difficult relative, almost like a conversion experience; the miraculous healing of a person given little hope by the medical profession, as though an answer to prayer; playing a game where it seems as though the "pull of gravity" has been removed, and one's relaxed body is felt floating effortlessly on air; certain blessed days when everything falls perfectly into place, as though foreordained; a total feeling of inner peace and assurance, as though visited by "an angel from on high."

• *Saying the right words at the right time.* Usually happens when someone has been "in tune with the Spirit"—the writing of a letter, the deliverance of a spontaneous speech, the chairing of a meeting, or leading a discussion when the right words are said in perfect sequence to express the exact meaning intended, and with the exact words entering the writer's/speaker's mind a phrase or two before their release; being a good listener to someone having troubles, and being led of the Spirit to say "the right encouraging word."

• *Expressing love.* Opportunities abound for serving as a channel for communicating God's Unconditional Love—accepting people we meet just as they are (warts and all), without their having to accept in advance our political and religious beliefs or life-styles; loving the unlovely neighbor across the street; trying to find the good in those we meet; forgiving those who have hurt us willfully and misused us; giving hope and encouragement to those seeking God's Love, and going the "second mile" when needed.

Opportunities also abound for being grateful and appreciative recipients of many loving-kindnesses shown to us: a birthday or anniversary celebration in our honor; an arrangement of flowers sent to the door; a dinner out; a letter of appreciation for community efforts; the forgiving love of a person for an injustice done; the loving esteem of close friends; and the reciprocal love of spouse and family members.

• *Helping one another.* Can happen on short notice, as in emergencies (flat tires, broken pipes), but usually lasts longer if part of a long-range, organized planning system, such as the "soup, soap, salvation" (in that order) program of the Salvation Army; the worldwide missionary outreach of the churches; the international Bible distribution program of societies like the Gideons and the American

221

Bible Society; the establishment of schools and hospitals in needy countries; the worldwide distribution of relief goods in times of disasters, as done by the Red Cross; and the millions of unreported good deeds of kindness done continually by "angels of mercy" in countless communities on a personal TLC (tender loving care) basis.

DEATH

None of us knows how long we are destined to live on this earth, nor do we know the manner of our death.

But this one thing we do know—we will all die. (There is surprisingly *one notable exception* for Biblical Christians—the coming of the Messiah back to earth whereupon our earthly bodies will be caught up in the air and instantly transformed into spiritual bodies, so that we will not experience death, as Enoch and Elijah did not.)

Except for this future earthshaking event, however, the great majority of us would willingly opt to postpone the final days of our earthly lives indefinitely. We reason that we know what life is like here on earth, with all its ups and downs, but we're not too sure what life will be like beyond death—in fact, most of us are quite hazy about it, are shaky about the next life, and therefore would prefer not to think about it too much.

Some of the reasons of this are obvious, others are not:

- We like to be in confident control of our lives, and the fact of death is one event that we cannot control (except through suicide) or overcome—it's one time we need outside help.

- We prefer to keep busy with things that are here-and-now, and postpone thoughts of the hereafter. We want to wipe death out of our minds—especially when we're feeling so fit and healthy. (If we hear that someone has died young, we rationalize it away by saying that at least he will never have to experience arthritis, blindness, or Alzheimer's disease.)

- Many of us are also led (often subconsciously) into postponing doing things that are associated with death: having our wills written, arranging for our burial plans in advance, visiting cemeteries, or even attending funerals.

- We think talking about death is rather morbid, and most of us would rather think about more pleasant things—like eating out, or going to a ball game or a play.

In this regard, our American culture seems to clearly display a preference for the start of life rather than for its ending. Some examples: we always celebrate the birthdates of famous Americans as holidays, not their death dates. The insurance industry packages its chief product as life insurance, not death insurance. Others in our culture would even deny the reality of death by saying it is an error of the mind. (Although there is nothing deader than a cold, stiff, spiritless dead body.)

But death need not be thought of as always morbid. There are some positive things to be said in its behalf. Consider the following:

• Attending funerals or memorial services, apart from the sadness and grief felt for the immediate family members, can be viewed as having some redemptive features:
  —The pastors are usually at their best.
  —Only the best things are said in remembrance of the deceased.
  —The Scriptures read are often among the most beautiful and comforting to be found anywhere. (Pss. 23, 46, 103, 121; John, ch. 14; Rom. 8:38,39; 1 Cor., ch. 15; and Rev. 21:1–4.)
  —The music is usually inspiring and meaningful—particularly if it has been selected in advance by the family.

• I have attended a few funeral or memorial services that have had an uplifting, joyous celebration ring to them. In one such poignant service, despite the premature death of a sixteen-year-old boy athlete from a three-month leukemia, the pastor set the tone for the packed church service at the very beginning by saying, "We are gathered here today to celebrate the homegoing of Andy Becker." The rest of the Christian one-hour service was like a glorious graduation held in celebration of Andy's going from his earthly home to his heavenly home.

• A different kind of memorial service was held outdoors under a warm June sun at Fordhook Farm, the residence of David Burpee, in his memory. There were abundant floral displays of his favorite multicolored marigolds in vases of many sizes. David Burpee (head of Burpee Seed Company), age 87, was eulogized by longtime friends and associates. The service was enhanced by the music of Joseph Haydn's *The Creation*.

• The increase in the number of funeral/memorial services being held in the houses of worship, with eulogies given when appropriate by family members or close friends, and the use of favorite music, hymns, and Scripture readings selected by the family in advance. (Less viewings and public interments; more *memorial gift plans*.)

• The Salvation Army has a positive, forward-looking way of announcing the deaths of their officers in its magazine. Instead of an obituary column, their headlines indicate that the officers were

Promoted to Glory! What an uplifting way of talking about the death of a loved one.

Some people seem to be helped by reading articles or books describing "near-death" experiences that are being reported in increasing numbers. Most of these experiences can be summarized as though the persons were:

- Floating about (out of the body).
- Going rapidly through a dark tunnel.
- Seeing a bright light at the end of the tunnel.
- Completely at peace (all-is-well feeling).
  "Indescribable peace and euphoria."
  "Consciousness becomes real clear." (Some astronauts in space report this also).
- Seeing a review of their lives pass by—like a panoramic view involving key events and people—or like having a scroll unrolled.
- Seeing loved ones (in most cases).

While most of the reportings seem to be positive and could be interpreted as pointing to a future life that is brighter and more peaceful than our present one—others report that some people have had extremely negative "near-death" experiences approximating Dante's *Inferno*, and are thus seldom published. Such reportings reveal the hellish equivalents of torment, frustration, weeping, isolation, and darkness.

Even though some people worry about being old by the time they reach forty, the Psalms tell us that the length of our days is seventy years—or eighty if we have the strength. Most people I know who reach seventy are pleased that they have arrived at that milestone—and hope they can push on to achieve eighty. If we arrive at this octogenarian goal, it is human nature to then want to live one more year (assuming relatively good health) and then another year after that—and maybe even reach ninety, or one hundred.

Ultimately, however, our bodies will lose their strength and will wear out, with some of us dying a natural death—having lived to a ripe old age. It has been reported that over half of us will die mercifully in our sleep.

However, it's what may happen to us before we draw our last breath that sometimes concerns us. Nurses working with terminally ill patients (those with six months or less to live) report that while some patients have a real fear of death, the larger fears are that they may not be able to bear the pain, or have the strength left to face death. Fortunately, in God's Providence, most of us will not know the exact manner of our dying too far in advance.

If my observations are correct, most people, if they had a choice and could bargain with God, would opt for a *fast death*as in a heart attack. For such persons, it is incumbent that they make advance preparations, have their house in good order, and be in a continual state of readiness.

Very few people would choose a *slow death*—as in most cancer cases. However, the spiritual benefits gained by some dear souls as they experience a slow death are immensely rewarding. They do have time to get their earthly house in order, to ask questions about their future existence in the heavenly realm, and thus have more time to discuss spiritual things with their loved ones before departure. Some precious dying patients have been known to ask such real questions as: What will happen to me when I die? Will I know my mother and father in Heaven? What will life in Heaven be like? Will I see angels? What does the Bible say about life after death?

The Bible contains many passages that are helpful to the dying, and comforting to the bereaved. Here are a dozen and more:

> *"I will pray the Father and He shall give you another Comforter, that He may abide with you forever. He is the Holy Spirit."* (John 14:16–17a, KJV, TLB.)

> *"Come to me, all you who are weary and burdened, and I will give you rest."* (Matt. 11:28, NIV.)

> *"I will never leave you or forsake you."* (Heb. 13:5b, NKJV.)

> *"In my Father's house are many mansions...I go to prepare a place for you. And when I go and prepare a place for you, I will come again and will take you to Myself, that where I am you may be also."* (John 14:2–3, KJV, RSV.)

If we live, we live to the Lord; and if we die, we die to the Lord. So, whether we live or die, we belong to the Lord. (Rom. 14:8, NIV.)

Precious in the sight of the Lord is the death of his saints. (Ps. 116:15, NIV.)

I have fought the good fight, I have finished my course, I have kept the faith. In Heaven a crown is waiting for me which the Lord, the righteous Judge, will give me on that great day of His return. (2 Tim. 4:7–8, KJV, TLB.)

All I want is to know Christ and to experience the power of His resurrection, to share in His sufferings and become like Him in His death, in the hope that I myself will be raised from death to life. (Phil. 3:10–11, TEV.)

Remain faithful even when facing death and I will give you the crown of life—an unending, glorious future. (Rev. 2:10c, TLB.)

But our citizenship is in Heaven. It is from there that we eagerly await the coming of our Savior, the Lord Jesus Christ. He will give a new form to this lowly body of ours and remake it according to the pattern of his glorified body. (Phil. 3:20–21, NIV, NAB.)

"Rejoice that your names are written in Heaven." (Luke 10:20, RSV.)

This is the promise that He Himself gave us, the promise of eternal life. (1 John 2:25, NEB.)

And God shall wipe away all tears from their eyes, and there shall be no more death, nor sorrow, nor crying, nor pain. (Rev. 21:4, TLB.)

O death, where is thy sting? O grave, where is thy victory? Death is swallowed up in victory. Thanks be to God who gives us the victory through our Lord Jesus Christ. (1 Cor. 15:55,57, KJV, RSV.)

"I am the resurrection and the life. He who believes in Me, even though he dies, yet shall he live; and whoever lives and believes in Me shall never die." (John 11:25–26, NKJV, P, RSV.)

So as we grow older day by day, let us pray that each of us will look to God, the author and finisher of our faith, to strengthen us by His Holy Spirit—and fill us with all joy in believing—so that we may appropriate the above Scriptures as our own, and overcome the fear of death through *the hope of the resurrection.*

And at the end of our days, may we have a transcending faith like Johann Sebastian Bach did when he wrote "Come, Sweet Death," so as to say:

Death is like the most brilliant sunset one can imagine.
Fierce colors fill the sky;
But through all these colors,
An even brighter light shines from the place which is after death.

THE RESURRECTION

From a Biblical perspective, the best way to overcome the fear of death is to have a firm belief in the resurrection.

There is no doubt that a person's religious faith (or lack of it) is paramount when facing the reality of the resurrection.

The hope of a future resurrection of our own bodies is a prime test of our faith—it's at the very core of our belief system.

At its best, "faith is being sure of what we hope for and certain of what we do not see." (Heb. 11:1, NIV.)

The witnessing of any Passion play drives home this very point. I have personally experienced a number of Passion plays, including the famous one in Oberammergau, Bavaria. All plays do a remarkable portrayal of Christ's life, with especially moving dramatizations of Palm Sunday, The Last Supper, Judas's betrayal of Jesus, Peter's denial, the arrest and "trials" of Jesus before Caiaphas and Pontius Pilate, the piercing crowd noises and shouts of "Crucify Him! Crucify Him!"—and finally the gripping scenes of the Crucifixion itself, with accompanying darkness, lightning, thunder, and shaking of the earth!

By contrast, the depicting of the historical resurrection visually is difficult, yes, impossible to portray in a dramatization—for the producers of Passion plays are faced with an impossible earthly task. They are asked to show us an event that we cannot see because it is of faith, the evidence of which we cannot show or see with our physical eyes because it's in the dimension of the spiritual world—invisible, silent, supernatural, indestructible, eternal.

But on Easter morning, millions and millions of the faithful will arise to attend the glorious celebrations of joy from early sunrise onward and echo the angelic voices of the choirs, the grand chords of the organs, and the crisp, clear notes of the trumpets and trombones—as together in one heralding voice they shout and declare by faith:

He is Risen!
Hallelujah! Hallelujah!
He is Risen Indeed!

Yea, if this be true, then let us reaffirm our faith by saying with Paul: "All I want is to know Christ and to experience *the power of His resurrection*...in the hope that I myself will be *raised from death to life*." (Phil. 3:10–11, TEV.)

"And if the Spirit of God, who raised up Jesus from the dead, lives in you, He will make your dying bodies live again after you die, by means of this same Holy Spirit living within you." (Rom. 8:11, TLB.) This experience is similar to what is demonstrated in nature each spring in the glorious appearing of new life—green grass, colorful flowers, budding leaves—from what appeared to be lifeless grass, dead bulbs, and barren trees in the winter.

HEAVEN

Now we know that when this [earthly] tent
    we live in is taken down—
    when we die and leave these bodies—
We will have a permanent house in Heaven,
    with wonderful new heavenly bodies—
    made, not by man, but by God.

                                    —2 Cor. 5:1 (TLB, P)

Are you someone who still believes that the only Heaven you will see and know will be what you experience here on earth? What a dim view of Heaven!

Scoffers similarly say: "All the hell we will ever experience is on this earth." What a dim view of Hell. For Hell full-blown must be *eternal frustration* in trying to achieve and accomplish self-goals, always desiring and struggling, yet always coming up short—as in our worst nightmares—and further complicated by *eternal separation* from God's help.

While all of us see through a glass somewhat darkly when it relates to Heaven, and the Bible does not contain an abundance of references on the details of "what Heaven is like" (perhaps because if it did we would all want to prematurely "jump ship" from this spaceship earth to get there before our appointed time)—yet we do gain occasional glimpses and insights about Heaven while here on earth that give us uplifting (and sometimes yearning) thoughts about the heavenly life to come.

Jesus once said to a skeptical Nicodemus, "I have spoken to you of earthly things and you do not believe; how will you believe if I tell you of heavenly things?" John 3:12 (NIV, KJV).

This same question might well be asked of us today, especially if we think in a halfhearted way that all the Heaven we will ever know is here on earth. For many might say they are contented enough in finding Heaven in misty clouds rising from the lake at dawn; in white fluffy clouds against a blue sky at noonday; in brilliant rainbows and sunsets; in starry skies at night; in great music recordings on a quiet Sunday afternoon; in dinner by candlelight; in the face of a child; in a good book and an easy chair beside the fireplace; in a hammock by a peaceful stream; and in a thousand other ways.

We sometimes say in lighthearted moments that we hope our favorite pets (cats, dogs, horses, whatever) will be in Heaven—or our favorite foods (bananas, strawberries, pecan waffles, lamb, lobster, asparagus with almonds, pumpkin pie, coconut ice cream, watermelon, peaches with whipped cream, chocolate nougats)—or our favorite pastimes (baseball, golf, tennis, swimming, skiing, gardening, sewing, painting, singing, reading, writing).

At the least, we expect Heaven to epitomize the equivalent beauty and majesty found in the best things we have here on earth: stately cathedrals with magnificent stained glass windows and the sounds of a grand organ echoing throughout its chambers; mighty choral-orchestral musical performances; and all the tranquil beauty of the earth's best vistas of sky, sea, and land—as witnessed in varied landscapes of mountains, plains, hills, and valleys, cheerfully adorned with flowers, grass, and trees and happily decorated with birds, butterflies, and fish.

As fascinating as living here on earth is, generally speaking, there are times when we all begin to feel a little uneasy in this world, that we sense we are only strangers and pilgrims here—especially with advancing years—and that we desire something better, a more permanent home.

A New York senior citizen said recently: "I am ninety years old, and looking forward to starting the next life in Heaven. That will be exciting." He is looking ahead to living life in a new dimension.

"For we have no permanent city (home) here on earth, but we are looking for one in the world to come." (Heb. 13:14, P)

Many believe that their real citizenship is in Heaven (see Phil. 3:20). Each day of earthly living brings them closer to their earthly departure through death. At the moment of death, their soul-spirits will take quick flight from their mortal bodies, and will escape to Heaven. Their souls and spirits will never die. (See John 11:25–26; 2 Cor. 5:1–2.) The Apostle Paul says in Rom. 8:18 (NIV, P): "I consider that our present sufferings [on this earth] are less than nothing compared with the glory that will be revealed in us, and the *magnificent future* God has planned for us."

We are further advised in Col. 3:2 to set our minds and affections on things above—on heavenly things—not on the passing things of earth.

With this admonition in mind, here are some thoughts and beliefs about Heaven and the heavenly life envisioned there:

We Will Have New (Transformed) Heavenly Bodies. Our new heavenly bodies will outperform all the marvels of earth's recent scientific discoveries as to speed and locomotion in space. Like the astronauts in orbit, we will not feel the pull of earth's gravity—but unlike the astronauts in their physical bodies, our spiritual bodies will be perfectly suited for experiencing weightlessness.

Our new bodies will be able to travel faster than the speed of light (186,000 miles a second)—yes, even travel at the speed of thought (infinitely fast).

These heavenly bodies will not be bound by three-dimensional living, or by time and space. They will be able to go freely through any so-called walls and doors (as Jesus did) without difficulty.

Our new bodies will never grow old. They will have perfect health. They will be energized by the unlimited power of the Spirit of God. They will be everlasting.

We Will Be Living in a Permanent Heavenly Home. It will be an eternal home, reserved for us—with no need of locks and keys, clocks and calendars. There will be no need of a sun or moon in Heaven, for the glory of God will give all the light needed.

The Apostle John describes his glowing vision of Heaven in Rev., ch. 21, where the City of God is described: 1500 miles in length, and as wide and high as it is long. The streets of the city are of pure gold, like transparent glass. The foundation of the city walls are decorated with every kind of precious stones, such as sapphire, emerald, and topaz—and the twelve gates are made of pearls.

While many may be turned off by this image of Heaven as a glittering place with streets of gold, on the other hand we may find it extremely difficult to improve upon this symbolism if we are trying to describe Heaven in a way that represents something rare, precious, and that will not rust away.

Of course, there are skeptics who disbelieve that Heaven is a place up there in space beyond the earth's atmosphere and the blackness of the starry heavens. They'll accept the first heaven (atmosphere) and the second heaven (stars) because they're visible—but not the third Heaven, which is invisible and hence unbelievable. Nor do they believe in heavenly mansions as told by Jesus in John 14:2–3.

Yet, the Apostle Paul tells in 2 Cor. 12:1–4 about being caught up into Paradise, the third Heaven, and experiencing "inexpressible things." Also Stephen, immediately before being stoned to death, was filled through all his being with the Holy Spirit. He looked steadily into Heaven. He saw the glory of God and Jesus Himself standing at His right hand. "Look," he said, "there is a rift in the sky; I can see the Son of Man standing at God's right hand!" (Acts 7:55–56, NEB.)

We Will Meet Loved Ones in Heaven. We'll look forward to meeting loved ones who have gone on before us, ancestral family and friends, and to meeting the saints of all ages (Abraham, Moses, David, Elijah, Luke, John, Peter, Paul, and the others) and Jesus Himself!

Some Biblical scholars believe that each of us has a guardian angel watching out for us here on earth, and at the time of our death will escort us into Heaven. If this be so, what a joy that would be to meet our guardian

232

angel in Heaven and compare notes.

It's also possible that we'll encounter millions of angels in Heaven.

We might even get to see God, our Heavenly Father, with our renewed spiritual eyes. What a stupendous thought!!

We Will Be Able to Explore God's Great Universe—For All Eternity. We will better understand the entire celestial cosmos, how it all exists in perfect harmony, and be able to travel on endless space explorations. It's conceivable we would be able to explore some of the oceans of stars (200 billion in the Milky Way alone) and reach some of the million other galaxies if we have such adventuresome spirits. We might even be sent to revisit earth on a special mission.

For those less desirous of space travel and exploration, there will be an abundance of things to do back home in Heaven.

Some believe that Heaven will be pure unbounded joy because its language will be music. So if you're musically inclined, there should be an abundance of angelic choirs, chorales, chamber music, organ recitals, harpists, and vast congregations singing Hosannas and Hallelujahs! Since the weather will always be clear and communications excellent, tuning in to the music of the stars would be a bonus ecstasy.

Others are looking forward to Heaven providing a time of "rest from earthly labors," when deep silence will be golden. Many times no words will need to be spoken, for love will be the silent language of life in the Spirit. There will be the peace of God that passes all understanding.

As for the more active realms, one can easily imagine billions of people moving about (as we do on streets, in malls, and in hotel lobbies)—except that in Heaven each person will have a distinctive loving personality. Everyone we meet will be filled with love stories. Heaven will be teeming with interesting people from every nation, language, race and historical period—with love being the common language on every street. We will be one Heavenly Family bound together in love.

One can also imagine a glorious array of other heavenly sights and sounds (using earth language): magnificent mansions, great banquet halls, continual art festivals, fountains, worshiping throngs, grand cathedrals, love celebrations, herald trumpet calls, cheering crowds, awards ceremonies (perhaps even marching bands and parades akin to Disneyland, or ceremonies like the opening of the Olympic games).

We Will Be Forever Surrounded by God's Glory and Majesty, Dominion and Power. Lest we think that Heaven will be just an upscaled version of the best things we have and desire on earth, with the added dimension of *enjoying them for ourselves forever*—the Scriptures are quick to point out that just the opposite will be true. In our heavenly bodies we'll be less aware of ourselves, our surroundings, our activities—but we'll be more aware of our love, worship, and communion with God and His Heavenly Kingdom, and *enjoying Him forever.*

God has a magnificent plan for us! He has made it possible for us earthly creatures who were made lower than the angels to rise higher than the angels and become the sons (and daughters) of God. He has made it possible for those who were bounded by earth's attractions and its pull of gravity, to be lifted up to Heaven and know the throne of God and the force of Heavenly attractions.

Just think of it! We'll be in the presence of the ultimate power and wisdom and knowledge of the entire universe (no need of libraries or daily newspapers)—the Creator of men and angels, of Heaven and earth, the Original Source of all ideas, feelings, and creativity, the Giver of all earthly blessings, and the Provider of all Heavenly glories.

What was hitherto supernatural and invisible to us while on earth will now become natural and visible in Heaven. Our souls and spirits, that were once heavily laden with sin's burdens and earthly cares, will now be filled to overflowing with praise and adoration to the Heavenly Father. We will finally be able to do God's will without repeated confessions for continual shortcomings because we'll be living the abundant life in the true Spirit of God.

What a bright, glorious future awaits us in Heaven! We'll have direct access to the Eternal Power and Godhead—to the Almighty God, to the Supreme Ruler of all history, to the God of the finite and the infinite, to Divine Providence, to the King of kings and Lord of lords, to the Great God and Heavenly Father of our Lord Jesus Christ. (See 1 Cor. 2:9)

Our wonderful new heavenly bodies will be shining reflections of God's dazzling glory and great majesty, His universal dominion and exalted power. Our new spiritual bodies will be holy and blameless and perfect before Him—and full of praise for all the new spiritual benefits and blessings that are ours because of our fully realized heavenly citizenship.

Well might we sing with Charles Wesley:

O for a thousand tongues to sing
My great Redeemer's praise,
The glories of my God and King,
The triumphs of His grace.

Or shout aloud with Donald Grey Barnhouse:

To *God* be the *glory.*
To *God* be *all* the *glory.*
To *God* be *all* the *glory for evermore!* Amen.

THE MESSIAH IS COMING!

A close Jewish friend of mine once told me that at the death of a loved one there was no hope of eternal life in Heaven for the deceased, since the Messiah had not come as yet.

Our conversation continued at some length and in some depth, whereupon I stated that as a Christian I believed that the Messiah had already come in Jesus Christ almost 2,000 years ago.

A close mutual understanding and appreciation of our respective faiths were realized when I suggested that his looking (as a Jew) for the Messiah to come for the first time in history, and my looking (as a Christian) for the Messiah to come for the second time in history might well be the *same person*—a kingly Messiah from the line of David. My Jewish friend smiled and nodded in the affirmative.

What glorious events to contemplate and anticipate! The *Messiah* is coming! The Messiah *is* coming! The Messiah is *coming again*!

But when? When?? When???

Scoffers say that all things are continuing as they have been from the beginning of creation, so let us continue to "eat, drink, and be merry" and not be concerned about the Messiah's coming. If things get a lot worse than they are now—say, like an earthquake toppling California into the Pacific Ocean, or a World War III engulfing the superpowers in a possible nuclear holocaust—then let the Messiah come to earth to straighten things out for both the Jews and the Gentiles.

It's so easy to procrastinate and put out of our minds any serious thoughts about the Messiah's coming—whether for the first or second time. It's in fact bothersome to most of us; it interferes with our own plans and timetables; it puts us "out of control" of our own lives and destinies.

Besides, most of us are not prepared to give up our prized earthly possessions of wealth and fortune—certainly not in the "twinkling of an eye," without any monetary compensation for all our hard-earned accumulations. Nor are we prepared to take quick flight from this earth without advance notice.

"One word of command, one shout from the archangel, one blast from the trumpet of God, and the Lord Himself will come down from Heaven! Those who have died in Christ will be the first to rise, and then we [the believers] who are still living on the earth will be swept up with them into the clouds to meet the Lord in the air. And after that we shall be with Him forever." (1 Thess. 4:16–17, P.)

What a swift escape from the earth! What a bold evacuation plan!

236

But *when* is the Messiah coming? Could it be *soon*? Before I get my house in order? Before I dig my fallout shelter? Before I get my promotion? Before I get married? Before I see my grandchildren? *In my lifetime??*

It is reported that Queen Victoria, after hearing one of her chaplains preach at Windsor on the second coming of Christ (the Messiah) said, "Oh, how I wish that the Lord would come during my lifetime. I should so love to lay my crown at His feet."

Throughout the centuries countless believers have wished and hoped that the Messiah would come while they were still alive on earth, and thus they would never experience physical death. Others yearn for the Messiah to come to earth again so that there might be world peace and tranquility finally brought to our "civilized" society. Still others would just like to see Him in person and behold Him, as Queen Victoria wished.

But *when is* the Messiah coming?

"No one knows when that day or hour will come—neither the angels in Heaven, nor the Son; only the Father [God] knows." (Mark 13:32, TEV.)

But *when* the Messiah comes, it will be a public event, a media explosion; the whole earth will know and will be greatly surprised. We are told in the Scriptures that it will be like a flash of lightning, like a thief in the night, in the twinkling of an eye, and no mistaking it—quick, unannounced, and unexpected.

Some Christians believe that Christ's second coming will be in two phases: (1) *for* his believers (the Church) at their rapture (departure) from the earth; and (2) *with* his believers to reign on earth during the millennium. In between these two events will be the seven-year tribulation that ends with the battle of Armageddon, and with the Antichrist (Antimessiah) taking control during this most troublesome period before the true Messiah finally rules with Supreme Authority.

Watch and Be Ready—for *the Messiah is coming* in the clouds with great power and glory!

He is coming to set free hundreds of millions of His believers from all nationalities in *the greatest airlift of all time*; and to forthrightly set things in motion for His direct bodily return to earth with His "heavenly armies" to deal with the nations and set our society free.

What a wonderful time that will be!

THE MILLENNIUM

Do you ever think about what a real Utopia would be like on this earth—a place of ideal perfection?

For some of you this could mean a retreat to a faraway Shangri-La island with your dearly beloved for a week or two, away from the hectic pace of life, with no interferences of any kind—no radio, TV, newspapers, telephones—only peace and quiet contentment.

Others of us, particularly after hearing the daily round of news events that buffet us from all sides, would increasingly yearn for a time that is less filled with violence, crime, death and destruction, natural catastrophes, international crises, false accusations, and gross injustices. We would rejoice if there were just a one-day reprieve from ugliness, prejudice, fear, and hatred.

Well then rejoice, you earthly citizens, for the good news is that there is not only one such day coming, but 365,000 such days—a thousand years, a whole millennium! All you have to do is to have patience and believe that God will eventually bring it to pass—a relatively long period of great happiness, the best government (better than democracy, and far better than atheistic communism), and swift justice to those scattered evildoers who may not care for holiness to reign so fairly and triumphantly.

Some Christians believe that during this period Christ will reign over all earthly nations as "King of kings and Lord of lords" and Satan will be removed from the earth and bound in some prisonlike place (see Rev., ch. 20). It is also believed that Jerusalem will be the seat of world government during this momentous period, and that nations will stop having wars (see Isa. 2:2–4).

Can you believe what earthly life will be like during those 1,000 years?

It is thought that there will be no wars, no crime, no terrorism, no diseases, no poisonous insects or snakes, only vibrant health and practically no death, beautiful crops (no thorns, thistles, or weeds), no weather extremes (no deserts), and longevity will be increased (perhaps with a life span similar to the days before the flood—like Methuselah's 969 years).

The age will be characterized by justice and an administration of righteousness; there will be fairness blended with loving mercy. Think of such an administration: no mistakes, no accidents, no misjudgments, no unfair decisions, no prejudices or biased opinions—only truth, justice, peace, full knowledge, comfort, and joy.

Throughout the past 6,000 years of human government, "kingdoms have come, and kingdoms have gone." The Babylonians, the Assyrians, the Persians, the Egyptians, the Greeks, the Romans—and many others since then—all eventually became weak with faded glory. But the Kingdom of the millennium to come will be a Kingdom that is unshakable and eternal, as strong at the end of the 1,000 years as at the beginning.

For such a Kingdom I'd give up the twenty-first century and the nine to follow it!

EPILOGUE

After reading this book, it is my hope that you have gained a greater awareness and appreciation of God's Spirit in *all* things, and are increasingly allowing the Spirit of God to guide your body, mind, and spirit so that your earthly life is full of love, joy, and peace—and a glowing witness to others that you belong on God's Team.

However, if you are still remorseful about the past, fear the present, and lack confidence in the future—it's possible that you have never experienced a personal relationship with God through faith in His Son Jesus, and allowed God's Holy Spirit into your life to comfort you, lift you up, and set you free. It may be that you still need to pour out your heart to God in repentance by saying something like this: "Lord, I admit what I'm doing is wrong. I'm sorry for what I've done. Cleanse me of my sins. Forgive me. Create a new spirit within me. Give me your Spirit to guide and renew my life—now, and always. In Jesus' Name, Amen."

It may also be that after receiving God's Spirit, you may go through seasons of unemployment, financial losses, family breakups, illness, or the death of loved ones. Fear not...for the Holy Spirit, God's gift to you on earth, will never leave you or forsake you...but will always give you encouragement to overcome all difficulties, enable you to love others, and empower you with a secure hope in eternal things.

Wherever your earthly pilgrimage may take you, and however many years your journey may last—I pray that you will be increasingly "filled with the eternal Spirit of the Lord" and enjoy living "the life of the Spirit" in this world with a growing faith and confidence, knowing all the while that God has planned a magnificent future for us in the glorious world to come.

May the grace of the Lord Jesus Christ, and the love of God, and the fellowship that is ours in the Holy Spirit be with you all! Amen.

—2 Cor. 13:14 (NIV, P)